Strategic Planning for Nonprofit Organizations

NONPROFIT LAW, FINANCE, AND MANAGEMENT SERIES

The Art of Planned Giving: Understanding Donors and the Culture of Giving by Douglas E. White
Beyond Fund Raising: New Strategies for Nonprofit Investment and Innovation by Kay Grace
Charity, Advocacy, and the Law by Bruce R. Hopkins
The Complete Guide to Nonprofit Management by Smith, Bucklin & Associates
Critical Issues in Fund Raising edited by Dwight Burlingame
Developing Affordable Housing: A Practical Guide for Nonprofit Organizations by Bennett L. Hecht
Financial and Accounting Guide for Not-for-Profit Organizations, Fifth Edition by Malvern J. Gross, Jr., Richard F. Larkin, Roger S. Bruttomesso, John J. McNally, Price Waterhouse LLP
Financial Planning for Nonprofit Organizations by Jody Blazek
Fund-Raising: Evaluating and Managing the Fund Development Process by James M. Greenfield
Fund-Raising Fundamentals: A Guide to Annual Giving for Professionals and Volunteers by James M. Greenfield
Fund-Raising Regulation: A State-by-State Handbook of Registration Forms, Requirements, and Procedures by Seth Perlman and Betsy Hills Bush
Intermediate Sanctions: Curbing Nonprofits' Abuse by Bruce R. Hopkins and D. Benson Tesdahl
The Law of Fund-Raising, Second Edition by Bruce R. Hopkins
The Law of Tax-Exempt Healthcare Organizations by Thomas K. Hyatt and Bruce R. Hopkins
The Law of Tax-Exempt Organizations, Sixth Edition by Bruce R. Hopkins
The Legal Answer Book for Nonprofit Organizations by Bruce R. Hopkins
A Legal Guide to Starting and Managing a Nonprofit Organization, Second Edition by Bruce R. Hopkins
Managing Affordable Housing: A Practical Guide to Creating Stable Communities by Bennett L. Hecht, Local Initiatives Support Corporation, and James Stockard
Nonprofit Boards: Roles, Responsibilities, and Performances by Diane J. Duca
The Nonprofit Counsel by Bruce R. Hopkins
The Nonprofit Guide to the Internet by Robbin Zeff
The Nonprofit Law Dictionary by Bruce R. Hopkins
Nonprofit Litigation: A Practical Guide with Forms and Checklists by Steve Bachmann
The Nonprofit Handbook, Second Edition: Volume I—Management by Tracy Daniel Connors
The Nonprofit Handbook, Second Edition: Volume II—Fund Raising by Jim Greenfield
The Nonprofit Manager's Resource Dictionary by Ronald A. Landskroner
Nonprofit Organizations' Business Forms: Disk Edition by John Wiley & Sons, Inc.
Partnerships and Joint Ventures Involving Tax-Exempt Organizations by Michael I. Sanders
Planned Giving: Management, Marketing, and Law by Ronald R. Jordan and Katelyn L. Quynn
Program Related Investments: A Technical Manual for Foundations by Christie I. Baxter
Reengineering Your Nonprofit Organization: A Guide to Strategic Transformation by Alceste T. Pappas
Reinventing the University: Managing and Financing Institutions of Higher Education by Sandra L. Johnson and Sean C. Rush, Coopers & Lybrand, LLP
Strategic Planning for Nonprofit Organizations: A Practical Guide and Workbook by Michael Allison and Jude Kaye, Support Center for Nonprofit Management
Streetsmart Financial Basics for Nonprofit Managers by Thomas A. McLaughlin
Successful Marketing Strategies for Nonprofit Organizations by Barry J. McLeish
The Tax Law of Charitable Giving by Bruce R. Hopkins
The Tax Law of Colleges and Universities by Bertrand M. Harding
Tax Planning and Compliance for Tax-Exempt Organizations: Forms, Checklists, Procedures, Second Edition by Jody Blazek
The Volunteer Management Handbook by Tracy Daniel Connors

Strategic Planning for Nonprofit Organizations

A Practical Guide and Workbook

Michael Allison

Jude Kaye

Support Center for Nonprofit Management

JOHN WILEY & SONS, INC.

New York • Chichester • Weinheim • Brisbane • Singapore • Toronto

This text is printed on acid-free paper.

Library of Congress Cataloging-in-Publication Data:

Allison, Michael (Michael J.)
Strategic planning for nonprofit organizations : a practical guide and workbook / Michael Allison, Jude Kaye.
p. cm. — (Nonprofit law, finance, and management series)
Includes bibliographical references.
ISBN 0-471-17832-2 (paper/disk : alk. paper)
1. Nonprofit organizations—Management. 2. Strategic planning.
I. Kaye, Jude. II. Title. III. Series.
HD62.6.A45 1997
658.4'012—dc21 97-9145

Printed in the United States of America

10 9 8 7 6 5

To my wife, Jennifer Chapman, in gratitude for your patient support, endurance and guest editing throughout this adventure. With love,

Michael Allison

In memory of Gregor E. McGinnis, a man of great vision who understood that the process is as important as the end product.

Jude Kaye

About the Authors

Mike Allison is the Director of the Consulting Group, Support Center for Nonprofit Management and he actively consults in the areas of strategic planning, boards of directors, organizational development, and program evaluation. He co-authored *The Collaboration Continuum,* published by the National Minority AIDS Council and *Why Boards Don't Govern,* a chapter in the University of Indiana's *Taking Trusteeship Seriously.* He is the former executive director of a community-based organization, has a Masters in Public and Private Management from the Yale School of Management, and teaches Program Evaluation at California State University at Hayward.

Jude Kaye is the Senior Staff Consultant for the Support Center for Nonprofit Management and a nationally respected trainer and consultant in planning, financial management, boards of directors, meetings, and organization development. Over the past two decades, Jude has worked with both large and small nonprofit agencies and has guest lectured at many Bay Area universities. She has authored not only Support Center training materials but also co-authored two handbooks on financial management: *Finance Manual,* published by the National Minority AIDS Council and *What a Difference Nonprofits Make: A Guide to Accounting Procedures,* published by Accountants in the Public Interest.

The Support Center for Nonprofit Management is based in San Francisco and seeks to develop and support the creative, important work of the nonprofit sector. The Support Center works with nonprofit staff and volunteers on all matters of organizational management including boards of directors, financial management, strategic planning, organizational development, program evaluation, and computer applications. Through consulting, workshops, and publications, the Support Center for Nonprofit Management holds over 500 workshops for Bay Area nonprofit managers and works with over 200 nonprofits in consulting assignments each year. Honored by *Inc.* Magazine as one of 1995's ten best-managed nonprofits in the United States, the Support Center for Nonprofit Management is a member of the national network Support Centers of America, the Nonprofit Management Association, and the Technology Resource Consortium.

Acknowledgments

The origins of this book lie in the strategic planning worksheets which were created by Jude Kaye for training she conducted on strategic planning. This training inspired Paul Kawata and the National Minority AIDS Council (NMAC), located in Washington, D.C. to produce a handbook which we published jointly with NMAC in 1994. This book is much expanded from that first work, but we owe its existence to the impetus created from these important beginnings.

Though the ideas and presentation of the strategic planning process have been put to paper by the two of us, we gratefully acknowledge our debt to the many other consultants and writers who have contributed to our learning and to the field of planning over the past many years:

- We have received invaluable support, inspiration, and input from many people around the country. Leaders in the Support Centers of America network include Consultants Jane Arsenault, Lane Erwin, Richard Fowler, Denis Greene, Gary Levinson, Barbara Miller, Antoine Moore, and Rick Smith, Executive Director of the Support Centers of America. Lee Allison, Marla Handy, Steve Hartranft, and Pat Noyes also made significant contributions. Thank you all.
- We have benefitted greatly from all the authors whose work we reference. In particular, we want to acknowledge Bryan Barry and John Bryson, whose books on strategic planning for public and nonprofit organization have contributed so much to the field.
- Jan Masaoka, Executive Director of the Support Center for Nonprofit Management, long-time colleague and friend to us both, has helped develop and refine much of our thinking over the past several years and has continually inspired us to make this Workbook as user friendly as possible. In particular, Jan contributed several of the planning tools in the appendix having to do with program evaluation and assessment of governance and the essence of several case illustrations included throughout the book.

- Finally, in the list of people to whom we are intellectual heirs, we would like to acknowledge a special debt to the late Jon Cook, founder of the Support Centers of America and a pioneer in bringing the practice of strategic planning to the nonprofit sector. Jon was an important teacher to both of us and many of our best ideas originally came from him.

In writing this book, we had the good fortune of working with two delightful editors at John Wiley & Sons. We want to thank and acknowledge Marla Bobowick and Martha Cooley who have been a joy to work with. We wish that all authors could receive as much patience, support, and understanding.

Contents

How to Use This Workbook

Strategic Planning for Nonprofit Organizations: A Practical Guide and Workbook offers a framework and detailed suggestions for doing strategic planning in nonprofit organizations. This book is the product of the authors' experience as planning and organization development consultants. The concepts, process design and language presented here have been shaped by our work over the years with scores of nonprofit organizations on strategic planning. Indeed, many of the Worksheets and approaches to formulating strategy were developed while working with individual clients in response to particular situations. The authors' goal has always been to provide clients with a practical conceptual framework that is comprehensive without being either overly complex or unduly simplistic, and user friendly tools and techniques. Those who have experience with strategic planning will find the book a useful refresher and "one-stop source book" of fundamental concepts and techniques; those without such experience will find it a valuable introduction to what strategic planning is—and is not—and how to make the best use of the process.

When done well, strategic planning is both a creative and a participatory process that engenders new insights and helps an organization pursue its mission. It is an important tool that can help nonprofit organizations achieve their goals. A tool's effectiveness, though, ultimately depends on how well it is wielded: a hammer is a very good tool for nailing together bookshelves, but just swinging a hammer doesn't mean the bookshelves will get built, nor does a failure to build bookshelves reflect poorly on the hammer. With this Workbook, the authors hope to help others understand enough about the potential and the requirements of this particular management tool to create sound strategic plans that contribute to the viability and success of their organizations' work.

PURPOSE OF THE WORKBOOK

This Workbook is written to help the leaders, both board and staff, of nonprofit organizations and other planning practitioners, do effective strategic planning. While the approach and process design here will serve a wide range of organizations, it is written with small to medium size organizations (those with no budgets to those with budgets of several million dollars) particularly in mind.

In addition, many government agencies and programs will benefit from the planning process described in these pages. Though there are certain important differences to note between nonprofit organizations and government organizations, the principles of successful planning which support effective organizations are identical.

We hope that consultants working with nonprofit organizations, students of nonprofit management, and others interested in this area will also find the Workbook useful.

STRUCTURE OF THE WORKBOOK

The Workbook is organized so that it can be easily followed and referenced during the course of strategic planning. There are four sections to the book: Getting Set Up for Success, Defining Your Challenge, Setting Your Course, and Keeping the Plan Relevant. Each section includes a discussion of the corresponding phases in the planning process and the planning steps associated with each phase. Note in the table below, WS indicates that a worksheet is included for the planning step. Tem indicates a sample(s) template is included to assist with implementation of the planning step.

Chapter	Section	Planning Phases
Two	Getting Set Up for Success	**Introduction**
		Phase 1: Getting Ready
		Step 1.1 Identify reasons for planning (WS 1)
		Step 1.2 Check readiness to plan (WS 2)
		Step 1.3 Choose planning participants (WS 3)
		Step 1.4 Summarize organization history and profile (WS 4)
		Step 1.5 Identify information needed for strategic planning (WS 5)
		Step 1.6 Write a "plan to plan" (Tem)
Three	Defining Your Challenge	**Phase 2:** Articulating Mission and Vision
		Step 2.1 Write (or revisit) your mission statement (WS 6)
		Step 2.2 Draft a vision statement (WS 7)

Chapter	Title	Phases and Steps
		Phase 3: Assessing the Environment Step 3.1 Update information needed for planning (WS 8) Step 3.2 Articulate previous and current strategies (WS 9) Step 3.3 Gather input from internal stakeholders (WS 10) Step 3.4 Gather input from external stakeholders (WS 11 and 12) Step 3.5 Gather information about program effectiveness
Four	Setting Your Course	**Phase 4:** Agreeing on Priorities Step 4.1 Analyze interplay of strengths, weaknesses, opportunities, and threats (WS 13) Step 4.2 Analyze competitive strengths of programs (WS 14) Step 4.3 Decide on priorities (WS 15) Step 4.4 Select core strategies (WS 16) Step 4.5 Summarize scope and scale of programs (WS 17) Step 4.6 Write goals and objectives (WS 18) Step 4.7 Develop long-range financial projections (WS 19) **Phase 5:** Writing the Strategic Plan Step 5.1 Put all the pieces together (Tem) Step 5.2 Submit to review process Step 5.3 Adopt the strategic plan
Five	Keeping Your Plan Relevant	**Phase 6:** Implementing Your Strategic Plan (Tem) **Phase 7:** Monitoring and Evaluating Your Strategic Plan (WS 20 and 21) Conclusion

Chapter 1 provides a brief introduction to the strategic planning process by defining the process and its components and by differentiating strategic planning in nonprofit organizations from other related topics. This chapter will give the reader a good overview of the subject.

Chapter 2, Getting Set Up for Success, discusses Phase 1, initiating a planning process. Phase 1 covers several steps which can greatly increase the chances for a successful planning process.

Chapter 3, Defining Your Challenge, covers the next two phases of the process. Phase 2 involves articulating mission and vision. Phase 3 reviews assessing the environment. Until this point, the process is organized around expanding the scope of possibilities and understanding the resources and capacities the organization brings to its potential challenges.

Chapter 4, Setting Your Course, covers Phase 4, Agreeing on Priorities, and Phase 5, Writing the Strategic Plan. In these phases, planners are focusing, analyzing, deciding, and summarizing which priorities to pursue.

Chapter 5, Keeping the Plan Relevant, covers the final two phases of planning: Phase 6, Implementing the Strategic Plan, and Phase 7, Monitoring and Evaluating the Strategic Plan. It is in the implementation of the plan where the value of planning is evident. If the planning process ends in a plan, but provides little direction to the work of the organization, the planning process may well have been a waste of time. On the other hand, if the planning process inspires the day to day work of the organization in the form of important reference points (values, strategic directions, and priorities) then the planning process will have had great value.

Worksheets

A integral feature of this Workbook is the series of worksheets which complement the text. The worksheets will help planners structure and focus the thought process involved with each planning step. Each worksheet is discussed in the text and includes process notes, which provide brief instructions for using the worksheet. Blank worksheets are included in Appendix A and on the disk included with this book.

Sidebars

Throughout the Workbook, short case studies drawn from real-life experience with nonprofit organizations are included to illustrate particular situations which may arise during a planning process. In some cases, the name of the organization is used; in others, for reasons of confidentiality, the name has been disguised.

ASO/USA

AIDS Service Organization/United States of America (ASO/USA) is a fictional organization. To illustrate the use of the worksheets in the context of the planning process, a strategic plan for this organization has been completed, in a step-by-step process, throughout the book. A completed case study worksheet follows each section that discusses a stage in the strategic planning process, and is a signal that

CASE STUDY: ASO/USA DESCRIPTION

NOTE: This case study of a fictional organization will be used to illustrate the use of the worksheets throughout the planning Workbook.

January, 1997

AIDS Service Organization/USA is an organization in a mid-size eastern city founded in 1988 to meet the needs of the growing number of people becoming infected and affected by AIDS. Ken Brown, the founding executive director has led the organization through a period of sustained growth. The organization started out doing a hotline and prevention work and won a federal grant to continue the work in their second year.

In subsequent years, under the direction of Program Manager Delores Molina, the organization expanded its programs to include case management services for persons with AIDS and support groups for people with AIDS and caregivers of people with AIDS; other support services include translation, transportation, benefits counseling, etc. ASO/USA has become known as a reliable community agency and serves men and women of all races. Most clients have low to moderate incomes. ASO/USA does a limited amount of advocacy and public education, supported by local foundations.

The organization's budget in 1996 was close to $645,000 with twenty full- and part-time staff and a core of fifty volunteers. $280,000 per year is from the Federal Centers for Disease Control, $190,000 is from the city, approximately $140,000 is from foundations, and $35,000 is raised from special events, individual donors, and other fundraising.

Two years ago, ASO/USA collaborated with the largest independent health clinic in the city, City Clinic, to conduct more aggressive outreach to people at high risk for contracting AIDS (intravenous drug users, homeless persons, and prostitutes), but who may not be receiving ongoing medical care. This project was funded by the city department of public health for $300,000 per year for three years, split between the two organizations. There have been significant problems coordinating the project between them.

Along with the good news of the new drug treatments available for people with HIV in the summer of 1996 came a whole new set of challenges. The complex protocols and costs associated with the medication make accessibility for marginalized populations difficult. And, with the prospect of better treatments has come an increase in high-risk behavior among individuals who think they don't have to worry about getting AIDS anymore.

The organization has developed detailed program plans associated with each funding source, but has never developed a comprehensive strategic plan for the agency. The board recognizes the need for planning, but tends not to be very active. Sam Green, the board president, is very supportive of the organization and of the staff, but has put little time into energizing the rest of the board.

The Executive Director and the Board President have decided that, given the changes happening in the external environment, increasing demands for services, and challenges facing the organization, it is time to do strategic planning.

ASO/USA is participating in—and can be used as a model for—this stage of the strategic planning process. A complete strategic plan is included as Exhibit 4–11.

Additional Resources

Additional resources to support strategic planning are included in the appendices including:

- Blank worksheets
- Workplan templates for a strategic planning process (Appendix B)
- A survey to assist with self-assessment of management systems (Appendix C)
- A self-assessment survey for boards (Appendix D)
- A set of techniques and tools to assist with program evaluation (Appendix E)
- A set of techniques and tools to assist with managing the group process (Appendix F)
- A template for an operational action plan (Appendix G)
- Selected bibliography for future reference (Appendix H)

PLANNING TIPS FOR SUCCESS

Each planning process is unique and has a slightly different focus; the authors have tried to be comprehensive and fully expect the Workbook to contain more suggestions and resources than any single organization will need for any given planning process.

- *Tip #1.* Focus on the most important questions during your strategic planning process. This will help you get the most value out of your effort. There are only a few critical questions which the plan needs to answer. (If you don't have any important choices to make about your organization's future, you don't need a strategic plan.) While many questions will be interesting, you won't have time, energy, or resources to do it all. Make sure that all of your planning work is related to developing strategic responses to these few critical questions.
- *Tip #2.* Produce a document! A useful strategic plan can be a few pages long. It can be written at the end of a one-day board and staff retreat. It doesn't have to be polished, it doesn't have to be pretty, but a document is a symbol of accomplishment and a guide for action. It is much better to com-

plete only an outline of a strategic plan with a summary of long-term and short-term priorities than to let someone with writer's block, intent on a beautiful and complete document, prevent you and your organization from getting your plan done.

- *Tip #3.* There is absolutely no need to use every worksheet in order to do a sound strategic plan. It is important to touch on the important points in each of the seven phases, but the level of detail each organization chooses for each phase will vary. The worksheets are an aid to the thinking process, not a set of hurdles to be surmounted. Use only those which will help your organization do the work it needs to do.

WHAT IF I HAVE ONLY ONE OR TWO DAYS?

This Workbook is designed as a do-it-yourself guide for organizations with limited time as well as for organizations intending to conduct an extensive planning process. Spend an hour or two to familiarize yourself with the planning framework and the approach presented in the Workbook. You should then be able to decide whether your organization is likely to choose an *abbreviated, moderate,* or *extensive* planning process.

The Workbook is organized to serve the *extensive* (most comprehensive) approach. The planning framework, however, will serve the *abbreviated* and *moderate* planning process equally well. The logic underlying each phase is articulated in the narrative and illustrated through the worksheets and suggested exercises included in the discussion of each planning phase. Based on the identical planning framework, the abbreviated and moderate planning process skips or shortens many of the steps without eliminating the fundamental planning questions. Draft workplans for all three levels are included in the appendices to help leaders choose where to spend their limited resources of time, money, and energy.

It is important to choose the right level of intensity for the planning questions facing your organization. There is no wisdom in choosing the path of an extensive process when the organization only requires a low or moderate process. At best, an organization will spend more resources than it needs to in developing a plan. More likely, the process will stall in the middle and leave a number of people feeling frustrated and defeated, rather than inspired and energized; sometimes that is worse than no planning process at all.

There are always trade-offs to be made in selecting a planning process. Even in a six- to twelve-month process, hard choices have to be made concerning which issues to explore and which to leave alone. Use Exhibit 1 and the Phase 1 Getting Ready worksheets to help you choose; don't be afraid to adjust the process as you go along if you find that a more, or less, intensive process will serve the organization better right now.

Exhibit 1 Levels of Strategic Planning

The *level* of our planning effort is likely to be:	**Abbreviated**	**Moderate**	**Extensive**
Time available:	One or two days	One to three months	Six months or more
Personnel Involved:	• If smaller organization, usually entire board and staff • If larger organization, usually entire board and staff representatives (usually only internal stakeholders)	• If smaller organization, usually entire board and staff • If larger organization, usually entire board and staff representatives • Some external stakeholders provide input (such as clients or funders)	• Large number, including extensive input from all major internal and external stakeholder groups
Depth of analysis/new information to be gathered:	Little or none	Some	A lot: at a minimum includes data from stakeholders and objective data about operating environment
Primary outcomes sought from strategic planning process:	• Consensus among board and staff on mission, core future strategies, list of long-term and short-term program, and management/operations priorities • Guidance to staff on developing detailed annual operating plans	• Consensus among board and staff on mission, core future strategies, list of long-term and short-term programs, and management/operations priorities • Articulation of program and management/operations goals and objectives • Greater understanding of the organization's operating environment (strengths, weaknesses, opportunities, and threats) • Some discussion of strategic choices • Guidance to staff on developing detailed annual operating plans	• Consensus among board and staff on mission, core future strategies, list of long-term and short-term program, and management/operations priorities • Articulation of program and management/operations goals and objectives • Greater understanding of the organization's operating environment (strengths, weaknesses, opportunities, and threats) • In-depth discussion of strategic choices • Guidance to staff on developing detailed annual operating plans

A WORD ABOUT WORDS: "CLIENT" AND "STAKEHOLDER"

Every citizen benefits from the work of nonprofit organizations every day. Both in the United States and abroad, our water and air are cleaner, civil rights have been advanced on many fronts, culture continues to be renewed and celebrated, people are cared for, and the policies and practices of both government and business have been greatly influenced—all though the work of nonprofit organizations. The beneficiaries or consumers of the goods and services nonprofit organizations produced are called by many names: legal service and human service organizations serve "clients," health care organizations serve "patients," arts organizations serve "patrons," advocacy organizations serve "constituents," other organizations serve customers, members, and so on. The authors have chosen to use the term "client" to serve as a representative name for the *primary beneficiaries or consumers* of the goods and services produced by nonprofit organizations. We recognize that it is not a wholly satisfactory solution, but it seems less distracting than using different names, and more appropriate than using a more generic name such as customers.

Nonprofit organizations are not "owned" as are private corporations, nor are they subject to the electoral process as are government organizations. Nonetheless, nonprofit organizations are accountable to many parties for their work, in addition to their clients. And, as with clients, the individuals and groups of people to whom nonprofit organizations are accountable are called by many names. We have chosen to call funders, clients, the public, other organizations, regulators, and so on *external stakeholders,* and to call board members, staff, and volunteers *internal stakeholders.* Simply stated, a stakeholder is anyone who cares, or should care, about the organization—anyone who has a stake in the success of its mission.

THE AUTHORS' APPROACH TO PLANNING

There are three values the authors hold in planning that should be clear to the reader.

1. We believe that an organization's chances for success are greater if the leader of the organization has a strategic plan (written or not). Although it is possible to be very successful and do much good without a strategic plan by being opportunistic and reactive, the authors believe that over the long haul, being *intentional* and *strategic* about the work of the organization will accomplish more than being only *reactive* and *opportunistic.*
2. We believe that an organization's chances for success are greater if the leaders of an organization commit to building a vision of success which is shared among board, staff, and volunteers. While a brilliant entrepreneurial leader may be able to direct the workforce of an organization without a

shared understanding of the vision, the authors believe that an organization whose members share a deep commitment to a vision of success will accomplish even greater things.

3. The authors believe that an *inclusive* strategic planning process is an excellent way to develop a strategic plan and to build broad-based commitment to a shared vision. Again, it is possible for one person, or a small group of people, to develop a plan and to sell the plan to all the people required to implement the plan. In the long run, an organization which includes many of its stakeholders in developing and renewing its strategic plans will come closest to achieving its true potential in pursuit of its chosen mission.

CHAPTER ONE

Introduction to Strategic Planning

What is strategic planning? Simply stated, strategic planning is a management tool, and like any management tool, it is used for one purpose only—to help an organization do a better job. Strategic planning can help an organization to focus its vision and priorities in response to a changing environment and to ensure that members of the organization are working toward the same goals.

In short,

> Strategic planning is a systematic process through which an organization agrees on—and builds commitment among key stakeholders to—priorities which are essential to its mission and responsive to the operating environment.

The particular use for strategic planning is to sharpen organizational focus, so that all organizational resources are optimally utilized in service of the organization's mission.

Several key concepts in this definition reinforce the meaning and success of strategic planning:

- The process is *strategic* because it involves choosing how best to respond to the circumstances of a dynamic and sometimes hostile environment. All living plants respond to the environment, but as far as we know they do not choose how to respond. Nonprofit organizations have many choices in the face of changing client or customer needs, funding availability, competition, and other factors. Being strategic requires recognizing these choices and committing to one set of responses instead of another.

- Strategic planning is *systematic* in that it calls for following a process that is both focused and productive. The process raises a sequence of questions which helps planners examine past experiences, test old assumptions, gather and incorporate new information about the present, and anticipate the environment in which the organization will be working in the future. The process also guides planners in continually looking at how the component programs and strategies fit with the vision, and vice versa.
- Strategic planning involves choosing specific *priorities*—making decisions about ends and means, in both the long term and the short term. Consensus on priorities must be reached at many levels, from the philosophical to the operational. While a strategic plan will stop short of the level of detail in an annual operating plan, it cannot be called a plan if it does not articulate the major goals and the priority methods the organization selects. Long-term goals have implications for short-term action: the two must be congruent with one another for the plan to be valid and useful.
- Finally, the process is about building *commitment*. Systematically engaging key stakeholders, including clients and the community, in the process of identifying priorities allows disagreements to be engaged constructively and supports better communication and coordination. The process allows a broad consensus to be built, resulting in enhanced accountability throughout the organization. This commitment ensures that a strategic plan will actively be used for guidance and inspiration, instead of serving as a dust cover for a remote corner shelf.

The strategic planning process can be complex, challenging, and cumbersome at times, but it is always informed by the basic ideas outlined above and one can always return to these basics to make sure one's own strategic planning process is on the right track.

WHAT DOES A "STRATEGY" LOOK LIKE?

Strategies are broad, overall priorities or directions adopted by an organization: strategies are choices about how best to accomplish an organization's mission. A few brief examples illustrate the point.

- The San Jose Museum of Modern Art is a relatively new institution. They chose an innovative acquisition strategy in pursuit of their mission to increase opportunities to experience world class art for their community: they chose to rent a collection, rather than buy one. Rather than slowly accumulate a collection, the traditional strategy for art museums, San Jose negotiated with the Museum of Modern Art in New York (which is only able to display some 10 percent of its collection at any one time) to borrow a museum full of art on a rotating basis, drawing on the best collection in the world.
- The mission of the NAMES Project Foundation, sponsor of the AIDS Memorial Quilt, is to help bring an end to the AIDS epidemic. In addition to memorializing the victims of AIDS and drawing public attention to the AIDS epidemic, the Quilt displays are designed to carry prevention messages as well. Early on, the NAMES Project organized public displays of the Quilt all over the country. In the past few years however, the organization was able to adapt its delivery strategy in order to reach more people. Rather than producing all community displays each year through its own network, the organization now also recruits collaborative hosts in high schools, corporations, communities of faith, and elsewhere which allow NAMES to display the Quilt in three to four times as many locations each year.
- One local Humane Society provided a wide range of services, including shelter and new homes for stray pets, a spay and neuter clinic, and euthenasia for unwanted animals. After many years spent caring for neglected animals, the society shifted its strategy toward prevention. To implement the strategy all programs were instructed to develop and implement an education component to their service, and the staff increased their efforts to pass legislation designed to prevent unwanted pets and animal abuse.

In each case, the organization has made a clear choice among competing options about how best to pursue its mission. It is easy to see how each of these core strategies might be translated into specific goals and objectives over a period of several years. What is not easy to see is how much effort, experimentation, and discussion were required to find these successful strategies. The strategic planning process outlined in this Workbook will help organizations identify various strategic options and to make intelligent choices in developing strategic directions and plans.

STRATEGIC PLANNING AND OPERATIONAL PLANNING

Strategic planning and operational planning involve two different types of thinking. Strategic decisions are fundamental, directional, and future-oriented.

Operational decisions, on the other hand, primarily affect the day-to-day implementation of strategic decisions. While strategic decisions always have long-term implications, operational decisions tend to have shorter-term implications. Exhibit 1-1 is a table illustrating this point.

Clearly, these two levels of planning overlap. For convenience, this overlap is discussed in terms of the planning horizon, the period of time covered by the decisions made. Strategic plans outline priorities to be achieved over the next several years, operational plans outline the actions to be taken in the next year which will lead to those strategic priorities. Both are important and need to be done well, however it is important not to confuse the two.

STRATEGIC PLANNING AND LONG-RANGE PLANNING

Although many use these terms interchangeably, strategic planning and long-range planning differ in their emphasis on the assumed environment. Long-range planning is generally considered to assume that current knowledge about future conditions is sufficiently reliable to ensure the plan's reliability over the duration of its implementation. In the 1950s and 1960s, for example, the U.S. economy was relatively stable and somewhat predictable, therefore long-range planning was both fashionable and useful. It was not uncommon for U.S. corporations to have large planning staffs developing long-range plans with highly detailed goals, strategies, and operational objectives identified over a twenty-year time period or even longer.

Strategic planning, however, assumes that an organization must be responsive to an environment which is dynamic and hard to predict. Strategic planning stresses the importance of making decisions which position an organization to successfully respond to changes in the environment. The emphasis is on overall direction rather than predicting specific, year-by-year, concrete objectives. The focus of strategic planning is on strategic management, that is, the application of strategic thinking to the job of leading an organization to achieving its purpose.

Exhibit 1-1 Strategic Decisions Versus Operational Decisions

Strategic Decisions	**Operational Decisions**
Fundamental, directional	Implementation-oriented
Long-term planning horizon	Short-term planning horizon (≤1 year)
Future-focused	Functional and current-focused

As a result, while some organizations may develop visions which stretch many years into the future, most strategic plans discuss priority goals no farther than five years out, with operational objectives identified for only the first year. A comparative illustration can be found in Exhibit 1-2.

How Is Strategic Planning with Nonprofit Organizations Different from Planning in Business or Government?

Strategic planning is interdisciplinary and incorporates concepts from military strategy, history, business practices, and organizational theory. It came to prominence as a distinct discipline in the 1950s and 1960s because of its popularity among many corporations' headquartered in the United States. Still, the essential concepts are applicable to any organizational setting.

What is *similar* about strategic planning in nonprofits, business, and government is the essence of strategic planning—in an organizational setting deciding what to accomplish, and how to go about it in response to a dynamic operating environment. What is *different* is the nature of the internal and external forces which bear on the essential task.

The governance of organizations in the three sectors is quite different and has significant implications for strategic planning. Both nonprofits and businesses are governed by a board of directors, whereas government organizations are governed by a wide variety of publicly elected bodies. The boards of

Exhibit 1-2 Long-Range Planning Versus Strategic Planning

Long-Range Planning	**Strategic Planning**
Views future as predictable	Views future as unpredictable
Views planning as a periodic process	Views planning as a continuous process
Assumes current trends will continue	Expects new trends, changes, and surprises
Assumes a most likely future and emphasizes working backward to map out a year-by-year sequence of events necessary to achieve it	Considers a range of possible futures and emphasizes the development of strategies based on a current assessment of the organization's environment
Asks "What business are we in?"	Asks "What business should we be in? Are we doing the right thing?"

(Adapted from Florence Green. *Strategic Planning: Blueprints for Success,* California Association of Nonprofits, February 1994.)

businesses represent, or are, the literal owners of the business. Nonprofit boards represent the public interest.

Businesses especially in the past twenty years have emphasized customer satisfaction to a greater degree than either nonprofits or government. Business has invested heavily in market research and in attempts to improve quality as they compete for customer business. Because the direct consumers of the products and services of nonprofits and government typically pay only a small portion of the cost, the funders, whether foundations or taxpayers, have had a much greater influence than customer satisfaction on the strategies of organizations in these two nonbusiness sectors. This is beginning to change; witness the popularity of the *Reinventing Government,* a book which emphasizes increased responsiveness of the government to the public and increased focus on accountability in the nonprofit sector.

Finally, values and an orientation to a mission have typically been the hallmark of nonprofits and less influential in business and government. This also is changing. In the past decade, much of the business sector literature, starting with *In Search of Excellence,* has emphasized the importance of values and mission statements in well-run companies. Similarly, it is not uncommon now to find government offices with mission statements which articulate the unique contribution the office aspires to make to the public welfare.

The strategic planning process outlined in this Workbook is designed to serve the wide range of organizations that make up the nonprofit sector: arts organizations, human services agencies, environmental groups, hospitals and other health organizations, advocacy organizations, religious institutions, and educational institutions. However, with minor translation to different contexts, much of the conceptual framework is equally applicable to organizational settings in either the business or government sectors.

What Strategic Planning Is Not

Everything said above to describe what strategic planning is can also inform an understanding of what it is not.

Strategic Planning Does Not Predict the Future or Make Decisions Which Can't Be Changed. Though strategic planning involves making assumptions about the future environment, the decisions are made in the present. "Planning deals with the futurity of current decisions. . . . Forward planning requires that choices be made among possible events in the future, but decisions made in their light can be made only in the present."[1] Over time, an organization must monitor changes in its environment and assess whether its assumptions remain essentially valid. If an unexpected shift occurs, major strategic decisions may have to be revisited sooner than they would in a typical three- to five-year planning cycle.

[1] George Steiner. *Strategic Planning* (New York: The Free Press, 1979), pp. 14–15.

Strategic Planning Is Not a Substitute for the Judgment of Leadership. Strategic planning is a tool—it is not a substitute for the exercise of judgment by leadership. Ultimately, the leaders of any enterprise need to sit back and ask themselves "What are the *most* important issues to respond to?" and "How shall we respond?" Just as the hammer doesn't create the bookshelf, so the data analysis and decision-making tools of strategic planning do not make the organization function—they can only support the intuition, reasoning skills, and judgment that people bring to the work of their organization.

Strategic Planning Is Not Always a Smooth, Predictable, and Linear Process. Strategic planning, though structured in many respects, typically does not flow smoothly from one phase to the next. It is a creative process, requiring flexibility—the fresh insight arrived at today might very well alter the decision made yesterday. Inevitably, the process moves forward and back several times before arriving at the final set of decisions. No one should be surprised if the process feels less like a comfortable trip on a commuter train than like a ride on a roller coaster. But remember, even roller coaster cars arrive at their destination, as long as they stay on track!

REASONS FOR DOING STRATEGIC PLANNING

Why should an organization embark on a strategic planning effort? After all, planning consumes resources, a precious commodity for any nonprofit, and defining the direction and activities of an organization, in an ever-changing environment, is a daunting endeavor.

Certainly planning alone does not produce results; it is a *means,* not an *end* in itself. The plans have to be implemented to produce results. However, well-developed plans increase the chances that the day-to-day activities of the organization will lead to desired results. Planning helps the members of an organization *focus* on the right priorities, and it improves the *process* of people working together as they pursue these priorities.

Successful strategic planning improves the focus of an organization in that it generates:

- An explicit understanding of the organization's purpose, business(es), and values among staff, board, and external constituencies; that understanding, supports an increased level of commitment to the organization and its goals.
- A blueprint for action. The plan is a conceptual framework that guides and supports the management and governance of the organization, a framework that orients board and staff as they go about doing the work of the organization.

- Broad milestones with which to monitor achievements and assess results.
- Information that can be used to market the organization to the public and to potential funders.

Successful strategic planning improves the process of people working together in that it:

- Creates a forum for understanding why the organization exists and the shared values that should influence decisions.
- Fosters successful communication and teamwork among the board of directors and staff.
- Lays the groundwork for meaningful change by stimulating strategic thinking and focusing on what's really important to the organization's long-term success.
- Most importantly, brings everyone together to pursue opportunities for better meeting the needs of clients.

HOW MUCH TIME AND MONEY DOES IT TAKE TO DO STRATEGIC PLANNING?

It depends! A useful strategic plan can be sketched out in a few hours for no cost, done at a one- or two-day retreat for several hundred or a few thousand dollars, or take over a year and cost up to $100,000.

What does it depend on? There are many factors which influence the cost and time frame for any given organization. Taken together, these factors can be weighed and balanced to assist in developing an appropriate planning process.

It sounds obvious, but the first factors are the amounts of time and money available to do planning. It pays to be realistic. There are usually relatively narrow ranges for both available money and time commitment. These ranges need to be respected and used as meaningful constraints. If a board and staff are heavily involved in a labor-intensive project or other immediate issues, they will not have the time or the energy to devote to an intensive planning process. And, while strategic planning is often supported through technical assistance grants, it is more appropriate for some organizations than others to invest a lot of money in strategic planning. One fifty-year-old organization with a multi-million dollar budget had not deeply examined its mission and program mix in decades. It received a $100,000 grant to support a two-year planning process which also covered the cost of staff time devoted to the planning process. A young organization may not be comfortable spending even $3,000 for a planning process when its entire operating budget is less than $100,000.

The experience level of the leaders of the planning process is another critical factor. It generally takes more time and requires more outside assistance if the organization's leaders have little experience with strategic planning. On the other hand, if an organization has a well-developed annual program and budget planning routine, much of the information needed for strategic planning may be readily available, thus shrinking both the time and cost of a strategic planning effort.

Other factors that will have an impact on the amount of time needed to do strategic planning include:

- *The degree of commitment to the current mission statement.* Is there a fundamental agreement as to the purpose, mission, and guiding principles which guide the organization? Is there a shared vision of the impact the organization wants to have in the world, and what the organization would need to do to accomplish that result? If so, the mission statement may only need polishing; if not, a full day or more may need to be devoted to this task.
- *The amount of new information.* The amount of new information that needs to be gathered in order to make informed decisions. How well do planners currently understand the strengths, weaknesses, opportunities, and threats facing the organization? How current is feedback on the organization's programs and services from outside stakeholders: clients, funders, community leaders, etc.? What information is needed to assess the competitive environment and the effectiveness of current programs?
- *The level of agreement on priorities.* How much agreement or disagreement currently exists regarding allocation of resources? Is there agreement over which clients to serve and what services are most important? Or are there power struggles going on over competing internal resource needs for program services, facilities, development, staff, etc.?
- *The level of trust.* The level of trust among and between staff and board. The level of trust among all the key stakeholders involved in the planning process can significantly hinder, or greatly support, the discussion of differences and the management of conflict.
- *Involvement of key stakeholders.* How much time and energy needs to be spent involving key stakeholders in the planning process in order to get both their input and their support for decisions made during the planning process?
- *The size of the organization.* Is there only one service provided, or does the organization provide a variety of services that need to be assessed? Does the organization have one department, or are there many departments that need to be involved in the planning process.

THE STRATEGIC PLANNING PROCESS

The fundamental phases of the strategic planning process, as outlined in this Workbook, are presented as a logical series of phases and related steps that allows for flexibility and creativity. A brief description of the seven phases in the process is illustrated by Exhibit 1-3. These recommended phases are not the only "recipe" for cooking up a strategic plan—other sources might recommend different steps or variations on these phases—but the Strategic Planning Process describes the essential ingredients to the planning process and the usual results. We encourage planners to add their own touches to the recipe, for example by spicing up opportunities for interaction among participants or giving elegance to the presentation, in order to create a plan which will not only sustain an organization but will help it to prevail.

Phase 1: Getting Ready

To get ready for strategic planning, an organization must first assess *if* it's ready. While a number of issues must be addressed in assessing readiness, that determination essentially comes down to whether an organization's leaders are truly committed to the effort, and whether they are able to devote the necessary attention to the "big picture" at the time. For example, if a funding crisis looms, or if the founder is about to depart, or if the environment is so turbulent that everyone is putting out fires, then it doesn't make sense to take time out for this effort at this time.

An organization that determines it is indeed ready to begin strategic planning must then do five things to pave the way for an organized process:

- Identify specific issues or choices that the planning process should address
- Clarify roles (who does what in the process)
- Create a Planning Committee
- Develop an organizational profile
- Identify the information that must be collected to help make sound decisions

The *product* developed at the end of Phase 1 is a Strategic Planning Workplan (Plan for Planning).

Phase 2: Articulating Mission and Vision

A mission statement is like an introductory paragraph: it lets the reader know where the writer is going, and it also shows that the *writer* knows where he or she is going. Likewise, a mission statement must communicate the essence of an

Exhibit 1-3 The Strategic Planning Process

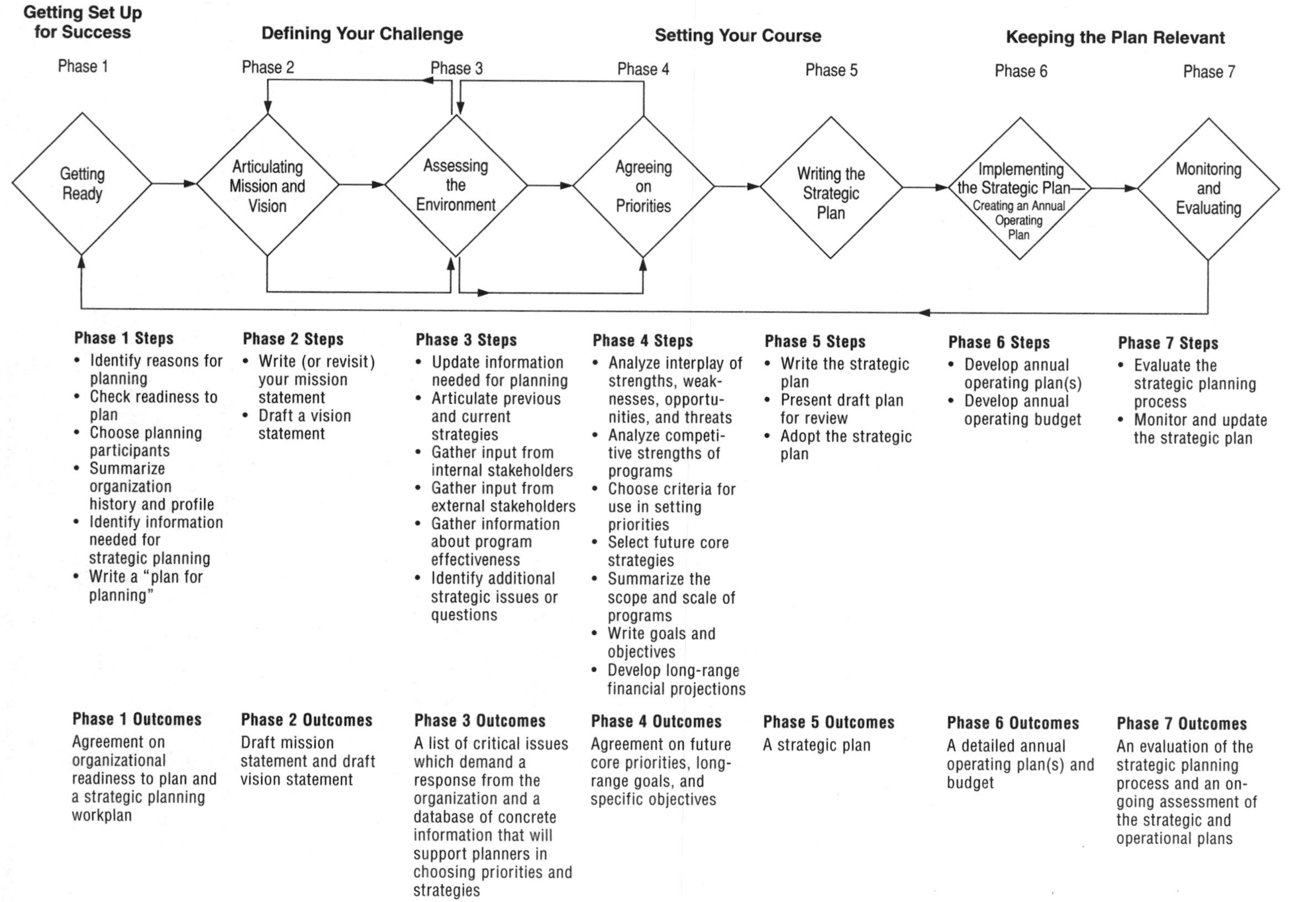

organization to the reader—and an organization's ability to articulate this indicates its focus and purpose. A mission statement typically describes an organization in these terms:

- *Purpose.* why the organization exists and what it seeks to accomplish
- *Business.* the main method or activity through which the organization works to fulfill this purpose
- *Values.* the principles or beliefs which guide an organization's members as they pursue the organization's purpose

Whereas the mission statement summarizes the what, how, and why of an organization's work, a vision statement presents an image in words of what success will look like.

"A vision is a mental model of a future state . . . built upon plausible speculations . . . reasonable assumptions about the future . . . influenced by our own judgments about what is possible and worthwhile. . . . A vision is a mental model that people and organizations can bring into being through their commitment and actions."[2]

With mission and vision statements in hand, an organization knows what it is doing, why it is doing it, and what it hopes to achieve. The next phases of the process discuss how to get the job done.

The product developed at the end of Phase 2 is a draft mission statement and a draft vision statement.

Phase 3: Assessing the Environment

Once an organization has established some clarity on why it exists, what it does, and what it hopes to achieve, it must take a clear-eyed look at its current situation. This step requires gathering up-to-date information about the organization's internal strengths and weaknesses, and its external opportunities and threats—assessments that will refine and possibly reshape the list of critical questions that the organization faces and that its strategic plan must address. These could include a variety of primary concerns, such as funding, new program opportunities, changing regulations or changing needs in the client population, and so on; the point is to choose the *most important* issues to address. Typically a Planning Committee will agree on no more than five to seven critical questions or issues around which to organize the strategic plan.

The products of Phase 3 are an understanding of the critical issues which demand a response from the organization—the most important issues the organization

[2] Burt Nanus. *Visionary Leadership* (San Francisco: Jossey-Bass, 1992).

needs to deal with—and a database of concrete information that will support planners in choosing priorities and strategies.

Phase 4: Agreeing on Priorities

Once an organization's mission has been affirmed and its critical issues identified, it is time to figure out what to do about them: the broad approaches to be taken (strategies) and the general and specific results to be sought (the long-term and short-term goals and objectives). Strategies, goals, and objectives may emerge from individual inspiration, group discussion, or formal decision-making techniques, but the bottom line is that in the end the leadership agrees on its top priorities.

This phase can take considerable time. Discussions at this stage may require additional information or a re-evaluation of conclusions reached during the environmental assessment. It is even possible that new insights will emerge which change the thrust of the mission statement. It is important that planners do not fear going back to an earlier phase in the process in order to take advantage of available information to create the best possible plan.

The *product* of Phase 4 is an outline of the organization's priorities: the general strategies, long-range goals, and specific objectives of its response to critical issues.

Phase 5: Writing the Strategic Plan

The mission has been articulated, the critical issues identified, and the strategies and goals agreed upon. This step essentially involves putting the pieces together into one coherent document. Usually one member of the Planning Committee, the Executive Director, or even a planning consultant, will draft a final plan document and then submit it for review by all key decision makers (usually the board and management staff). The reviewers should make sure that the plan answers the key questions about priorities and directions in sufficient detail to serve as a guide for the organization's members. Revisions should not be dragged out for months, but action should be taken to answer any important questions raised at this juncture. The end result will be a concise description of where the organization is going, how it should get there, and why it needs to go that way—ideas that are widely supported by the organization's staff and board.

The *product* of Phase 5 is your strategic plan!

Phase 6: Implementing the Strategic Plan

All of the work described above is for naught if it doesn't align the day-to-day work with the strategic priorities so carefully chosen. The interface between the strategic directional thinking embodied in the strategic plan and day-to-day work is a concise and easy-to-use operating plan. It should coincide with the organization's fiscal year and accommodate the need for other, more detailed program-level planning related to funding cycles or other reporting cycles.

The nature of a particular organization's operating plan will be influenced by its strategic priorities, its organizational structure, and its previous planning process. The essence of the operating plan, though, remains the same: a document which defines the short-term, concrete objectives leading to achievement of strategic goals and objectives, and which is easy to use and monitor. Ironically, the level of detail is not the deciding factor in how useful the operating plan is; the most important factors are the clarity of guidelines for implementation and the precision of results to be monitored. The operating plan should be closely tied to the operating budget.

The *products* of Phase 6 are a detailed annual operating plan and budget.

Phase 7: Monitoring and Evaluating

The strategic planning process is never really finished. There are cycles, and periods of more and less intense activity, but the process of being responsive to a changing environment is ongoing. Each organization needs to choose the appropriate length of time for planning and re-evaluating. Many nonprofits use a three-year planning cycle. The first strategic plan is completed with a three year time horizon and a one year annual operating plan. At the end of years one and two, progress toward the priorities of the strategic plan are assessed and adjusted as necessary, and a new annual operating plan is developed. During year three a renewed strategic planning process is undertaken. Depending on the extent of change in the organization's internal and external environment, the strategic planning workplan is more or less intensive. By the end of year three a new three-year plan, as well as a new annual operating plan of course, is approved and the cycle begins again.

What is important is that the planning process is ongoing and remains responsive to the changing environment. The documents are less important than the quality of the thinking and the degree of commitment to the core strategies and priorities of the organization.

If the core strategies and priorities agreed to for the future remain valid, which is not uncommon, the time frame outlined briefly above works well. On the other hand, if the environment changes in ways that are fundamentally different from the assumptions underlying the strategic plan, then it is necessary to regroup and re-strategize earlier.

The *product* of Phase 7 is a current (quarterly or annual) assessment of the ongoing validity of the decisions made during the strategic planning process.

THE LANGUAGE OF STRATEGIC PLANNING

In professions like accounting and law, the language is fairly well-defined. Every accountant knows what a debit is. Every lawyer knows what a tort is. There is no such agreement on the definitions of planning words used by planners: goals and objectives are used conversely by nonprofit organizations and the for-profit business sector; within the nonprofit sector *mission* sometimes gets used to describe the ultimate result an organization is trying to achieve, while other times the word describes an organization's primary business(es) or activities.

Is there a difference between mission and purpose? Why distinguish between external and internal vision? What is a strategy? What distinguishes goals from objectives and programs from activities? The planning process presented in this Workbook is built on the relationships between several related concepts. Because different individuals use different terminology, Exhibits 1-4 and 1-5 defines the language to help make the thinking behind this process clear and useful.

"TIGHT ON ENDS, LOOSE ON MEANS"

A successful strategic planning process supports an organization involving its stakeholders—paid and volunteer staff, board, clients, funders, and the community—in reaching consensus about what end results they are trying to achieve (external vision, purpose, goals, and objectives), and the means to accomplish those results (internal vision, business(es), programs, and activities).

An organization's strategic plan is not an end in itself, but rather a means of achieving its purpose. Tom Peters *(In Search of Excellence),* John Carver *(Boards That Make a Difference),* and many others have emphasized the need for the people implementing a strategic plan to have enough flexibility and authority to be creative and responsive to new developments—without having to reconstruct an entire strategic plan. This flexibility is required most in adjusting means. In other words, the purpose of an organization and the priority goals are much less likely to change than are the programs and activities necessary to achieve them.

For example, an organization decides it wants to achieve a particular goal and decides to set up a program to achieve that goal. If another organization has decided simultaneously to set up a similar program, the first organization may collaborate with the second organization or in some other way adjust its program plan without changing its original goal.

Peters calls this being "tight on ends," that is, building strong commitment to the purpose and goals of an organization, while allowing the people in the organization to creatively adapt their methods to best achieve the goals, or staying "loose on means."

Exhibit 1-4 The Language of Planning in the Nonprofit Sector—Focusing on Ends and Means

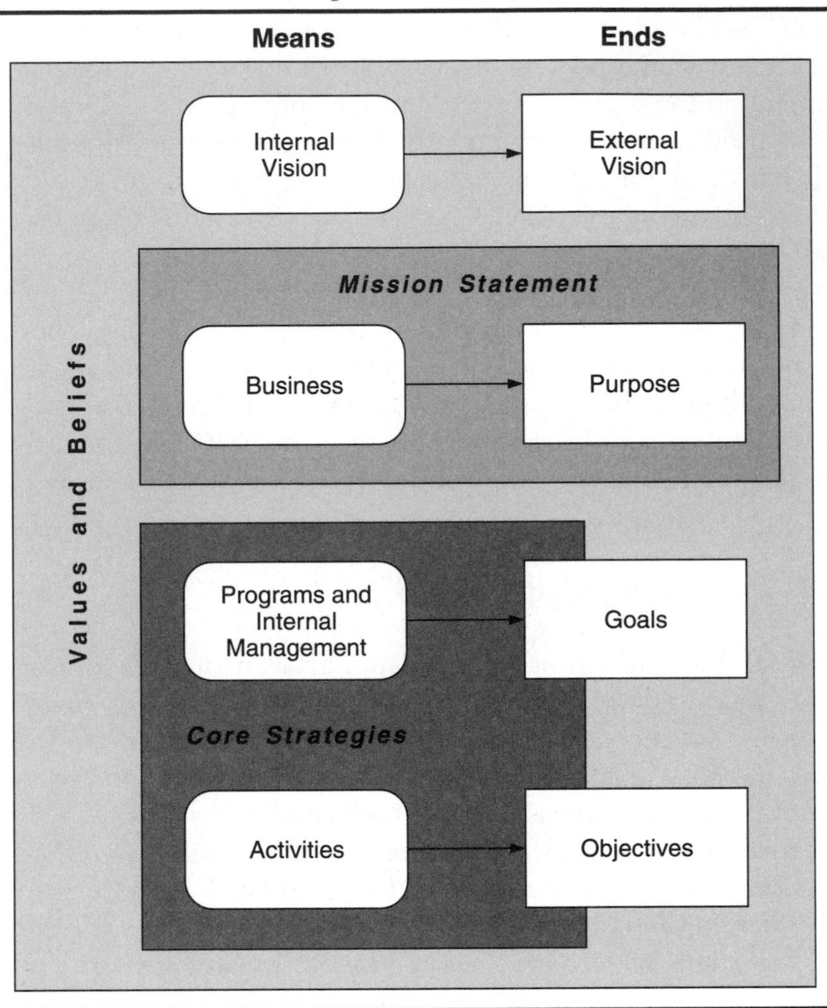

Exhibit 1-5 Definitions

Means	Ends
Internal Vision A description of the organization operating at its most effective and efficient level	**External Vision** A statement that describes how the world would be improved, changed, or different, if an organization is successful in achieving its purpose
Business The primary method(s) used by the organization to achieve its purpose	**Purpose** The ultimate result an organization is trying to achieve (Answers the question "Why does the organization exist?")
Programs and Internal Management A description of services and products that an organization offers, and the internal operations that support the delivery of services or products	**Goals** Outcome statements that define what an organization is trying to accomplish both programmatically and organizationally
Activities The specific actions required to produce services and products	**Objectives** Precise, measurable, time-phased results that support the achievement of a goal
Core Strategies Broad, overall priorities or directions adopted by an organization	

Mission Statement
A succinct statement that articulates the organization's purpose, business, values, and beliefs

Values and Beliefs
The basic, guiding principles that provide guidance and inspiration to the board and staff

C H A P T E R T W O

Getting Set Up for Success

HOW DO WE GET STARTED?

Strategic planning is a good idea in theory, but it is only a good idea in practice if the right people in an organization believe it is a good idea and the organization is ready. The initial worksheets to be used in the Getting Ready phase specify prerequisites for successful planning, as well as potential pitfalls to look out for. Chief among the prerequisites is a true commitment to the planning process by the executive director and board leadership. In other words, regardless of how much an organization needs to do some strategic planning, a sole program manager, or member of a board will not be able to initiate a planning process alone, nor see that it happens successfully; top leadership must spend significant time and energy on the process, or it will merely amount to going through the motions.

Does this mean that a lonely visionary on the staff or board has no opportunity to initiate a strategic planning process? No, but it does mean that such an individual must actively recruit support from leaders by identifying the potential benefits to the organization and helping them see the need for planning. For example, is the staff confused about how their programs relate to each other? Does the board shy away from seeking community support for the organization? Is it unclear what the organization has accomplished and how it should measure the success of its efforts? If the answer to these kinds of questions is "yes," then a compelling case for doing strategic planning can be made to the organization's

Initiating a Planning Process

A new executive director of a large multi-service community center in southern California wanted to initiate a strategic planning process because of her past successful experience in using strategic planning to help set priorities and galvanize staff and board. In addition, one of the community center's major funders had proposed partially funding such a planning process. The director hired a consultant and set up initial meetings with board and staff.

Much to her surprise, the board and staff resisted the idea of strategic planning. Some staff felt that their concerns and input had been ignored during a planning process with the previous director. The Board, on the other hand, had not seen any tangible results from the prior planning efforts, and therefore was reluctant to approve the use of resources to support any new planning.

The executive director and consultant took a step back and convened a Planning Committee of both board and staff to identify reasons for planning and a process that all could support. The group crafted a "Plan for Planning" that would make good use of input from both staff and clients. The workplan also ensured that concrete plans, and concrete measures of success, would be developed so that the Board's work of governing the organization would be aided. The revised strategic planning process resulted in the development of both strategic and operational plans that had the active support of both board and staff.

leadership. (Similarly, an enthusiastic executive director working with staff and board members who are reluctant to commit time, energy, or money to strategic planning must look for ways to understand the organization's needs from their perspective.) It's important to take the time to build board and staff commitment to the process up front, because it will pay off down the line.

Whoever initiates the strategic planning process must recognize that its success lies in getting involvement from all parts of the organization. Therefore, the executive director and board president must be committed to planning and be willing to both participate fully and invest the necessary organizational resources (time and money) to support the planning process. These two individuals, at a minimum, need to be clear on what they would like the planning process to accomplish and assess the organization's readiness to do successful planning. If it makes sense to go forward, then proceed with forming a Planning Committee and get ready to succeed!

PHASE 1: GETTING READY

Step 1.1: Decide What to Accomplish through Strategic Planning

The best place to start the process of strategic planning is to establish the context for the effort: what do we want to accomplish through strategic planning? This is not the time to do a formal evaluation of the organization as will be done later (Phase 3: Assessing the Environment). As can be seen from the actions taken by the model organization in the case study, it is simply a way to get a handle on the concerns and expectations that will inform the planning effort at the outset.

Usually, an organization considering a strategic planning process is facing one or more important issues or choices. "Are our services still relevant? Should we buy a building or should we lease more space? What do we do about a potential loss in funding? Should we close down a program, change its focus, or explore a collaborative partnership?" Sometimes the need for a plan is more vague (we don't really know where we're going), sometimes more concrete (our biggest funder is requiring a three-year plan).

The reasons for planning have a major impact on how to go about planning, who to involve and even whether or not a strategic plan is needed. The planning process notes highlighted in Exhibit 2-1 provide a framework for determining these issues. It is okay for the key issues and choices to be somewhat vague and/or overlapping; the planning process is designed to help bring clarity to the questions as well as to develop answers. But if the reasons for planning aren't important ones, the process will probably fizzle for lack of commitment. And, if the

Exhibit 2-1 Worksheet 1: Planning Process Outcomes and Issues

Process Notes	
How to do this activity	Use the Planning Process Outcomes and Issues Worksheet to • List your expectations: what success would look like at the completion of the planning process, what you hope to accomplish by the end of this process. • List some of the general or specific issues, questions, and choices that you think the planning process needs to address. • Briefly explain why the issues are of importance and what the consequences are of not responding to them. • Sort issues appropriate for strategic planning and those operational issues that need immediate attention. • Clarify whether any issues are non-negotiable.
Why do this activity	• You have to agree on "ends" (what you wish to accomplish during the planning process) before you can agree on "means" (how you will go about doing planning).
Who to involve in the process	• Executive director and board president (plus other key board and staff members if their input would be helpful).

Case Study—ASO/USA

◆ **Worksheet 1** **Planning Process Outcomes and Issues**	☐ What does your organization wish to achieve from a planning process? ☐ What issues or choices do you think need to be addressed? ☐ Are there any non-negotiables or constraints that need to be articulated up front?

What would success look like at the completion of the planning process? What does your organization wish to achieve from a planning process?

- *A 3-year plan and vision*
- *Get everyone on the "same page," get Board involved with fund-raising*
- *Solve the internal struggle over the outreach program*

What are the issues facing your organization? What questions need to be answered during the planning process?

Issue	Why is it an issue? What are the consequences of not responding?	Check (√) whether the issue is strategic or operational Strategic	Operational
1. *Overdependence on federal funding*	• *Concern that we could bankrupt quickly if funding priorities shift* • *We could get caught unprepared*	√	
2. *Medical advances in AIDS treatment are challenging us to change our services and our prevention efforts*	• *The new treatments are causing a lot of confusion* • *We could get left behind*	√	
3. *Collaboration on the outreach program is problematic*	• *Not producing the results we'd hoped* • *Funder and community are getting upset about program*	√	√
4. *Financial management is a mess*	• *We don't have the right staff* • *We don't have good information about income and expenses, and it is becoming a problem for us with our funders*		√

Are there any questions which are non-negotiable (not up for discussion)?

It is a given that we will focus on prevention and care.

goals for planning aren't clear in the beginning, it will be hard at the end to determine if the process was successful!

Once these issues and questions are drafted, it is important to make sure that strategic planning is the appropriate way to deal with them. A pressing need to hire a new executive director, respond to a request for proposals, or address a cash short-fall may well have strategic implications, but the urgency of the decisions requires immediate executive action by the board and/or senior staff. Therefore, it is necessary to sort the issues into (1) *strategic issues,* questions that have a longer range focus (1 to 3 years) and are more geared to fundamental questions regarding organizational ability to meet the needs of the community, (2) *operational issues,* the questions that are primarily shorter-term (less than 1 year) in focus and implementation oriented, and (3) *crisis situations,* whether strategic or operational, which have to do with the immediate survival of the organization.

Both strategic issues and operational issues are important and will need to be addressed by the organization. However, separating them out can help determine whether certain operational issues need to be addressed before serious attention can be paid to the strategic issues (or whether they can be handled concurrently). Any crisis situation will have to be brought under control before beginning a strategic planning process.

Finally, if there are certain decisions that are not up for discussion, then those issues or decisions should be put on the table at the beginning of the planning process as non-negotiable. The non-negotiable issues may be program-oriented ("we are not going to expand our geographic boundaries") or business-oriented ("any new program effort must be revenue-generating"). Articulating non-negotiable issues up front will help avoid wasting people's time or setting them up for unrealistic expectations about what they can and can't change. (Please review case study on page xxi.)

Step 1.2: Check Your Readiness to Plan

As with any major effort, a strategic planning process has its proper time and place in the life of the organization. Certain conditions must exist (and others must not) if strategic planning is to be a creative, collaborative, successful endeavor—so it is important to be honest when analyzing an organization's readiness to plan. It is not uncommon for a planning process to be initiated before an organization is truly ready to meet the challenges and demands of the job. When an organization initiates a planning process before being ready and able to do so, that organization may either go through an inadequate process and arrive at unsatisfactory results, or have the planning process stall abruptly or stop completely.

In thinking through the conditions that encourage an effective planning process, the two most important components are committed leadership and sufficient information. However, there are several other important criteria to consider in determining readiness. The following two check lists, conditions for success and pitfalls to avoid, together form the readiness assessment.[1]

Conditions for Success. An organization should make sure the following conditions are present before deciding to initiate a strategic planning endeavor:

- Commitment and support from top leadership, especially the executive director and board president, throughout the entire process
- Commitment to clarifying roles and expectations for all participants in the planning process, including clarity as to who will contribute input to the plan and who will make final decisions
- Commitment to gather and use relevant information for assessing current programs and evaluating how to meet current and future client needs—sufficient market research
- At least one visionary and at least one "actionary" (someone focused on making sure that the projected goals and objectives are realistic) who are willing to actively participate on the Planning Committee
- Willingness to be inclusive and encourage broad participation, so that people feel "ownership" and are energized by the process
- An adequate commitment of organizational resources to complete the planning process as designed, for example, staff time, board time, dollars, and so on
- A board and staff that understands the purpose of planning, realizes what it is and is not able to accomplish, and has consensus about the desired outcomes of the planning process
- A willingness to question the status quo, to look at new ways of doing things; a willingness to ask the hard questions, face difficult choices, and make decisions that are best for clients
- Good working relationships and no serious conflicts between key players

These are the conditions that an organization ideally should have in place before committing to a strategic planning process; equally important are the pitfalls to be avoided when considering a planning effort.

Pitfalls to Be Avoided

- Top management's assumption that it can completely delegate the planning function to other staff or a planning consultant and not remain actively involved

[1] Adapted from George Steiner. *Strategic Planning* (New York: The Free Press, 1979), pp. 290–293.

- Executive director, senior managers, and the board so engrossed in current problems (such as a financial crisis or other extreme circumstance) that they have neither the time nor the energy to look far enough ahead to plan for the future
- Top management's tendency to reject the decisions made during the planning process in favor of its own intuitive decisions
- Board or executive director's unwillingness to involve line staff, management staff, and board in the planning process
- Failure of the board and executive director to articulate constraints and non-negotiables up front
- Reluctance to create a realistic strategic plan that will provide guidance to current operational decisions
- Lack of an organizational climate that inspires forward thinking and rewards creativity and strategic thinking

In addition to assessing current circumstances, it is useful to assess past efforts at planning and apply any lessons learned. Clues to the presence or absence of conditions for success and/or the likelihood of pitfalls can be found in the examination of past planning efforts. If an organization's previous planning processes were successful, then it will want to try to duplicate that success by using similar processes this time around. If prior planning efforts have not worked well, or if the plans that resulted from prior efforts were not followed, then an organization needs to spend some time figuring out why this is so and what changes might benefit future planning efforts. The process notes in Exhibit 2-2 and the Case Study will provide guidelines for conducting this exercise.

What if We Don't Pass the Readiness Assessment? If any of the conditions for success above are missing, or if any of the pitfalls are likely, then an in-depth strategic planning process may *not* be appropriate at this time. Even if an organization is halfway through the planning process before realizing that it isn't really ready to plan, it should stop right there and reassess how to proceed. Consider the following situations:

- "Fall is our busiest time of the year; we should wait until spring." This is easy: wait.
- "We won't know what is going to happen to our most important funder (competitor, constituency, customer base, etc.) until 'X' happens next year." In this case, program planning for the coming year is appropriate, but a longer-range plan will be difficult to create without serious work on contingency planning.

- If the lack of readiness has to do with the lack of commitment to planning, lack of commitment to inclusiveness, or lack of willingness to consider new possibilities, the situation is more difficult. Sometimes it is possible to influence the individuals in question regarding their orientation to strategic planning. However, sometimes it just doesn't make sense to do strategic planning until the players change. An executive director might wait until after the next board election, a board might have to assess whether lack of leadership by an executive director in this area is enough of a problem to find a new executive director. Clearly, in these situations the readiness assessment is a judgment call, as is the decision about how to respond to a suspected lack of readiness.
- If current problems exist that might interfere with the ability of top leadership to focus on the future, then either delay the strategic planning process or choose an abbreviated planning process instead. Alternatively, there could be two parallel planning processes taking place, one that addresses the immediate issues and one that focuses on the larger, strategic issues.

In most cases, though, the readiness assessment serves as a guide to *potential* problems in the process. The value in discussing the readiness criteria lies in

Exhibit 2-2 Worksheet 2: Check Your Readiness to Plan

Process Notes	
How to do this activity	• Before embarking on a strategic planning process, make sure the conditions for successful planning are in place and pitfalls can be avoided. Check "yes" or "no" in the Conditions and Pitfalls checklists. Explain any negative responses. • Review past planning documents and talk to participants of prior planning processes at your organization. Describe what has worked or not worked in the past. • Decide whether to proceed with planning: "Go" or "No Go." If significant barriers exist that might impede the process, deal with those barriers before continuing.
Why do this activity	• Helps you decide whether you are ready to embark on a planning process.
Who to involve in the process	• Executive director and board president (plus other key board and staff members if their input would be helpful).

Case Study—ASO/USA

♦ **Worksheet 2** **Check Your Readiness to Plan**	☐ Assess your organizational readiness: • What crtieria for successful planning are in place? • Which pitfalls can be avoided? • What can you learn from your prior experience with planning? ☐ Answer the question: • Are you ready to plan? Go or No Go

The Following Criteria for Successful Planning Are in Place

Yes	No	Criteria
√		1. Commitment and support from top leadership, especially the executive director and board president, throughout the entire process
√		2. Commitment to clarifying roles and expectations for all participants in the planning process, including clarity as to who will contribute to the plan and who will be the decision makers
√		3. Willingness to understand and respond to the organization's internal and external environment (strengths, weaknesses, opportunities, and threats); a commitment to gathering relevant information for assessing current programs and evaluating how to meet current and future client needs—sufficient market research
√		4. At least one strategic thinker and at least one actionary (someone to make sure the projected goals and objectives are realistic) who are willing to be active participants on the Planning Committee
	?	5. Willingness to be inclusive and encourage broad participation, so that people feel "ownership" of and are energized by the process
√		6. An adequate commitment of organizational resources to complete the planning process as designed, for example, staff time, board time, dollars spent on the process (for market research, consultants, etc.), and so on
	?	7. A board and staff that understands the purpose of planning, realizes what it is and is not able to accomplish, and has consensus about the desired outcomes of the planning process
	?	8. A willingness to question the status quo, to look at new ways of doing things; a willingness to ask the hard questions, face difficult choices, and make decisions that are best for the clients
√		9. Good working relationships and no serious conflicts between key players

Comments to explain and respond to "No" or "Questions" answered:

5. Not sure all board members are committed to an inclusive process

7. Don't yet have consensus between staff and board about process

8. Have some "old timers" on the board—not sure how open to change they really are

(Continued)

Worksheet 2 *(Continued)*

The Following Pitfalls Can Be Avoided:

Yes	No	Pitfalls That Can Be Avoided
√		10. Top management's assumption that it can completely delegate the planning function to a planner and not remain actively involved
√		11. Executive Director and Board President so engrossed in current problems (such as a financial crisis or other extreme circumstance) that they have neither the time, nor the leeway, to look far enough ahead, to plan for the future
√		12. Top management's tendency to reject the decisions made during the planning process in favor of its own intuitive decisions
√		13. Board or Executive Director's unwillingness to involve line staff, management staff, and Board in the planning process
	?	14. Failure of the Board and top management to articulate constraints and non-negotiables up front
√		15. Reluctance to create a realistic strategic plan that will provide guidance to current operational decisions
√		16. Lack of an organizational climate that inspires forward thinking and rewards creativity

Comments to explain and respond to "No" (pitfalls cannot be avoided) or "Questions" answered:

14. Concern that board will not be clear up front about any concerns

Prior Experience Doing Planning: What Has Worked? What Hasn't Worked? Why?

- *Program planning by staff has worked okay*
- *Board retreats generally get low turnout*

Other Issues:

- *Board involvement must be focused into relatively limited time blocks*
- *Management wants board to look at its role as part of planning*
- *Have to have clarity about Outreach Program*

Organizational Readiness: Go or No Go?

Go

Barriers to Planning in Government Agencies

Government agencies have built-in obstacles to effective planning. Some of the obstacles are similar to those found in any large institution: entrenched bureaucratic procedures; dense and complex decision-making processes; the challenge of involving large numbers of staff in order to foster staff participation in planning; and the logistical difficulties of uniformly implementing a plan over time.

In addition, however, government has inherent practices, values, and structures that make long-term strategic planning particularly difficult.

- *The Political Arena.* All organizations operate in some form of political context. Government programs, however, are especially affected by the electoral process. Partisan politics drive the timing and types of policy-making in government. And, since policy drives strategic planning—in terms of an organization's identity, philosophy, values, and method of operation—then it is clear that strategic planning in government must reflect policy that has a political base. When partisan politics change, so too may an agency's policies and plans. The greater the visibility factor in the political environment, the more difficult it is to plan and execute for the long term because of the varying concerns (philosophies and values) of both the elected body and the stakeholders outside the agency.
- *The Decision-Making Process.* Two factors make decision-making in government programs difficult. First, the uncertainties of the election process make it difficult to commit to strategies which will take longer to implement than the length of an election cycle. Second, where policies are defined by statute, the flexibility of program-level decision-makers is strictly bounded. This makes it difficult to be responsive to changes in the environment.
- *Leadership.* The highest level of management in government is elected. It is not uncommon for newly elected officials to have no working knowledge of a government agency's purpose and programs, or for their views of what an agency should do to differ from those of agency staff. Elected officials may set policy, both administratively and through legislation, without involving the agency in planning for any changes. Obviously, agencies strive to continually educate elected officials about their activities in an effort to improve the quality of decisions that will come their way.

Despite these obstacles, agencies at all levels of government do strategic planning and many of them do it well. One government agency was able to overcome some of the barriers by adopting and implementing a planning process that incorporated the following planning principles:

- Top management shall exert strong leadership in valuing and committing to a planning effort.
- Management will participate in and support planning efforts with adequate time, budget, and staffing.
- Adequate background work or research will be done to include client or constituent needs, as well as a record of the public's use of agency services.
- The planning effort must be inclusive of staff in some form that is both informative and meaningful to both staff and management.
- A good strategic plan must define the agency, clearly indicate goals and objectives, lay out a range of activities that meet the agency's mission, and benchmark success.

- A good strategic plan must be used and results measured against the benchmarks.
- Our agency must update and/or renew its planning efforts annually.

During this agency's initial "getting ready" meeting, staff identified the following benefits of engaging in a strategic planning effort:

- Effective planning that targets and achieves results can build a base of support with constituencies outside of the agency, who in turn can advocate for continuation of services, assuming that the constituents' needs are being addressed. The more our agency tracks client response and need and uses that information to build its programs, the greater the likelihood that elected officials, regardless of which party is in office, will have a reason to continue to support our plans. The more public our agency makes its plan and the more it involves client participation, the more client satisfaction will be realized in the long run.
- A good strategic plan can help staff keep focused, productive, and in good spirits during times of political uncertainty. Planning can enhance morale, hone staff skills, and maintain program credibility with the public.
- The more effectively our agency plans, the more credibility it has with its top management, particularly in the sensitive environment of new management under a new administration. A good plan gives guidance to newly elected officials and appointees, which in turn minimizes reasons for introducing change that may seem arbitrary or even destructive.

---

focusing a prospective planning group's discussion around the commitment and concerns of its members, developing a planning process that addresses those concerns and setting the planning process up to be successful.

Step 1.3: Choose the Participants for Your Planning Process

Strategic planning should be an inclusive effort that engages key stakeholders at appropriate stages. Who are stakeholders? A stakeholder is simply defined as anyone who cares, or should care, about the organization—anyone who has a "stake" in the success of its mission. This encompasses those who must implement the strategic plan, those who benefit from its implementation, and those who could significantly help or hinder its implementation. Internal stakeholders include board members and staff (part-time and full-time, salaried personnel, and volunteer staff). External stakeholders include clients (existing, past, potential), previous staff and board members, funders (existing, potential), community leaders, competitors, potential collaborators, and other agencies in parallel or related fields.

Part of the thoughtfulness and creativity of the strategic planning process is identifying those individuals and groups who traditionally might not be regarded as key stakeholders. This might include those who could contribute unique and valuable perspectives (not to mention those who should be included because of other substantive or political reasons). A truly inclusive process can accomplish the following:

- Help build internal and external enthusiasm for and commitment to the organization and its strategies—those who feel they have contributed to the planning process then feel invested in it and are more likely to take ownership of the organization's goals and efforts
- Add objectivity to the process—outsiders can identify jargon or ask critical questions about issues that insiders might assume common knowledge of or simply take for granted
- Develop foundations for future working relationships
- Establish a continual information exchange among staff, management, clients, and other key stakeholders
- Ensure an adequate depth and breadth of data from which to make informed decisions

Stakeholders' Roles in Planning. Determining how to include all these stakeholders can prove trickier than identifying who they are, for there are many different kinds and levels of participation in the planning process:

- Leadership: taking the initiative to see that decisions get made and things get done
- Facilitation: paying attention to the process rather than content (a role played, for example, by an outside consultant or neutral participant)
- Input: providing information and opinions
- Decision-making: deciding on strategies, goals, objectives, etc.

It is especially important to delineate between those stakeholders who provide input and those who make decisions. Being asked an opinion is not necessarily the same as having a final say in related decisions, but stakeholders sometimes lose sight of that distinction. It is the responsibility of those who do make the decisions to let participants who provide input know what was done with their information and the rationale for decisions that were made.

The nature of stakeholders' participation will depend on any number of factors—an organization's size, culture and management style, range of constituents, breadth of services, and so on—but below are some general understandings of specific stakeholders' roles in the strategic planning process.

Internal stakeholders include:

- *Executive Director.* The executive director (Chief Executive Officer or CEO) is usually the chief planner and prime "mover" of the plan through the entire process. Even if he or she is managing the planning process, the executive director works closely with the chair of the Planning Committee and often serves as the prime liaison between the staff and the Planning Committee. Sometimes the executive director writes the plan, but larger organizations may delegate that responsibility to someone else. Finally, the executive director plays the crucial role of being ultimately responsible for the implementation of the plan.

- *Board of Directors.* Strategic planning is at the intersection of governance (the board's role) and management (the staff's role). Both the board and the staff have different contributions to make and perspectives to bring to the process: the staff know individual clients' needs, understand day-to-day operations and other service providers, but may not always be willing or able to think "big picture" or long-term. The board, in its governance capacity, has the responsibility to think about what is of importance for the entire community and not just one particular client. The board has within its governance role the responsibility to practice what Harvard Professor Regina Herzlinger has referred to as "intergenerational equity," that is, the needs of both current and future clients are responded to within the strategic plan. The board must make sure that the plan's goals are consistent with resources and that the organization is sustainable.[2]

  The board should make sure an effective planning process is in place, contribute its perspective on the organization's strengths, weaknesses, opportunities, and threats, and work with staff to reach consensus on overall program and administrative priorities. The board should provide input into the organization's mission statement and approve any changes that need to be made. The board, either as a whole or through their representation on a Strategic Planning Committee, should be involved in strategy discussions, setting long-term program and administrative priorities, and setting goals for the board itself. The Board can help gain access to external stakeholders so as to gather their perceptions.

  The board needs to be kept informed throughout the planning process, not just at the end when they are presented with the final planning document. It is important for the Chair of the Planning Committee to keep the entire board involved and informed through reports at board meetings.

- *Staff.* Paid and volunteer staff have programmatic expertise and familiarity with the field and clients which are vital to shaping a relevant and workable strategic plan. Their involvement not only ensures "buy-in" to

[2] Regina Herzlinger. "Effective Oversight: A Guide for Nonprofit Directors." *Harvard Business Review,* July–August 1994, pp. 52–60.

Board of Directors' Participation in a Planning Retreat

"The process of holding an annual planning retreat has benefits far beyond even the significant advantage of giving a clear idea of where you're going. For instance, the very nature of the session provides the [board] with a common grasp of existing commitments and resources . . . and [their participation will help them] feel a commitment to the goals for the year. . . . Planning retreats are not easy sessions; properly organized, they should be designed to decide what *not* to attempt to accomplish or what should be assigned a low priority. . . . "

Source: *Brian O'Connell.* The Board Member's Book *(New York: The Foundation Center, 1985), p. 79.*

the organizational goals and strategies, but is also the link between the plan's vision and the realization of that vision on a day-to-day basis. As such, staff should be involved in identifying current and future client needs and able to give their perceptions regarding the organization's strengths, weaknesses, opportunities, and threats, and possible short-term and long-term program and administrative priorities.

Staff might also be asked to collect data (do market research) and evaluate programs. Program managers should have significant input into setting long-term program objectives and assist in the development and monitoring of operational plans. Ideally, staff should be represented on the Planning Committee.

External stakeholders include:

- *Clients.* The sole reason for most nonprofits' existence is the betterment of society, whether that means providing a top-notch and well rounded education, enriching cultural life, feeding the hungry, providing quality health care, or protecting the freedom of individuals. In a planning process, then, it is critical to evaluate what kind of job the organization is and should be doing in this regard. Directly involving past and present clients (and perhaps future clients) in the planning process, and soliciting their unique first-hand experience of the organization, is one of the best ways to gain such insight into the organization's performance and guidance for future services. Some organizations include client representatives on the Planning Committee.
- *Funders.* Past, current, and potential funders provide another valuable perspective on client needs and how others in the community are either meeting or failing to meet those needs. They may be able to shed some light on the funder community's inclination to fund a specific new program; likewise, discussions with funders might enable an organization to design "fundability" into a program at the outset. Funders' input should be sought

primarily during the assessing the environment phase of the planning process; current and prospective funders should also receive an executive summary of the strategic plan.

- *Previous staff and board members.* Staff who were previously employed with the organization or board members who had prior participation on the board, can offer a historical perspective that can be helpful in informing the future choices facing the organization. As such, their input might be sought regarding the organization's strengths, weaknesses, client needs, the external environment, and possible future program and administrative priorities.
- *Community leaders.* Community leaders, including political officials, can also offer a valuable opinion of an organization's strengths and weaknesses, as well as insight into the needs of the community and knowledge of the competition. Their buy-in and support may be needed to secure funding and other forms of support; therefore, their input is valuable. Some organizations include a key community leader on the Planning Committee, thereby building in community commitment to the organization and its mission.
- *Competitors and potential collaborators.* Competitors (those who compete for funding as well as those who compete for clients or other customers) might also be approached to contribute to an organization's assessment of its environment—not just to get another outside opinion, but also to garner information to help the organization to be more competitive or to develop collaborative relationships.
- *Other agencies in parallel or related fields.* When individuals from related fields are involved in an organization's planning process, their knowledge and experience can be leveraged not only for the benefit of the clients being served, but can help foster cooperation and decrease unnecessary competition.

Participation: Top-Down, Bottom-Up, or Hybrid Planning. A basic influence on the nature of stakeholder participation will be whether an organization uses a top-down or bottom-up planning process. A top-down process assumes that those with the highest level of responsibility in an organization are in the best position to be "big picture" thinkers and plan what is best for the organization; the main drawback to this approach is that it often results in plans that do not have the understanding and support of line staff (those most directly involved in providing services to clients), and the plan may not prove feasible or in the best interests of the clients. A bottom-up planning process, on the other hand, compiles plans from individual staff members or departments, thereby addressing the need for staff input and investment. Such a process, however, can produce a patchwork plan that lacks coherence for the organization as a whole and results in an uncoordinated, even wasteful, use of resources.

In assessing top-down or bottom-up planning and involving outside stakeholders, the organization will need to decide what perspectives need to be heard and how important it is to involve those individuals whose opinions are not usually sought, but whose perspective is valuable. Including these stakeholders may slow down the process, but in the end will make for a better plan. If the organization is community-based, it will especially need to have more involvement and representation from that community.

For most organizations, the best approach seems to be a hybrid that strikes a balance between the need for decisive leadership and productive collaboration, featuring the open communication of a bottom-up planning process as well as the clear coordination of a top-down process. The net result is an effective combination of the best of both models of participation; the planning process described in this Workbook is such a hybrid.

The Planning Committee. The authors of this Workbook recommend the use of a Planning Committee. An effective committee can ensure appropriate involvement, perspective in weighing issues, and add credibility to the process. The Planning Committee spearheads the planning process—which means that committee members are not responsible for doing all of the work, but they are responsible for ensuring that the work gets done. Basically, the Planning Committee is the quarterback for the strategic planning effort, deciding which stakeholders to involve and how to involve them, coordinating and making assignments to staff or board, providing linkages and liaison with constituencies, and prioritizing or narrowing information for the organization to discuss and evaluate. In addition, the Planning Committee will normally discuss some of the strategic issues, make recommendations regarding strategies and priorities, create initial drafts of planning documents for approval by the board, and so on. The Planning Committee should:

- Consist of approximately 6–10 individuals (could be larger if need exists to include broader representation of stakeholders; however, too large a committee (more than 15) may make it more difficult to coordinate meetings and have discussions)
- Be a combination of visionaries (people who see what the organization can be and can rally the organization around that vision) and actionaries (people who will ensure that the projected goals and tasks are realistic)
- Be a group that has informal power and the respect of the entire organization
- Be a diverse group of stakeholders who are committed to a vision for the common good, rather than just advocating for the particular population they represent

- Be a combination of board and staff members, including the executive director, Board president, and whoever has responsibility for writing the final planning document

The Planning Committee is typically selected by the executive director and the board president. The committee should be convened once a decision to go ahead has been reached. At the first meeting of the Planning Committee, their responsibilities should be delineated and any milestones or deadlines confirmed. The Planning Committee should state the principles and values that will broadly govern the strategic planning effort.

Planning principles and values serve as a framework for assessing the integrity and responsibility of the planning process. Some typical planning process principles and values may include:

- *Inclusiveness.* Input will be sought from all levels within the organization
- *Meaningful participation.* Staff should feel that their participation is substantive with the potential for real influence on the outcome of the plan; if an individual is expected to implement a strategy, that individual should participate in shaping that strategy
- *Share the work.* The successful completion of the planning process should not depend on one or two people
- *Focus on the "big picture."* There should be no expectation that every concern or complaint will be addressed by the strategic planning process. We will, however, address all critical issues, regardless of how difficult those issues may be
- *Ownership.* We will seek to develop deep ownership of our mission, vision, critical issues, and corporate strategies
- *Strategy.* Our strategies should be responsive to the environment and based on our understanding of the probable future environment. Much of this understanding will come from in-depth market research
- *Set benchmarks.* Our strategic plan must be used and results measured against set benchmarks; we must update and renew our planning efforts annually

Finally, everyone involved in the planning process should have a basic understanding of strategic planning, what it can and cannot accomplish, and an overview of the language of planning. All members of the Planning Committee must talk the same planning language. As stated previously, words such as purpose, mission, business, strategy, strategic, goal, objective, vision, and long-range have different meanings to different people and even the nonprofit and for-profit sectors sometimes use these terms in different ways. Committee members should be given some training material on the language and process of planning, perhaps a copy of Chapter 1 of this Workbook. At the first meeting, the Committee should agree on the definitions they will use for such words as "purpose," "business," "mission statement," "strategy," "goal," and "objective." The process notes in Exhibit 2-3 highlight the roles and responsibilities of the Planning Committee. The board as a whole, and staff, should also be given a presentation on the strategic planning process and understand the extent of their involvement.

Exhibit 2-3 Worksheet 3: Participation in the Planning Process

Process Notes	
How to do this activity	• The Executive Director and Board President (and others if applicable) usually will select the Planning Committee members, making sure that appropriate key stakeholders are represented, and select a Planning Committee Chair. • At the first meeting of the Planning Committee, identify all the people who are considered stakeholders, and decide whether each stakeholder should have input, lead the activity, and/or be a final decision-maker. • Review the Committee's primary responsibilities, planning principles, milestones and/or deadlines. Brainstorm and get consensus on the principles and values that will be followed during the planning process. • If an outside consultant has been hired to work with the Planning Committee, delineate the consultant's responsibilities from those of the Chair and the Committee.
Why do this activity	• Helps ensure that you have included the right players in the process and have done so appropriately; involvement of stakeholders increases the knowledge base and commitment to the plan. • Provides data for making sure that your Planning Committee has the right membership, and is clear on its responsibilities and commitments.
Who to involve in the process	• Initially, Executive Director and Board President. Process to be expanded to include entire Planning Committee.

Case Study—ASO/USA

♦ **Worksheet 3** **Participation in the Planning Process**	☐ Create a Planning Committee and clarify its mandates. ☐ Identify who to involve in the planning process.

Planning Committee Responsibilities:

- *Lead the planning process to a successful conclusion*
- *Ensure all stakeholders' perspectives are heard in the process*

Milestones and Deadlines:

- *By June, we need to decide whether to renew our joint program to conduct the outreach program*
- *Budget planning starts in October; we want to have the plan done by September*

Planning Principles and Values (e.g., the planning process is as important as the plan itself):

After lengthy discussion with participating board members!

- Inclusiveness: *input will be sought from all levels of the organization as well as from external stakeholders*
- Share the work: *this planning process cannot succeed if it depends on only one or two people*
- Focus on the big picture
- Ownership*: we want to develop a plan that has the buy-in of all*
- Strategy: *we will be strategic and responsive to our changing environment*

Chair of the Planning Committee:
Sam Green, Board President

Who Will Write the Plan:
Ken Brown, Executive Director, and Delores Molina, Program Director

Planning Committee Membership:

Name	Representing what key stakeholder
Sam Green	*Board*
Juan Hernandez	*Board, former client*
Tom Washington	*Board*
Ken Brown	*Executive Director, management*
Delores Molina	*Program Director, management*
Jon Nguyen	*Outreach Coordinator, line staff*
Lori Smith	*Volunteer Representative*

Who Should Be Involved in the Planning Process? (Circle all those who should have some involvement)

(Board of Directors) (Executive Director) (Management Team) (Line Staff)

(Volunteers) (Current Clients) (Past Clients) (Donors) (Funders)

Other: *City Clinic* Other: *Department of Public Health—AIDS Office*

Role of Outside Consultants. Many organizations include an outside consultant in part or all of the planning process. For example, it is quite common to have a consultant facilitate retreats and meetings, serving as a "conversation traffic cop" so that good ideas do not get lost among the emotions or personalities of the participants. A consultant can also provide objectivity by asking clarifying questions, challenging assumptions, encouraging the group to question the status quo, and seeing that organizational jargon is kept to a minimum. Organizations can also look to consultants for information or training on planning language, tools, and processes.

When working with consultants, it is important to clearly define the scope of the project identify the benefits expected for each party, agree on responsibilities and mechanisms for accountability. The relationship must be one you can depend on.

Different situations allow for different ways to involve consultants. The following are some examples of how consultants can help strategic planning efforts:

- *Facilitator.* Consultants often help facilitate discussions between the members of a planning committee, freeing the participants from having to focus on the process of their interaction. A consultant in this role can break the ice on difficult topics, ensure that all viewpoints are heard, encourage accountability, and keep things moving and focused.
- *Researcher.* An organization doing strategic planning might ask a consultant to do research or analysis that is either unfamiliar, too time-consuming for staff, or is best done by an outsider. For example, a planning process with a heavy emphasis on fund-raising may have a consultant research funding prospects, while a process focused on program development may ask a consultant to conduct focus groups among clients.
- *Extra pair of hands.* In some cases, a consultant can be useful carrying out tasks that the organization staff and board members simply don't have time to do. Examples include writing grant proposals, investigating sites for program events, writing publicity materials, and writing up notes from group meetings.
- *A neutral set of eyes.* In some cases, groups can spend all their time on conflicts real or imagined, or on the other hand, be overly polite and avoid dealing with important differences or conflicts. A consultant can serve groups by bringing an objective, neutral perspective to the mix, going beyond the facilitative role to offer input into the discussions and helping to manage conflict.
- *Expert.* An organization may find it helpful to have an expert "on retainer," or brought in to advise on a particular topic. For example, a managed care consultant can help an organization assess its ability to compete for service

contracts with HMOs, or a fund-raising consultant can help an organization develop a development strategy.

When hiring consultants, consider the following tips:

- Interview at least two consultants. You'll be able to explore different approaches to the project and may find yourselves utilizing the ideas of more than one consultant.
- For substantial projects, ask for references and a written price bid from each consultant interviewed.
- Agree on one person to whom the consultant will report. The consultant will get confused if different people are asking for different things.
- Have a written memorandum of understanding (MOU) or contract with the consultant, with payments based on the consultant's performance of agreed tasks.
- Throughout the project, give the consultant feedback about his or her work.
- Don't expect a consultant to make tough decisions or value-based choices for you. A consultant can help articulate alternative courses of action and the implications of various choices, but the organization's decision-makers should make the decisions themselves.
- Agree in advance on how you will pay the consultant's fees, including any overruns.

Step 1.4: Summarize the Organization's History and Profile

Part of the context for an organization's strategic planning effort is the organization's history: where it came from, how it arrived where it is today, and what lessons from history are either the keys to stability and growth or causes for organizational instability. The Planning Committee should have a common understanding of this historical context so that all committee members are building the plan on the same foundation and the lessons from history can be incorporated into everyone's thinking. Therefore, as part of Getting Ready for strategic planning, an organizational history and organizational profile should be prepared. The history is simply a brief summary of the events that have shaped the organization; for example, when the organization started, a timeline that shows when programs were first offered, milestones reached in the organization, important events in the organization's history, and shifts in priorities, as well as significant external events that affected the organization's course.

An organizational profile should also be prepared. (The process notes can be found in Exhibit 2-4.) The organizational profile is a summary of all the organization's current programs and related infrastructure. This can be accomplished in three basic steps (which might be accomplished even more quickly by using documents that already present this information, such as annual reports or brochures):

1. List all specific program activities and services (for example, counseling and support, housing, information and referral, speaking engagements at corporations, public policy updates, and so on). Note current levels of activity and scale of current programs (including production data such as

Exhibit 2-4 Worksheet 4: Organizational Profile

Process Notes

How to do this activity	• Summarize the organization's history using a timeline format. • List and group all program activities into broad program groupings (goals). Describe current scope and scale of services. Add related management and operations data (infrastructure). • Take advantage of any documents that already explain the organizational profile, such as annual reports or brochures. • This information should be distributed to all members of the Planning Committee at the first or second meeting. • After the information has been reviewed, Board and staff should identify lessons from history: keys to stability and growth and recurring themes that show causes for instability.
Why do this activity	• Helps ensure that all members of the Planning Committee are operating from the same knowledge base about the organization. • Organizes and presents programs for discussion of mission statement.
Who to involve in the process	• Individual or individuals who have in-depth knowledge of the organization's programs and history. Alternatively, to construct a group member history timeline, have attendees at an initial planning retreat reconstruct the organization's history using chart paper hung on the wall. • Both Board and staff should have the opportunity to review the lessons from history—the keys and obstacles to stability and growth.

Case Study—ASO/USA

◆ Worksheet 4

Organizational History and Profile

- ☐ Summarize your organization's history and identify lessons from your history.
- ☐ Describe your programs and related infrastructure.

Presentation of Organization's History

Timeline	1980	1989	1990	1991	1992	1993	1994	1995	1996	1997	1998	1999	2000

List Key Organizational Events and Shifts in Priorities (use the timeline to place in chronological order)

- *Organizing committee formed, Ken Brown hired*
- *ASO/USA incorporated*
- *1st federal grant (for prevention work)*
- *City funding begins (expansion of support services)*
- *Moved to current office*
- *World AIDS Day—city-wide event—big success*
- *Outreach program begun*

List External Events Impacting the Organization (use the timeline to place in chronological order)

- *Bush elected*
- *National study shows high rates of new infections among people of color and IV drug users*
- *Increasing numbers of homeless people in Ourtown*
- *Clinton elected*
- *Scare with change in Congress, that federal funding would be cut (it wasn't)*
- *New drug treatments become widely available*

Lessons from History: Keys to Stability and Growth	Lessons from History: Recurring Themes That Show Causes for Instability
• *Consistent leadership of executive director* • *Steady support from federal and city funders* • *Excellent volunteer program and community support*	• *Financial management has always lagged behind the complexity and volume of work* • *Board has been an inconsistent presence for the past few years*

List all programs, projects, and services (and note their current scope and scale of service)	Group the activities into categories (sort by common outcome; write program goal for each grouping)	Note any related management and operations data (infrastructure data such as number of staff, number of board members, breakdown of revenue and expenses, etc.)
• *Public Education: 6 staff work with about 15 volunteers to educate the public about the risks of HIV, ways to prevent its spread, and the advantages of early treatment; Outreach Program is a component of Public Education; education takes place in schools, businesses, bars, and includes street outreach; each year 100 presentations are made in schools, 35 to corporations, 50 at bars, 5 media campaigns are held, and 80 other speaking engagements are presented.*	*Public Education Division* *Goal: Prevent new HIV infections.* • *Schools Program* • *Outreach Program* • *Media Program* • *Speakers Bureau*	*Financial Support* *1996 budget $645,000* • *$280,000 Centers for Disease Control for prevention outreach, support groups, media campaigns and public education in schools, businesses* • *$190,000 city Department of Public Health for case management services* • *$140,000 from 5 foundations for advocacy work and outreach to high risk populations* • *$35,000 from fund-raising*
• *Public Policy: 4 staff work with a few volunteers to staff a city-wide network of organizations concerned with HIV and AIDS and to develop research and policy positions for ASO/USA. We don't do "lobbying" in an official capacity, but we do a lot of advocacy with the city council and at the state level. We also work with the city Department of Public Health staff to track the epidemic in the city.*	*Public Policy Division* *Goal: Improve public policy as it affects HIV and AIDS issues.* • *City HIV/AIDS Network (we coordinate and staff the Network)* • *Research and Policy Program*	*Staff and Board* • *20 staff, of whom 5 are part-time* • *9 board members* • *50 volunteers* • *Communications: monthly staff meetings, twice-a-month department meetings, monthly board meetings*
• *Support Services: 7 staff work with about 20 volunteers in conducting a wide range of support services. Case management serviced 300 individuals in 1996, an average of 10 hours per client per month; 12 ongoing support groups for both people with AIDS and caregivers are staffed with both staff and volunteers; our hotline is managed by staff but volunteers take most of the calls—we get over 5,000 calls per year. In the last few years we have begun to provide translation as part of case management, which grew into an English as a Second Language program for our clients; we provide limited transportation support.*	*Support Services Division* *Goal: Improve the quality of life and health for people living with HIV and AIDS.* • *Case Management Program* • *Support Groups* • *AIDS Hotline* • *Translation Program* • *ESL Classes* • *Transportation Program*	*Systems* • *Bookkeeping partly computerized* • *10 computers* • *Excellent phone system supporting the hotline and the office*

Organizational Profile of a Red Cross Chapter

Program Activities Grouped By Common Outcome

1. **Prevention of Disasters.**
   Goal: To prevent disasters that are caused by lack of awareness

Courses

- Sailing
- Canoeing
- Vital signs
- Parenting
- AIDS
- Baby-sitting
- Alcohol abuse
- Facts of life
- Seat belt safety
- Food safety
- Swimming
- Tornado/hurricane/flood

Information

- Newsletter
- Exhibits
- Public speakers bureau

Service Level

- 240 courses, 4,800 participants
- 10 newsletters
- 20 public speeches

2. **Intervention in the Midst of Disasters.**
   Goal: To decrease the impact of disasters which they are occurring

Direct Services

- Life-saving CPR
- First-aid stations at public events
- Blood pressure screening
- Blood drives

Service Level

- 100 courses, 2,000 participants
- 2 blood pressure screenings, 500 participants
- Ongoing blood drives at Red Cross office, and 52 blood drives at office sites.

3. **Relief of Suffering After Disasters Occur.**
   Goal: To decrease the human suffering caused by disasters after they have occurred

Direct Services

- Services to military families and veterans
- Mass feeding
- Bone and tissue transplantation
- Transportation services
- Emergency communications
- Disaster damage assessment
- Service in hospitals and health centers

Service Level

- 15 services to military families and veterans
- 280 bone/tissue units transplanted
- 1,000 persons transported
- 5,000 hrs. of volunteer service in hospitals
- 50 damage assessments
- 6 mass feedings
- 6 emergency communications operations

Summary of Volunteer Usage

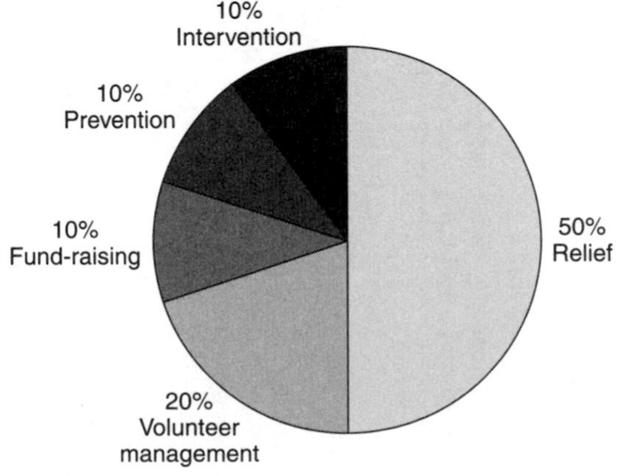

4. **Fund-raising**

Goal: To ensure donations are adequate to support programs

Production:	• Individuals $150,000 • Corporations $150,000 • Foundations $100,000
Volunteer usage:	• 1,000 = 10% of volunteer hours
Expenses:	• $100,000 = 10% of gross expenses
Income:	• $400,000 = 40% of income

5. **Marketing**

Goal: To increase public understanding of the organization

Production:	• 10 newsletters, 12 PSAs
Expenses:	• $10,000 = 10% of gross expenses

6. **Personnel**

Goal: To have a knowledgeable and experienced staff to manage and deliver services

Production:	• 15 FTE (full time equivalent)
Expenses:	• $600,000 = 60% of gross expenses (subset of other expenses)

Goal: To maintain a pool of trained volunteers to deliver services

Production:	• Recruit 6,000 volunteers • Train 4,000 volunteers • Place 2,000 volunteers • Produce 10,000 volunteer hours worth $200,000
Volunteer usage:	• 2,000 hours = 20% of volunteer hours
Expenses:	• $40,000 = 40% of gross expenses

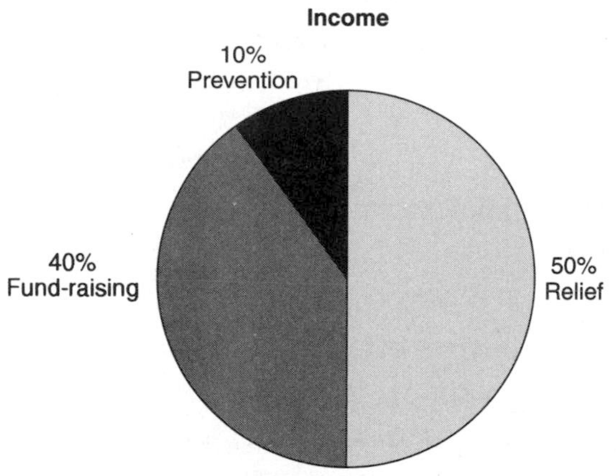

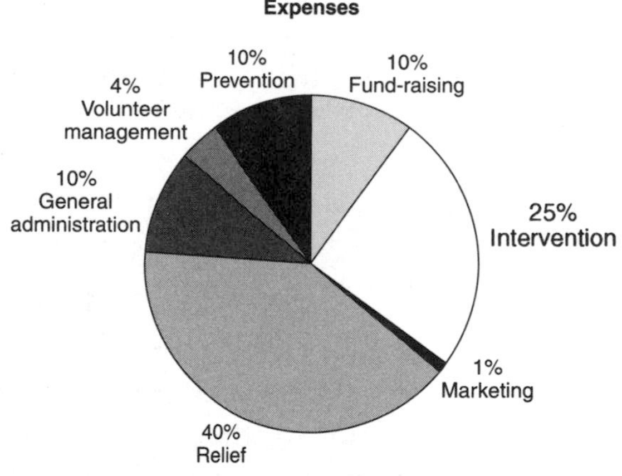

number of clients served, cost per unit of service, geographic locations serviced, etc.).

2. Group these program activities and services according to common outcomes, categories, similar services, or the like (think of these groupings as goals; for example, education, direct services, advocacy); list each program activity or service under the most appropriate program grouping.
3. Prepare an infrastructure profile. This will include information on basic management and operation functions that support the current programs, such as personnel management, fund-raising, marketing, facilities, financial management, and board of directors. This information will include current paid and volunteer staffing levels for all programs and for the entire organization, as well as the size of the board of directors. Also, briefly summarize sources and use of funds, analysis of financial condition, and other related organizational and management data. Charts and diagrams are useful visuals to help present data.

Step 1.5: Identify Information Needed for Strategic Planning

Effective strategic plans are the end product of discussions by informed individuals. Much of the information will be gathered and analyzed during Phase 3: Assessing the Environment. This is the time to draft the list of information that will be needed to respond to the critical issues and questions. Based on the critical questions around which the planning process is organized, this information may include:

- Key trends in the program environment, plans and attitudes of major existing funders, views of key community informants, demographic changes within the target population, regulatory changes
- List of competitors, including what services they offer, prices charged, etc.
- Client statistics and other information needed to evaluate programs: client data trends for the past five years, changes in client mix based on staff observation, consumer attitudes, quality indicators, changes in the program base for the last five years, and known client needs
- Financial trends of the organization for the past five years
- Any other data that should be gathered to help develop responses to the initial list of strategic issues

In addition, surveys and in-depth interviews with different groups or individuals other than Board or staff might take considerable time. It would be helpful to gather this information in advance and present it at a planning retreat attended by some or all Board and staff. If the information gathering should or can be done earlier in the process rather than later in process, then the Information Gathering Plan should be started at this point in the planning process. See Sidebar on page 82 "Sample Types and Sources of Information for Strategic Planning" for ideas on information to be collected to support the strategic planning process.

The information gathering plan worksheet has two components. The first asks planners to identify information needed to address the critical questions. The second page asks planners to think of all the important stakeholders and decide what to ask them. It is important to be open to new ideas and to the possibility that there are additional critical questions which the Planning Committee has not yet articulated. Asking open-ended questions of important stakeholders is a good way to expand the perspectives represented in the planning process. The process notes found in Exhibit 2-5, as well as the case study, provide a plan and a model for gathering this information.

Exhibit 2-5 Worksheet 5: Information Gathering Plan

Process Notes

How to do this activity	• At the first meeting of the Planning Committee, review the initial list of strategic issues and identify any other issues that must be addressed during the planning process. Brainstorm a list of information that the Planning Committee and management will need during the Phase 3: Assessing the Environment discussions. • Prioritize data needs. Develop a plan for how and when data will be collected and who will collect it. Summarize information gathering plan on Information Gathering worksheet. • Start to list all the different groups or individuals (external stakeholders) who need to be involved in the planning process, what questions you might ask them, and how and when should you collect the data.
Why do this activity	• Good information helps make (good) informed decisions.
Who to involve in the process	• All members of the Planning Committee brainstorm the list of data that needs to be collected; collection of data delegated to appropriate individual(s).

Case Study—ASO/USA

◆ **Worksheet 5** **Information Gathering Plan**	☐ Identify which strategic issues need to have information gathered. • What information do we need? • Who will collect it? • How will it be collected? ☐ List key external stockholders. • What questions can they help answer? • How should we collect this information?

What are the strategic issues about which we need to gather information about (refer to Worksheet 1)	What information do we need?	Who will collect it?	Format for collecting this information; time
1. Overdependence on federal funding	• *Assess potential to increase independent fundraising* • *Develop assumptions regarding federal funding (two or more possible scenarios)* • *Look at cost structure to see if there is any room for savings*	*Development Director*	*Basic research, by end of February*
2. Medical advances	• *Contact several experts and practitioners to project changes likely for program needs* • *Assess our own client data to look for trends in use of new treatments, changes in health status* • *Talk with all our case managers*	*Program Director to supervise*	• *Interviews, by end of February* • *Records review, by end of February* • *Focus group with case managers in early February*
3. Collaboration with City Clinic	• *Review and summarize total benefits and costs/ problems of relationship* • *Investigate alternatives and implications of ending/ continuing relationship*	*Executive Director and Outreach Coordinator*	*Analysis by end of February*
4. Financial management	*Resources required to support a revamped financial management system need to be assessed and evaluated, presented to the board as an operational issue. Long-term financial management and information systems need to be addressed as part of strategic planning*	*Not applicable*	*Not applicable*

Worksheet 5 *(Continued)*

List external stakeholders	**What questions can they help answer?**	**How should we collect stakeholder feedback? Who should collect this information and by when?**
Current clients	• *Quality of services* • *Utilization of services* • *Alternatives to our services*	*Three focus groups with clients; Delores to organize and assess by end of March*
Past clients	• *Quality of services* • *Utilization of services* • *Alternatives to our services*	*Series of phone interviews where possible to reach clients; Delores to organize and assess by end of March*
Funders	• *Anticipated changes in priorities* • *Likelihood of ongoing support* • *Other funding sources to consider*	*Face-to-face interviews with current funders and at least five potential funders; Development Director, by end of March*
Community leaders	• *Feedback on public image regarding effectiveness, etc.* • *Input about new and emerging priorities* • *Input about consequences of continuing/discontinuing relationship with City Clinic (for select individuals only)*	*Interviews; Board members and Executive Director, by end of March*
Potential collaborators/competitors (both competitors for clients and competitors for funding)	• *Feedback on public image regarding effectiveness, etc.* • *Input about new and emerging priorities* • *Brainstorm opportunities for collaborative action*	*Interviews; Board members and Executive Director, by end of March*
Other		
Other		
Other		

Step 1.6: Write a "Plan to Plan"

Last but not least, the Planning Committee will need to develop an overall workplan for managing the planning effort (also referred to as a "Plan to Plan"). The workplan should outline the activities involved over the course of the entire planning process, the processes to be used for all activities (such as interviews, retreats, etc.), persons responsible for executing or overseeing those tasks, desired outcomes, resources required (e.g., time and money), and time frames.

It is at this point that the Planning Committee will need to decide the extent of the planning process. On the following three pages is a guide to developing the planning workplan describing three levels of intensity in the planning process: an abbreviated planning process, a moderate planning process, and an extensive planning process. Use this guide to select the depth of the process appropriate for your organization. In Appendix B, sample workplans are included for each type of process.

Why develop a workplan? As a wise consultant once said: "Failure to plan is planning to fail."

Abbreviated Workplan

Type of Process	Depth of Analysis during the Planning Process	Personnel Involved	Typical Format	Typical Time-Frame	The Strategic Plan: Typical Products to Come out of the Strategic Planning Process	Suggested Worksheets
Abbreviated workplan	Abbreviated analysis	• If a smaller organization, usually the entire Board and staff • If a larger organization, usually the entire Board and staff representatives (management team)	• Day-long retreat (plus time to plan retreat) • Follow-up meeting(s) by staff to develop detailed annual operating plan to implement Strategic Plan	• One day* • Time for staff to develop annual plan	• Strategic planning document that is 3–8 pages in length and includes: • Mission statement • Summary of strategies and list of long-term and short-term program and management/operations priorities • Detailed annual operating plan (as prepared by staff)	Homework assignment to be filled out and brought by all participants to the retreat: #4 Organizational history either filled out by one or two individuals before the retreat or done on wall using large piece of butcher paper #6 Mission statement #7 Vision statement #8 SWOT

May need additional meeting(s) if more time is needed to discuss all issues and agree on priorities.

Moderate Workplan

Type of Process	Depth of Analysis during the Planning Process	Personnel Involved	Typical Format	Typical Time-Frame	The Strategic Plan: Typical Products to Come out of the Strategic Planning Process	Suggested Worksheets
Moderate workplan	Moderate analysis	• If a smaller organization, usually the entire Board and staff • If a larger organization, usually the entire Board and staff representatives (management team) • Usually includes some external stakeholders input (such as clients or funders)	• One or two days of larger group meetings; smaller meetings of entire Board and line staff may meet prior to larger group meetings • A few Planning Committee meetings to discuss past strategies, current issues, and future priorities • May include some collection of data regarding the external environment and stakeholder expectations and needs	• One to three months to complete process • Time for staff to develop annual plan	• Strategic planning document that is usually 8–12 pages in length and includes: • Mission statement • Summary of strategies • List of long-term and short-term program and management/operations priorities • Program and management /operations goals and objectives (optional) • Summary of environmental assessment (optional) • Detailed annual operating plan (as prepared by staff)	• For first retreat: homework assignments to be brought by all participants to the retreat: #4 Organizational history either filled out by one or two individuals before the retreat or done on wall using large piece of butcher paper #6 Mission statement #7 Vision statement #8 SWOT • Other worksheets will depend on the issues facing the organization and the detail of information needed to assess the environment and set priorities, but at a minimum would include: #8 Previous and current strategies #13 Interplay of SWOT #15 Core future strategies #16 Long-term and short-term priorities • Additional worksheets may be used, depending on the products that the organization wishes to produce as part of the strategic planning process

Extensive Workplan

Type of Process	Depth of Analysis during the Planning Process	Personnel Involved	Typical Format	Typical Time Frame	The Strategic Plan: Typical Products to Come out of the Strategic Planning Process	Suggested Worksheets
Extensive workplan	Extensive analysis	• Entire Board • Entire staff • Clients/ customers • Others, including funders, other organizations, community leaders, government officials, actual or potential competitors, and collaborators	• Meeting(s) to assess strategic issues, organizational readiness, and participation in the planning process • Meeting(s) to orient Planning Committee regarding planning process and planning language; review of organizational history and profile, previous and current strategies, and development of an information gathering plan • Retreat(s) of Board and staff to review organization's history, mission and vision statements, SWOT analysis, and discussions of issues, possible strategies, and priorities • Planning Committee meeting to identify external stakeholders and how to involve them in the process • External stakeholder input through surveys, interviews, or focus groups; staff input through assessment of programs, and program evaluation; other data collection will depend on information needs • Meeting(s) of Planning Committee to review external and internal environment information collected above, the interplay of SWOT, and competitive analysis of programs • Meeting(s) of Planning Committee to discuss strategic issues and determine core future strategies and possible long-term and short-term priorities • Meeting(s) of Planning Committee to review proposed future program portfolio and short-term and long-term program and management/operations priorities • Meeting(s) of Planning Committee to develop and review goals and objectives • Meeting(s) of Planning Committee to review and modify Strategic Plan • Board of Directors meet to approve Strategic Plan • Follow-up meeting(s) by staff to develop detailed annual operating plan to implement Strategic Plan	Four to eight months to complete process	• Extensive Strategic Plan that is usually 12–40 pages in length and includes: • Mission statement • Strategic issues and core strategies • Program goals and objectives • Management/operations goals and objectives • Summary of planning process • Appendices: summary of environmental assessment, in-depth analysis from client/customer surveys and stakeholder comments • Detailed annual operating plan (as prepared by staff)	All worksheets might be used in completing the extensive workplan

CHAPTER THREE

Defining Your Challenge

This chapter is called Defining Your Challenge because once you have decided you are ready to plan, Phase 2: Articulating Mission and Vision guides you through defining the essential reason for your organization's existence and Phase 3: Assessing the Environment analyzes both the forces assisting you and those which must be overcome.

PHASE 2: ARTICULATING MISSION AND VISION

One of the primary reasons for creating a strategic plan is to establish a common understanding of, and ambition for, an organization's work. The most succinct reflection of this shared understanding lies in the organization's mission and vision statements—declaration of intentions, hopes, and expectations.

Why Do We Need a Mission Statement?

"Who are you, as an organization? Why do you exist? What do you do? Whom do you serve?" Anyone coming into contact with your organization has these questions. A mission statement should provide the answers. In just a few sentences, a mission statement should be able to communicate the essence of an organization to its stakeholders and to the public: one guiding set of ideas that is articulated, understood, and supported by the organization's board, staff, volunteers, donors, and collaborators. For example:

> At the Developmental Studies Center we develop, evaluate, and disseminate programs that foster children's ethical, social, and intellectual development. While nurturing children's capacity to think skillfully and critically, we also strive to deepen children's commitment to prosocial values such as kindness, helpfulness, personal responsibility, and respect for others—qualities we believe are essential to leading humane and productive lives in a democratic society. *(Developmental Studies Center, Oakland CA)*

Another Word about Words

A word of clarification: words such as "mission," "purpose," and "mission statement" are not used consistently by people in either the nonprofit sector or the for-profit sector. The authors of this workbook recommend the definitions used in this section. Participants in the planning process should not get hung up on words, but understand the difference between ends and means and what each concept refers to. Ultimately, it doesn't really matter what the concepts are called as long the end result is a document that clearly defines what the organization seeks to achieve, what it does, why it does it, and what are the overall priorities for the achievement of the organization's purpose. However, all participants in the planning process need to agree to call the concepts by the same name and as such, definitions should be clarified during the Getting Ready phase.

In *Profiles of Excellence,*[1] a book about the best practices of nonprofit organizations, published by the Independent Sector, the researchers stress that a "clear, agreed-upon mission statement" is one of the four primary characteristics of successful nonprofit organizations (the other three are a strong, competent executive director, a dynamic board of directors, and an organization-wide commitment to fund raising).

[1] E. B. Knauft, Renee Berger, and Sandra Gray of the Independent Sector. *Profiles of Excellence* (San Francisco: Jossey-Bass Publishers, 1991).

The Example of Alice

Lewis Carroll's *Alice's Adventures in Wonderland* speaks indirectly to the importance of mission statements:

Said Alice, "Cheshire Puss . . . . would you tell me, please, which way I ought to go from here?"

"That depends a good deal on where you want to get to," said the Cat.

"I don't much care where—" said Alice.

"Then it doesn't matter which way you go," said the Cat.

"—so long as I get *somewhere,*" Alice added as an explanation.

"Oh, you're sure to do that," said the Cat, "if you only walk long enough."

Source: *Lewis Carroll.* Alice's Adventures in Wonderland *(London: William Heinemann Ltd., 1907, pp. 75–76).*

Step 2.1: Write (or Reaffirm or Rewrite) Your Mission Statement

A mission statement should include:

- *Purpose.* One sentence that describes the end result an organization seeks to accomplish (and for whom)
- *Business.* A description of the primary means (program, action, services, etc.) used to accomplish the purpose
- *Values.* A list of values and beliefs or guiding principles shared by members of an organization and practiced in their work

Creating a Purpose Statement by Identifying the Focus Problem. The development of a purpose statement may be developed by simply asking the question, "why do we exist?" For example, when asked why their organization existed, members of the strategic planning committee of the California Child Care Resource and Referral Network developed a statement that read: "to achieve a quality child care system which meets the needs of all children and families."

This direct approach to defining an organization's purpose may not be as easy for all organizations. Therefore, in order to define or clarify an organization's purpose—the ultimate result an organization is working to achieve—individuals may need to step back from the day-to-day activities and try to identify the focus problem that the organization is trying to solve. The focus problem is the need or opportunity the organization exists to resolve, and the purpose statement describes how the world would be changed if that problem or condition were solved or improved. For example, the focus problem for a Big Brothers/Big Sisters chapter might be that "children from single-parent families are increasing in number without same-gender positive role models. These children are at a higher risk of developing adjustment/delinquency problems than children with same-gender positive role models." The ideal future impact if the problem was solved would be "that every little brother or sister will become a happy, productive member of society." The purpose of Big Brothers/Big Sisters is: "to decrease the problems experienced by children in single parent families."

Why Is Clarifying Purpose Important? Failure to state and communicate clearly an organization's purpose (in "ends" terminology) can lead an organization to inadvertently restrict its effectiveness. For example, one program whose stated purpose was to provide counseling to youth ages 13–18 (a means statement), inadvertently shut off any hope of innovation by too narrowly restricting the scope of its programs and vision. Because its focus was only on counseling, the staff and board did not look at what they were hoping to achieve and whether they were being effective. When they rewrote their purpose to reflect an "end" statement: "to increase the mental health of youth in our county," they expanded their vision to include new programs such as a hotline, after-school programs, workshops on coping with stress, etc.

Or, organization members can waste time "barking up the wrong tree" or "letting the tail wag the dog." For example, a Native American community organization had long owned a building with several small programs and an often-used meeting room. The meeting room was rented out to other organizations and provided a small but steady income. As long as the purpose was vaguely defined as "meeting the needs of the community," renting out the room took a higher priority over new activities because it was a revenue-generating activity. A strategic planning process led the organization to sharpen its focus on meeting the cultural needs of the Native American community. As a result, many new uses were found for the meeting space involving youth groups, senior citizen cultural activities, and programs celebrating Native culture targeted at the general public. Because of the importance of these activities to the organization's purpose, new funding was developed off setting the loss of the rental income and in the process making much better use of one of the organization's primary assets: its building.

Finally, an organization may not realize when it is time to go out of business. For example, the initial purpose of the March of Dimes was "to eliminate polio." Because the purpose statement was quite clear, once polio was eliminated, the organization had to choose whether to go out of business or to refocus its mission. The board of directors of the March of Dimes chose to change the purpose of the March of Dimes to the broader effort "to eliminate birth defects."

Writing Your Purpose Sentence. The "purpose" component of the mission statement explains the solution the organization seeks to accomplish with respect to the focus problem. It describes, in one sentence, why the organization exists and the end result of its efforts, i.e., what the organization aspires to achieve. A purpose statement usually includes two basic elements:

- An infinitive verb that indicates a change in status (such as to increase, to decrease, to eliminate, to prevent, etc.)
- An identification of the problem to be addressed or condition to be changed (such as access to healthcare, public policy on the environment, cultural assets in the community)

An agency's purpose might be "to decrease infant mortality rates in our city," or "to increase appreciation of accordion music." The United States Department of Agriculture, Forest Service purpose is "to achieve quality land management under the sustainable multiple-use management concept to meet the diverse needs of people." Note that these examples focus on outcomes and results rather than methods. They describe how the world is going to be different—what the organization intends to change. Thus, the purpose of an agency serving the homeless should not be described in terms of their method "to provide shelter for homeless individuals." The purpose should be described in terms of a broader end result, such as "to eliminate the condition of homelessness in our region."

From Focus Problem to Ideal Future to Purpose Statement

Identify focus problem	Youth who are involved in the juvenile justice system, homeless, inner city dwellers, poor, or otherwise at risk have special needs for their physical and emotional well-being. Among the issues these youth face in their environment are violence, racism, sexism, poverty, lack of education, and substance abuse. These factors are often obstacles to accessing and utilizing services effectively, as well as elements that affect their higher rates of morbidity and mortality.
Articulate ideal future impact if the problem were to be solved	In concert with the constellation of service providers who work with these youth, it is necessary to have quality comprehensive healthcare designed to meet their special needs.
Draft the purpose statement	Improve the health of at-risk kids.

Define the Business of Your Organization. The statement of "what business you are in" is not the same as the purpose statement. The purpose is an end, the business is a "means." Business statements often include the verb "to provide," or link a purpose statement with the words "by" or "through."

For example, the purpose of the above youth-serving agency is to improve the health of at-risk youth. The business must define what methods the organization will use to pursue that purpose; for example, offer direct medical services, counseling, and health education to youth at Juvenile Hall.

An organization dedicated to the purpose of eliminating homelessness might choose one or more of the following three methods: by constructing housing for homeless individuals, by educating the public and advocating for public policy changes, or by providing counseling and job training to homeless individuals. Try the exercise in Exhibit 3-1 to help your organization determine the difference between ends and means.

Exhibit 3-1 Purpose v. Business

Examine the statements below. Which are statements of purpose and which are statements of business?

Statements	Purpose	Business
1. Eliminate the causes of birth defects		
2. Provide counseling and support to victims of crime		
3. Make a profit		
4. Increase the effectiveness of nonprofit organizations		
5. Conduct biomedical research		
6. Heal the wounds of crime		
7. Increase the mental health of our clients		
8. Provide leadership training and legal assistance to migrant workers		
9. Decrease the problems of single-parent children		
10. Provide food and shelter to the homeless		

If you identified statement numbers 1, 3, 4, 6, 7, and 9 as purpose statements, you understand the difference between purpose (ends) and business (means).

Clarifying Purpose and Business

The logic of the mission statement says that your ends (the purpose) determine your means (the business). However, it is sometimes easier for people to relate to the business of the organization because that is what is more visible. "We build housing," "We put on art shows," "We do public advocacy." After the business is defined, then the group can take a step back to ask why. "We build housing in order to decrease homelessness, etc." Whatever works best for your group is the right way to go!

Articulate the Fundamental Values, Beliefs, and Assumptions That Guide Your Work. The driving values of an organization exist, whether spoken or not, in all organizations, but in most successful organizations, they are spoken.

Spoken values usually focus on service, quality, people, and work norms. Values and beliefs are about faith, about trust, about giving people guidance with regard to means to achieve a clearly stated purpose. The values and beliefs component describes the basic principles shared by members of the organization and practiced in their work; for example, integrity, quality, and excellence in service provision must always be maintained; individuals should be empowered to make educated decisions about their health choices; we are client-centered; etc. Values might also state related beliefs, such as a vegetarian association's assertion that "eating vegetables is more economically efficient and ecologically responsible than eating beef."

While beliefs and values articulate fundamental principles, assumptions are statements that guide the choices that the organization makes. For example, a fundamental belief might be that "everyone deserves shelter from the elements and a roof over their heads." Three assumptions related to this belief may be: "there are too many people in our city who don't have roofs over their heads; not everyone may want a roof over their head, but choice is important; and there are sufficient resources available in this city so no one should have to go without shelter from the elements."

Sample Value, Belief, and Assumption Statements

The purpose of *Squeezebox Synthesis* is to promote accordions as a vital cultural link between the past, the present, and the future.

Value and belief statements	• Culture is essential to a fully lived life • It is a good thing for people to understand their roots
Assumptions	• Accordions help people find their European roots • An accordion is a maligned and misunderstood instrument

The values, beliefs, and assumptions component of the mission statement highlights the important connection between the nature of the organization's work and the inspirations guiding the individuals involved. Ideally, the personal values of staff, as well as external constituents and supporters, will align with the values of the organization. When developing a written statement of the organization's values, stakeholders will have a chance to contribute to the articulation of these values and evaluate how well their personal values and motivation match those of the organization. This process will help build stakeholders' commitment to the organization and will provide the foundation upon which individuals can do their work.

Other examples of values, beliefs, and assumptions:

- Self-confidence is not taught or learned; it is earned by surpassing your own self-set limitations (Outward Bound)
- Appreciating the differences among people is essential to building mutual understanding and respect (Berryessa Union School District)
- Doing art (painting, sculpting pottery, etc.) is a great way to develop the whole brain (City Arts Center)
- Good role models give kids a greater opportunity to achieve their mental, emotional, and moral potential, and that helps all of society (Big Brothers/Big Sisters)
- We exclude no one from our concern, but are especially sensitive to youth and women and are impelled to prefer the poor (School Sisters of Notre Dame)
- We value collaborating with other service providers (Special Programs for Youth)
- Understanding the world geographically as a youth is a prerequisite to acting with global responsibility as an adult (National Geographic Association)
- Economics and economies should be guided by principles of moral justice (Center for Ethics and Economic Policy)
- The vitality of life depends on the continued addition of new perspectives, new beliefs, and new wisdom (Center for the Arts, Yerba Buena Gardens)

One valuable exercise that can be undertaken during this phase is to perform a gap analysis on the core values, making a list that compares real values (values

Shared Core Values of the American Heart Association

Integrity:	Highest ethical standards, trustworthy, honest, financially and morally accountable, efficient and effective use of all resources
Excellence:	Premier experts and leaders in all that we do, leadership, professionalism
Visionary:	Proactive, innovative, creative, progressive, willing to take prudent risks
Dedicated:	Conviction, perseverance, high motivation, working together toward a common mission and goals
Inclusive:	Broadly reflective and representative of all peoples and communities
Sensitive:	Respectful of the unique qualities of others, open and responsive, treating all with dignity and equality, appreciative

that are currently being modeled) with the core values that an organization wishes to personify.[2] This is especially important if an organization's staff is currently operating with a different set of values than what they wish to personify in the future. The strategic plan then becomes the vehicle to bridge the gap between what is and what they wish to be.

Old Values, New Values

HOPE Rehabilitation Services, an organization whose purpose is to enhance the quality of life of individuals with disabilities and their families, articulated within their strategic plan such values as "empowering clients to be the best they can be, valuing family, and placing high value of honesty, ethics, integrity, respect, equality, and commitment." During a planning retreat, HOPE's planning consultant suggested a process that would support a fundamental shift in how HOPE did business. The process entailed Board and staff articulating old mental models/mindsets/assumptions they would like to discard, and replacing them with the new mental models they would like to embrace.

Old mental models/mindsets/assumptions we'd like to discard (abbreviated list)

- We'll do what we need to do to get by.
- We focus on disabilities rather than abilities.
- Government should give HOPE money because we run good programs.
- The staff knows what is best and makes decisions for clients.

HOPE's new mental models we'd like to embrace (abbreviated list)

- HOPE Rehabilitation Services is driven by a "quality first" mentality with regard to internal and external customers.
- We focus on abilities rather than disabilities.
- HOPE is more independent/self-reliant—it operates as a business.
- Clients are involved/make their own choices.

Put the Components of the Mission Statement Together. The mission statement, when completed, should be a simple yet powerful and inspiring statement that communicates to both internal and external stakeholders what the organization is all about. The mission statement can be one or two sentences long, or it can take up an entire page. Examples:

- The YMCA of San Francisco, based in Judeo-Christian heritage *(values)*, seeks to enhance the lives of all people *(purpose)* through programs designed to develop spirit, mind, and body *(business)*.

[2] Karl Albrecht. *The Northbound Train: Finding the Purpose, Setting the Direction, Shaping the Destiny of Your Organization* (New York: American Management Association, 1994), p. 159.

- Institute for Food and Development Policy works to eliminate injustices that cause hunger *(purpose)* by providing analysis and education *(business)* aimed at awakening people to their own power to participate in bringing about change *(vision)*.
- The Berryessa Union School District mission is to educate and inspire students *(business)* to become leading world citizens *(purpose)* by achieving their personal best and contributing to the community *(vision)*. This mission will be accomplished through the partnership of our staff, students, parents, and community *(values)*.
- The state division of the American Cancer Society is financed by voluntary contributions and its purpose is to control cancer and minimize its burden on people *(purpose)* through innovative, organized volunteer action *(values)* by funding research directed at cancer prevention, detection, treatment, and cure; sponsoring, supporting, or directly operating educational and advocacy programs to prevent, detect, treat, and cure cancer; and providing the cancer patient and family with services and rehabilitation programs *(businesses)*.
- In order to enhance the capacity of California communities to develop and manage their local and regional economies, the Office of Business Development's mission is to work cooperatively with the public and private sectors to provide strategic financial and technical assistance for economic development *(business)* to local organizations and businesses, resulting in job creation and retention, diversification, and an increased tax base *(purpose)*. The mission is based upon the following *(assumptions and values)*:

  1. Community is defined as the inter-relationship of the business, government, and nonprofit sectors at the local level.
  2. Healthy communities contribute to the overall economic, social, and cultural well-being of their region and the state.
  3. The majority of economic development activity happens on site at the local level; therefore, communities have a significant amount of control over policies, strategies, and systems that support job creation and growth.
  4. All communities can enhance their economic, social, and cultural environment using relevant economic development policies and strategies.
  5. Local empowerment to manage the local economy ensures greater economic stability for the region and the state in the long run.
  6. There is a need at the local level for financial and technical expertise, information, and resources for developing and implementing economic

development strategies and programs. That need is able to be met only partially by the for-profit private sector.

7. The state can play an important role in leveraging available resources to help local government develop and operate successful economic development programs by establishing effective state-wide strategies, programs, and services, in partnership with our stakeholders.

There is no simple formula for efficiently crafting a definitive mission statement for an organization. In *Reinventing Government,* the authors state that "the experience of hashing out the fundamental purpose of an organization—debating all the different assumptions and views held by its members and agreeing on one basic mission—can be a powerful one. When it is done right, a mission statement can drive an entire organization from top to bottom. It can help people at all levels decide what they should do and what they should stop doing."[3] The process of creating a mission statement usually takes considerable time, but the effort is almost always worth the end result. Exhibit 3-2 highlights key issues in the process.

Exhibit 3-2 Worksheet 6: Mission Statement Worksheet

Process Notes	
How to do this activity	Two options: 1. Have board and staff fill out Worksheet 6 in advance of a planning retreat and then discuss the key components at a retreat. Or, 2. Have one or two designated writers from the Planning Committee review the current mission statement (if the organization has one), redraft it as necessary and present first to the Planning Committee, then to Board and staff for feedback.
Why do this activity	Clarity about your mission statement is vital—you need to know where you're going before you can figure out how to get there. Expect to go through a few drafts before getting one that everyone likes.
Who to involve in the process	Input from Board and staff (and possibly other key stakeholders); one or two people write the draft(s). Formal approval of the Mission Statement by the Board of Directors.

[3] David Osborne and Ted Gaebler. *Reinventing Government* (Reading, MA: Addison-Wesley, 1992), pp. 130–131.

Case Study—ASO/USA

◆ **Worksheet 6** **Creating a Mission Statement**	☐ Draft Your Mission Statement (Note: Please write legibly. Use only the space provided.)

What is the *focus problem(s)* that our organization exists to solve? What need or opportunity does our organization exist to resolve? (In considering the focus problem or need, you might want to consider the following questions: Who is affected by the problem? How are they affected?) Describe how the world would be improved, changed, or different if our organization was successful in solving the problem or responding to the need.

AIDS and HIV have greatly impacted our society. Greater attention must be spent not only educating people regarding how to prevent HIV infection, but also in helping people who are living with HIV. In addition, many low income, homeless, IV drug users are not being seen through traditional healthcare services. Also, there is a continuing need to do aggressive prevention work within marginalized communities.

Our vision of the world would be that we would be successful in preventing the spread of HIV in our community and that people who have AIDS would be able to lead quality, productive lives. Our ultimate vision is that AIDS would be eradicated and we would go out of business.

What is the *purpose* of our organization (answers the question of why we exist, does not describe what we do)? This should be a short succinct statement that describes the ultimate result we are hoping to achieve; make sure to indicate outcomes and results (e.g., to eliminate homelessness), not the methods of achieving those results which is your mission (e.g., by constructing houses).

The purpose of our organization is to increase the quality of life for people living with HIV and prevent the spread of HIV in our community.

What is our business? Describe the business or businesses we are in—our primary services or activities.

- *Prevention and education*
- *Research and public policy*
- *Supportive services to improve the quality of life for people living with HIV*

Worksheet 6 *(Continued)*

What are the *fundamental values and beliefs* that should guide us in our day-to-day interactions with each other and our constituencies? What are the *major assumptions* upon which our organization provides its services?

We believe:

- *All people deserve quality health care*
- *Self-empowerment*
- *Value of diversity, equal rights, and non-description*
- *Cooperation is crucial—we need to work together*

We assume:

- *We can make a real difference in this epidemic*
- *There is a need for ongoing advocacy*
- *This disease will be with us for the next several years*
- *Government funding will continue, though probably at a diminishing level*

Our Mission Statement

(Combine the information above to create a compelling mission statement about *who* the organization is, what the organization does, and why the organization does it.)

AIDS Services Organization/USA (ASO/USA) is dedicated to reducing the impact of HIV. We do this by providing services to improve the quality of life for people with HIV, advocating for responsible public policies, and striving to prevent the spread of HIV in our communities. We believe that AIDS education programs and services to people with AIDS must be culturally sensitive and linguistically appropriate. ASO/USA is committed to the value of indigenous leadership, the value of all human life, and the possibility of success in achieving our mission.

Drafting Mission Statements: Role of Groups

Note: In writing a mission statement, it is useful to realize that while groups are good at many things, writing is not one of them! Staff, Board, and Planning Committee members might all participate in generating and discussing ideas, but it usually proves most efficient to leave one or two Planning Committee members in charge of actually getting the words on paper.

One way to start the process is to discuss the key components of the mission statement (either revisions to the organization's current statement or the creation of a brand new one) at a board or staff retreat; a broad preliminary discussion of the concepts to be included in the statement will quickly demonstrate areas of consensus and disagreement. The designated Planning Committee members might then write a first draft of the statement and redraft it as it goes through the process of review, discussion, refinement, and final approval by the Board of Directors. Furthermore, as a result of assessing the environment or discussing the strategic issues facing the organization, the mission statement may need to be revised. However, a draft of a working mission statement should serve as a basis for guiding the discussions and decisions.

While the Planning Committee is primarily responsible for hammering out the details of the mission statement's format and wording, the evolving draft should also be circulated several times through Board, staff, and perhaps other stakeholders as well. Some consultants also advise organizations to seek an outside opinion from someone unfamiliar with the organization to gauge how accessible the statement is to the uninitiated. The great advantage of hashing over the statement this way is that the discussion and debate introduces newcomers to the nuances of the organization's mission, refreshes old-timers' understanding, fosters stakeholders' sense of participation and commitment, and results in a mission statement that genuinely expresses a collective intention and common ideas. With a measure of passion, humanity, and an eye on the big picture, a Planning Committee can keep refining the mission statement until it has a version that stakeholders can actively support.

Step 2.2: Draft a Vision Statement

A vision is a guiding image of success. If a mission statement provides a blueprint for an organization's work—the what, why, and how of what it does—then the vision is the artist's rendering of the realization of that mission. While a mission statement answers the questions about why the organization exists, what business it is in, and what values guide it, a vision statement answers the question, "What will success look like?" It is the pursuit of this shared image of success that inspires and motivates people to work together.

Martin Luther King, Jr. said "I have a dream," and then offered a vision that changed a nation. That famous speech is a dramatic example of the power that can be generated by a person who communicates a compelling vision of the future. While John F. Kennedy did not live to see his vision for NASA come to fruition, he set it in motion when he said, "By the end of the decade, we will put a man on the moon." When it came time to appropriate the enormous funds necessary to accomplish this vision, Congress did not hesitate. Why? Because this vision spoke powerfully to values the American people held dear: America as a pioneer and America as a world leader.

An organizational vision statement might not put a man on the moon, but it should be compelling in the same way that Kennedy's and King's visions were: it should challenge and inspire the group to stretch its capabilities and achieve its purpose. An effective vision statement should convey both an external and an internal vision for the organization.

The *external vision* focuses on how the world would be improved, changed, or different if the organization achieved its purpose. Too often, vision statements merely focus on the internal vision—what the organization itself would look like sometime in the future ("We will have doubled the staff; we have now"; "We will have our own building"). But these statements avoid answering the question: "So what?" Why should we have doubled the staff; why do we need our own building? An exclusively internally focused vision statement is rather self-serving and can encourage the organization to focus on perpetuating itself rather than making sure that a problem will be solved or a need in the community will be met. The focus of an effective vision statement should first of all be on the client to be served or the constituency whose lives are to be impacted by the organization. For example,

- All people in our state will have access to quality health care, regardless of ability to pay (Health Care for All, Inc.).
- We, the citizens of Oakland, commit ourselves to creating a city of healthy, well-educated people; safe, vital neighborhoods; a dynamic economy; and a vibrant quilt of cultures where the future will work for all (Oakland Sharing the Vision).

While the external vision defines how the organization plans to change the world, the internal vision describes what the organization will look like when it is operating effectively and efficiently to support the achievement of that external vision—the organization's service or product mix, it's image or reputation, funding, partnerships, use of technology, board, staff, and facilities. The internal vision also defines what distinguishes the organization from its competitors. Examples of internal vision statements:

- We will have a 100,000 square foot gallery that has all the great neon artworks of the 20th century on display (Museum of Neon Art).
- All victims of felony assaults in Oklahoma County will receive information and counseling from a Victims' Assistance Fund (VAF) staff member or volunteer within 24 hours of their assault (Victim's Assistance Fund).
- The Chorus will be the best gay men's chorus in the world and the equal of any performing arts organization in San Francisco, and will be a leader in the development of gay culture and gay pride in the United States (San Francisco Gay Men's Chorus).

- We are recognized nationally and internationally as a leader in caring for the land and serving people. We are a multicultural and diverse organization. Employees work in a caring and nurturing environment where leadership is shared. All employees are respected, accepted, and appreciated for their unique and important contribution to the mission. The work is interesting, challenging, rewarding, and fun—more than just a job! We are an efficient and productive organization that excels in achieving its mission. Responsibility and accountability for excellence are shared by employees and partners. The American people can count on the Forest Service to perform (United States Department of Agriculture—Forest Service).
- We will achieve a diversified funding base which will adequately support all of our programs (Every nonprofit organization the authors have ever worked with!).

Drafting a Vision Statement. Like the mission statement, drafting a vision statement begins with intuition and ideas, evolves through discussion, and results in a shared sense of direction and motivation. All of the board and staff should be involved in initial brainstorming and some subsequent discussion; the Planning Committee should more fully engage in the process. As with any such process, differing ideas don't have to be a problem: people can spur each other on to more daring and valuable ideas—dreams of changing the world that they are willing to work hard for, encouraging each other to dream the possible. As with the mission statement, the organization will probably refer back to its vision statement

Combined Mission and Vision Statement of a Department of Obstetrics and Gynecology

The mission of the Department of Obstetrics and Gynecology is to conduct significant research, develop and maintain a scholarly educational environment, and provide quality, state of the art healthcare for women and their families *[business]*. Our vision is that the Department shall be internationally recognized for its efforts in research, education, and patient care *[vision]*. We dedicate our efforts to basic and applied research and clinical investigation that will optimize the health of our patients and families *[purpose]*. We will develop exemplary leadership and educational programs so that our students, fellows, residents, faculty, and staff may reach their fullest potential. We adopt and embrace innovations in the healthcare delivery system that will better our program. Our care is accessible, efficient, and effective. We strive to create and sustain an environment that inspires trust, stewardship, integrity, collaboration, and personal responsibility *[values last three sentences]*.

Note: This is an excellent example of a compelling statement. In this case the organization uses the word "mission" instead of "business." We include this example to again stress the point that what these ideas are called is not the important thing—there simply is no such thing as the common usage for these words in our sector yet. It doesn't matter! What matters is being clear about why your organization exists, what it does, and its guiding philosophy.

throughout the planning process and may modify it as it becomes clearer where the organization can and should be in the future.

The challenge is to create a vision that is grand enough to inspire people, but also a vision that is grounded in sufficient reality that people can start to believe that it can and will happen. No Olympic athlete ever got to the Olympics by accident; a compelling vision of his or her stellar performance helped surmount all the sweat and frustrations for many years. Without that powerful, attractive, valuable vision, why bother? Sometimes organizations far surpass their initial visions; as progress happens, what is possible expands. Nonetheless, the picture we carry around to remind us of why we are working so hard continues to inspire this success.

The Value of a Visioning Process within the Strategic Planning Process. The creation of a vision statement and the process of visioning (outlined in Exhibit 3-3) can not

Exhibit 3-3 Worksheet 7: Vision Statement

Process Notes	
How to do this activity	• Visioning is a powerful activity to do at a meeting of Board and staff. Distribute the vision statement worksheet to participants in advance of the retreat and ask them to describe their external and internal vision of success. If the number of participants at the meeting is small, have people read their visions and record key ideas on butcher paper (both where there is agreement and where there is disagreement); if a large group, break into smaller groups and work as teams. • You may need to refine or change this initial vision statement after you have completed Phase 2 and Phase 3 of the planning process.
Why do this activity	• An inspiring shared image of success will galvanize the efforts of your organization's staff and Board and help to start defining program and organizational strategies, goals, and objectives.
Who to involve in the process	• Ideally, all Board and staff should have some opportunity to give input into the organization's vision statement. The Planning Committee would review that input and designate one or two people to craft a powerful vision statement that could be included in your plan.

Case Study—ASO/USA

◆ Worksheet 7

Vision Statement

☐ Dare to dream the possible. What is your organization's realistic but challenging guiding vision of success?

External vision: Describe how the world would be improved, changed, or different if our organization was successful in achieving its purpose.

Our vision is that all people with HIV get the appropriate care they need in a comfortable, accessible setting, and that we see the day soon when HIV is no longer a killer in our community.

Internal vision: Envisioning our organization's future.

What is your programmatic vision for our organization for three to five years from today? (What would be our ideal program mix/service? List in order of priority—top priority services at the top of the list.)	**Describe your administrative vision for our organization for the next three to five years in terms of: staffing and benefits, Board of directors, our image in the community, our funding, our infrastructure and use of technology, facilities, information systems, planning and evaluation, quality control, or other**
• *The leading, comprehensive case management service in the city for people with HIV* • *A successful, independent outreach program operating city-wide* • *A spectrum of support services for people living with HIV* • *An aggressive and highly successful prevention program*	• *Increase our staff to 35 full-time equivalent positions* • *Strong, active board of 15 members* • *Image in the community of a well-run, aggressive, and effective community organization* • *No more than 60% of our funding from government in three years, with steady, renewable funding sources making up the remaining 40%* • *Sufficient internal resources, including space, computers, etc., to do our jobs well* • *A vital, ongoing planning process which incorporates quality assessment on a frequent basis*

only help to inspire board and staff, but can also be used as a basis for setting priorities. The visioning exercise can be referred to during Phase 4: Agreeing on Priorities to provide guidance to defining the ideal scope and scale of services and products. Visioning can help the organization be better able to answer the questions:

- What services and products should we be offering now and in the future that would best enable us to achieve our external vision of the future?
- Should we make changes in the services or products we are currently offering or how we go about doing our business so as to be better able to achieve our preferred future?

Suggested Visioning Exercise

During a retreat, put up a series of large, easel-size wall charts, scattered around the room. There would be one wall chart for each of the following ten questions:

- How would the world be improved or changed if we were successful in achieving our purpose?
- What are the most important services that we should continue to provide, change, or begin to offer in the next three years?
- What staffing and benefits changes do we need to implement to better achieve our purpose?
- What board of directors changes do we need to implement to better achieve our purpose?
- What resource development (fund-raising) changes do we need to implement to better achieve our purpose?
- What facilities and technology changes do we need to implement to better achieve our purpose?
- What infrastructure, systems, or communication changes do we need to implement to better achieve our purpose?
- How could we more effectively or efficiently provide our services? If you could only make three changes which would significantly impact our ability to provide quality services to our clients/customers, what would those changes be?
- What makes us unique (distinguishes us from the competition)?
- What do our clients/customers consider most important in our provision of services? What do our clients/customers need from us?

Divide the retreat participants into groups of three to six members and give each group thirty 3 × 5 inch Post-it Notes. Have each group fill out no more than three Post-it Notes for each question. When each group is finished, their responses to the questions should be posted on the wall charts. Individuals should be encouraged to walk about the room and read everyone's responses.

Likewise, the internal vision statement could be used to clarify what the organization would need to do from a management and operations level to ensure that there was an infrastructure in place to support the effective and efficient provision of goods and services to meet the needs of clients and customers. The internal vision can be used during the Setting Priorities phase as a basis for looking at some of these questions:

- What should be our long-term and short-term priorities regarding staffing, benefits, board, facilities, funding, partnerships, management, and financial information systems?
- What do we need to do now and in the next three years to distinguish us from our competition and to ensure that we are known and respected by our clients and the community?
- What can we do to increase cooperation and networking with agencies doing similar work so that limited resources are used in the most effective and efficient way?

Regardless of whether an organization is involved in an abbreviated, moderate, or extensive planning process, the above questions need to be answered. The process of visioning can provide a framework for answering those questions and therefore provide guidance in making the choices as to how an organization might best accomplish its purpose. ASO/USA's visioning process provides a good example of the creation of this framework.

PHASE 3: ASSESSING THE ENVIRONMENT

No organization exists in a vacuum. The definition of strategic planning offered earlier stresses the importance of focusing on the future within the context of an ever-changing environment—taking into account the myriad political, economic, social, technological, demographic, and legal forces that affect our world daily. In addition to assessing the external environment, it is important to understand the organization's internal environment—what resources and capacities the organization brings to the work of its mission. Skill at assessing the environment and then being pro-active in responding to that environment—in other words, strategic thinking—determines which organizations are most likely to be successful and effective in using their resources.

Phase 3: Assessing the Environment outlines the process of gathering and analyzing the information needed to make such an explicit assessment of an organization in its environment. At the end of Phase 3, you will have focused your understanding of the issues in the environment and the issues within the organization to which the organization must respond in order to be successful. These critical issues form the basis for the priority-setting process in Phase 4.

Assessing the situation includes the following three information-gathering activities:

1. Collecting input from internal stakeholders (board, staff, and volunteers)
2. Collecting input from external stakeholders (clients, funders, community leaders, and other key informants)
3. Reviewing more objective data such as government or other reports on projected demands for service, documented statement of client needs and changes in client mix, analysis of census and other public statistics, financial trends over the last few years, etc.

Planners have three information analysis tasks in Phase 3:

1. To understand the current and previous strategies which led the organization to its current situation
2. To assess the organization's programs, their effectiveness and competitive position, and the opportunities and threats in the environment relative to meeting client or customer needs
3. To identify any additional strategic issues or challenges facing the organization, based on the information gathered from internal and external sources

At the conclusion of this phase, the Planning Committee will have a database of concrete information that can be used to make decisions about program and administrative priorities and develop overall strategies. Part of the challenge of this information-gathering and analysis phase is that the information gathered may not be complete, or information gathered from one source may conflict with information gathered from another source. During this phase the Planning Committee will continually have to assess whether they have sufficient and accurate information to make informed decisions regarding short-term and long-term priorities.

Information gathering and analysis can be time consuming, and it will be natural to jump to solutions as issues, problems, and questions emerge and are clarified. While a given issue may appear to require an obvious response ("We're running a deficit; we need to bring in more revenue and cut costs!"), most issues have more than one level of complexity ("If we cut costs, how will that affect the quality of our programs? If we want to bring in more revenue by charging for certain services, how will that affect accessibility?"). Try to hold back from deciding how to respond until you have gathered most of the information you will work with. Don't be afraid to begin discussing possible responses; just wait to decide until Phase 4 of the planning process, Agreeing on Priorities. The Assessing the Environment phase is a creative process of gaining new insight into your organization's internal and external forces. If we think of each stakeholder and source of information as casting votes for which issues are most critical, the value of the creative thinking in this phase will be reduced if decisions are made before all the votes are in. It is only when you have gathered sufficient information about the environment that you will be able to employ strategic thinking in your planning and be strategic in your actions.

The assessment of the environment can be abbreviated (such as a planning group sitting down together and identifying strengths, weaknesses, opportunities, and threats) or it can be extensive (gathering lots of new information from stakeholders about their views with respect to the organization's strengths, weaknesses, opportunities, and threats). The depth of the information gathering and analysis in Phase 3 is the primary variable in differentiating an abbreviated process from an extensive process. This section of the workbook describes the steps to be taken in an extensive process. Refer back to Phase 1: Getting Ready for guidance about which steps to include in an abbreviated or moderate strategic planning process.

Step 3.1: Articulate Previous and Current Strategies

What does it mean to be strategic and employ strategic thinking? Being strategic means making conscious choices as to how you are going to use your limited resources to achieve your purpose in response to a dynamic environment. Strategic thinking therefore includes making decisions regarding what you *will* do and what you *will not* do, where you should focus your energies, and what your overall priorities should be. In this process, the goal is to capitalize on the strengths, core capabilities, and unique attributes of the organization in pursing its mission. Strategic thinking embodies the currently popular concept of leverage; how can we focus our energy to do the most good with our limited resources. The strategic planning process requires translating this strategic understanding into core program and organizational strategies and developing goals and objectives that support these overall strategies. See Exhibit 3-4.

Exhibit 3-4 Worksheet 8: Previous and Current Strategies

Process Notes	
How to do this activity	Review the history of the organization and articulate previous and current strategies. Discuss effectiveness of the strategy and implications for future.
Why do this activity	Understanding how your organization focused its resources in the past and present is critical to learning from your experience and setting future strategies.
Who to involve in the process	Planning Committee.

Case Study—ASO/USA

◆ **Worksheet 8** **Previous and Current Strategies**	☐ Identify and assess your organization's previous and current strategies.

Previous and Current Strategy	Was or is the strategy effective? Why or why not? Should it be considered as a strategy for the future? Why or why not?
Be a very grassroots organization, many volunteers, community-based	*This has been an important part of our success because the people we are trying to reach trust us and can relate to us.* • *Continue this strategy overall, but improve coordination and efficiency of our operations*
Focus on the people at greatest risk for HIV	*While this has been a selling point, we are increasingly serving people who are not at greatest risk because we are accessible and community-based.* • *We need to reconsider this approach*
Go after large grants so that we don't have to spend all our time fund-raising	*This has been successful to date; it now leaves us in a vulnerable situation, though it is not clear that we should change the basic strategy.* • *Investigate and decide*
Do any service for which we can get funding	*We never would have said it this way, but basically that is what we have been doing. As a result, our programs have grown in unpredictable ways. We need to make sure all our programs still fit together.* • *Change this strategy; we should not be teaching English classes or providing transportation because there are other groups better able to provide these services*
Be collaborative at any cost	*Again, we probably would not have said it this way, but the value of cooperation is so strong that we have tended to collaborate when it might have served our clients better to do it ourselves. The Outreach program may be an example of this.* • *We need to change this strategy; there are some times when it is best to provide a program by ourselves*

A strategy is a broad overall priority or direction adopted by an organization so as to best achieve its purpose. A strategy defines your overall program and organizational priorities and therefore suggests where your organization should be investing its resources now and over the next few years.

A good place to start the Assessing the Environment phase is to step back and look at the previous and current strategies that the organization has either successfully or unsuccessfully used. The organization's history, developed using Worksheet 4, identified what was happening in the organization's internal and external environment during its history. What the organization did in response to its environment were in actuality strategic choices. All organizations make strategic choices, although often these have neither been recognized nor articulated as actual strategies. Once an organization is in the process of strategic planning, however, it is important to make explicit these unspoken strategies and incorporate

How the Arts Organization Changed Its Strategy

Storytelling Songbirds is a two-person performing arts group that tells dramatic stories through a combination of drama, dance, and song. Two years ago, both members of the group gave up their part-time day jobs to devote all their time to the Songbirds. During this time they have made a modestly successful CD and completed a national tour as well as a brief tour in Europe.

Storytelling Songbirds, centered on the artistic vision of the two writer/performers—Carlos and Fran—is nonetheless governed by a nonprofit board of directors. When the board of directors insisted on developing a strategic plan, an important insight emerged during the discussion about previous strategies.

They realized that an important part of their business strategy, and indeed a point of pride, is that they have never sought contributions to cover the cost of their performances. "We're making a decent living and paying all our expenses," says Fran, "with a budget purely on box office, performance contracts, and CD sales. For a performing arts organization, that's astounding success!"

Some of the board members of Storytelling Songbirds have been on other arts boards and felt a responsibility to warn Carlos and Fran about the financial unpredictability of arts income. When Carlos sprained his shoulder last month, the Songbirds realized that they had to reevaluate their long-term strategy.

"I hate it when I see other arts organizations begging for money," says Carlos. "But I've also realized how much we've just been scraping by. What we want to do—taking these stories to new audiences—just won't ever be completely supported by contracts. We need time to develop new concepts, work out collaborations with other artists, and explore our own boundaries and visions. I realize now that it costs more to put on a season than people can afford to pay."

Along with their board, Carlos and Fran are beginning to think about raising a modest proportion of their budget from grants and donations. "Moving away from a box office-only strategy has meant changing our self-image," comments Fran. Carlos is quick to add, "This new strategy will let us grow in new ways. I'm feeling good about it."

them into the deliberate consideration of the organization's future directions. As part of the Assessing the Environment, the Planning Committee should look for past patterns of operation or allocation of resources—these are the organization's previous strategies. The Planning Committee should analyze whether the organization's past and present strategies were and are effective, and then consider whether they should be part of future strategic thinking. ASO/USA goes through this process in Worksheet 8.

Step 3.2: Gather Input from Internal Stakeholders

Now that you have an understanding of your organization's past environment and strategic responses, you are in a position to gather information regarding the current environment and future trends. A useful organizing framework for this assessment is the SWOT analysis (which stands for Strengths, Weaknesses, Opportunities, and Threats). The SWOT analysis is a broad overview of the most important internal Strengths and Weaknesses and the most important external Opportunities and Threats.

S W O T — What are the organization's internal *Strengths?* ("What do we do well?")

S **W** O T — What are the organization's internal *Weaknesses?* ("Where can we improve?")

S W **O** T — What external *Opportunities* exist with respect to pursuing our mission? ("What changes are taking place in our environment which might allow us to better achieve our mission?")

S W O **T** — What external *Threats* might hinder the pursuit of our mission? ("What changes in the environment do we need to guard against or prepare for in doing our work?")

The SWOT analysis can be done at the level of the whole organization or at the level of each program. Use the SWOT framework (see Exhibit 3-5) to help gather and organize information in assessing the operating environment.

As can be seen in the case study, evaluating an organization's strengths and weaknesses typically includes gathering perceptions about the effectiveness of program services; the relationship of revenue to expenses; customer service and quality control; program delivery; reputation of programs and the organization and staffing (sufficient paid and volunteer staff, wages and benefits, training opportunities); board governance; resource development; organizational structure; planning and evaluation; information and financial systems; office facilities and equipment; intergroup, intragroup, and individual working relationships; communication; decision-making; and so on. Successful organizations are those that exploit strengths rather than just focus on weaknesses—in other words, this process isn't just about fixing the things that are wrong, but also nurturing what goes right.

The same should apply to how an organization approaches its opportunities and threats—the external forces that influence the organization. These are usually categorized into Political, Economic, Social, Technological, Demographic, and Legal (sometimes known as the acronym PESTDL) trends. These encompass circumstances such as changing client needs, increased competition, changing regulations, new interest in a particular focus problem that the organization tries to address, and so on. These are forces that can help an organization move forward (opportunities) or forces that can hold an organization back (threats): opportunities that are ignored can become threats, and threats that are dealt with

Exhibit 3-5 Worksheet 9: Staff and Board Perceptions of SWOT

Process Notes

How to do this activity	• Brainstorm and record on flip charts a list of SWOTs. This activity can take place at meeting(s) of staff and Board; staff and Board may meet separately or together (such as at a planning retreat). You may want to distribute the worksheet to staff and Board ahead of time in order to get people thinking about the organization. • Alternatively, you may distribute Worksheet 8 and collect and summarize results. Participants should be encouraged to be as specific as they can and not generalize (e.g., "at least 3/4 of all staff have been with the agency for at least six years," rather than "great staff"). • Gather lists of SWOTs, sort into categories, select most important items, and summarize results.
Why do this activity	• Individuals' perceptions provide a starting framework for perceiving the organization's current situation. • One of the key aspects of strategic planning and management is being proactive—making decisions that take advantage of strengths and opportunities, overcome weaknesses, and try to turn threats into opportunities.
Who to involve in the process	• Board and staff. The extent and format of their involvement to be decided by Planning Committee.

Case Study—ASO/USA

◆ **Worksheet 9** **Staff and Board Perceptions of SWOT**	☐ List our program and administrative strengths and weaknesses (star [*] the top three internal forces). ☐ List the external opportunities and threats (political, economic, social, technological, demographic, and legal trends) that may impact the organization (star [*] the top three external forces).

Internal Forces	**External Forces**
Strengths	**Opportunities**
**Strong track record of achievement* • *Good reputation in the community* • *Solid volunteer program* **Excellent executive director* • *Dedicated, talented staff* • *Good relationships with funders financial base*	**New AIDS treatments could greatly help our clients* • *There are still many people not served by our programs; we could expand services* • *We have good relationships with many other organizations; we could develop additional collaborative partnerships* • *Our case management services could potentially be expanded to include other clients, not only people with HIV*
Weaknesses	**Threats**
**Our financial management is really a problem* • *Board not as active as it could be* • *Staff are feeling overwhelmed* • *Lack of a long-range strategic direction* • *Program record keeping*	**New AIDS treatments could make our services obsolete* **Outreach program threatens our credibility in community because of inconsistent quality* **Overly dependent on federal grant; federal funding could dry up* • *Funders are requiring increased accountability and better record-keeping* • *Managed care continues to be a confusing presence in our field*

Sample Types and Sources of Information for Strategic Planning

Type of Information	Possible Sources	Comments
Key trends in the field in which the organization operates	Industry journals; notes from latest conferences; local or state planners for the field; experts or advocates (lobbyists) and client advocates (consumer groups)	Information from individuals can be gathered via interviews or inviting key individuals to speak to the Planning Committee
Plans and attitudes of major existing funders	Personal interviews or annual reports	Some funders may be reluctant to talk about future funding commitments or give feedback to current grantees about their performance
Demographic changes within the target population	Census data; public health data; housing stock studies; city, state, or national planning offices	Staff and volunteers can often provide additional informal perspectives
Regulatory changes	Journals, conferences, state associations of nonprofit organizations, independent sector, state regulators	Presentation should focus on the impact such changes have on the organization
Financial trends for the past five years	Organization's audited financial statements	Preferred presentation mode is through use of graphs that delineate trends and key ratios
Client data trends for the past five years	Program reports, annual reports, funder reports, and other internal records	Presentation should be graph of key relationships among programs, shifts in characteristics or needs/wants of clients
Client satisfaction	Client surveys and/or focus groups	Such feedback should ideally be built into the organization's ongoing commitment to quality and meeting client needs
Quality indicators	Existing evaluation data, surveys of referral sources, consumer satisfaction, and staff perceptions	Such evaluation should ideally be built into the organization's ongoing commitment to quality and meeting client needs
Future program opportunities	Information from sources above; focus groups among potential consumers; market studies or needs assessments done by organization or others; interviews with other service providers	Once data has been collected, staff will need to put together a business plan with two or three year demand projection; staffing pattern; equipment and space needs; and first year financial pro forma

appropriately can be turned into opportunities. During the strategic planning process the organization wants to figure out how it can best use its scarce resources to take advantage of strengths and opportunities, and use resources so as to overcome weaknesses and threats.

In using the SWOT technique, the Planning Committee should involve as many staff and board as possible in this process. Their ideas and opinions might be collected through questionnaires, telephone or in-person interviews, facilitated organization-wide or small group meetings, or a combination of these methods; some organizations have board and staff in the same meeting to discuss these ideas, while others have them meet separately.

One way to do this is to brainstorm ideas on flip charts during a retreat. After the lists of strengths, weaknesses, opportunities, and threats have been recorded, the listed ideas can be grouped into logical topic or issue groups to make the data easier to present and analyze. For example, all the ideas related to fund-raising, staffing, or program development would be grouped together. Smaller groups (preferably mixed groups of board and staff) might then take that data and brainstorm ideas about how the organization might respond to the various challenges presented during the SWOT exercise.

Other Information-Gathering Tools for Use with Internal Stakeholders

It may be helpful to examine individual dimensions of the internal organization in more detail than the above SWOT assessment. The following three tools provide guidance in looking at management, financial performance, and governance.

Self-Assessment of Management. A tool that can be used to identify how effectively the organization is managed and what specific areas need attention is "Elements of an Effectively Managed Organization" (EEMO™). EEMO™ is a framework for looking at what it means to be effectively managed and can be used by an organization's managers to identify areas that are perceived as strengths and areas that are real or potential perceived weaknesses. EEMO™ defines eight elements that make up an effectively managed organization: Mission, Priorities, Structure, People, Systems, Program Evaluation, Leadership, and Relationships.[4] Appendix C has a copy of Elements of an Effectively Managed Organization.

[4] There are many different frameworks that have been used to assess organizations. The McKinsey 7-S Framework identifies seven elements: structure, systems, style, staff, skills, shared values, and strategy. Marvin R. Weisbord developed a six box model of organizational diagnosis: purposes, structure, relationships, rewards, helpful mechanisms, and leadership. Peters and Waterman listed eight characteristics of excellence: a bias for action; close to the customer; autonomy and entrepreneurship; productivity through people; hands-on, value driven; stick to the knitting; simple form, lean staff; and simultaneous loose-tight properties.

Assessment of Financial Performance. Organizations have several sources of data with which to assess financial performance. Most organizations have audited financial statements to review. In addition to the statements of revenue, expenses, and assets and liabilities, the management letter included with an audited set of financial statements can be a source of information about systems and structures that support effectiveness and efficiency. While the audit is useful for looking at a whole year's activity, organizations typically have monthly and/or quarterly reports prepared showing revenues and expenses compared with the budget. The following questions may be helpful in suggesting the dimensions of financial performance relevant for your organization:

- How much does the organization spend per unit of service?
- Is the organization living within its means and maximizing its program services within its available resources?
- Are there financial reserves available for hard times or to take advantage of new opportunities? (A reserve of three months of operating expenses is a relatively prudent goal.)
- Given comparison of current financial data to similar data for prior periods, is the organization better or worse off than before, and what are the possible future trends?
- To what extent are services being subsidized from other revenue sources, and what does this mean for future ability to provide services?
- How diversified are the organization's funding sources?
- What is the organization's overall financial health? Are financial management systems and personnel adequate?

Self-Assessment of Governance. The effectiveness of the board is of major strategic importance for any organization. The board is expected to assess its own work on an ongoing basis, so the strategic planning process may or may not provide an appropriate opportunity for assessing its effectiveness. An annual self-assessment has several important advantages:

- Determining the criteria for the assessment is a good mechanism by which the board can develop its values and set standards for itself
- By conducting a survey of all board members, the board can take a look at itself as a whole, including those who are quiet at meetings
- Over time, assessments provide feedback to the board officers and to the executive director on how well the board is working together

One example of a board self-assessment survey is included in Appendix D. This or a similar assessment can be completed by each board member anonymously. The results for each question then can be tallied and presented using bar graphs to show the spread of the board members' opinions. An example of a bar graph tally is presented at the end of the survey. The results of such a self-assessment would then be one more source of information in developing a comprehensive statement of the organization's strengths, weaknesses, opportunities, and threats.

Step 3.3: Gather External Stakeholders' Perspectives

Just as the above SWOT assessment allows an organization to garner a wide variety of perspectives from internal stakeholders, an assessment of SWOT by those outside the organization can also add a great deal to the assessment of the environment (see Exhibit 3-6). Relying only on internal stakeholders will provide an incomplete picture of the organization's situation. (Refer back to Worksheet 5: Information Gathering Plan where the Planning Committee identified external stakeholders from whom to gather input.)

Exhibit 3-6 Worksheet 10: External Stakeholders' Perceptions

Process Notes	
How to do this activity	• Gather information directly from stakeholders. All interviews and/or surveys should be completed before discussion of strategies, goals, and objectives. Refer back to Worksheet 5. • Once all the data is gathered, you may choose to fill out Worksheet 10: External Stakeholders' Perceptions, summarizing key findings.
Why do this activity	• To incorporate outside perspectives into an understanding of current situation. • To make explicit the expectations and needs of various stakeholders so that the organization can decide whether and how to meet them. • To provide a chance for stakeholders to have input into the planning process, to provide an opportunity for the organization to tell key stakeholders about current services, and to promote buy-in by stakeholders.
Who to involve in the process	• Key external stakeholders provide input. Planning Committee reviews findings.

◆ Worksheet 10

External Stakeholders Perceptions and Expectations

☐ Summarize findings regarding stakeholders' perception and expectations of the organization

Constituency	• What does this constituency say about or organization's strengths and weaknesses? • What trends do they perceive as either opportunities or threats?	• What does this constituency need or expect from our organization? (What is the criteria they use to judge our performance?) • How well does our organization perform against those criteria (excellent, good, fair, or poor)? Why such a rating? • What does this constituency want us to do more of or less of? • What additional or increased programs or services do they think we should be offering if resources were available?
XYZ Foundation	• Strength: *Provide needed services* • Strength: *Respect Executive Director* • Weakness: *Not happy with financial reports* • Opportunity: *Work together with other AIDS service organizations* • Opportunity: *Get financial systems technical assistance from Support Center or other management support organization* • Threat: *Increased competition for charitable funds* • Threat: *Ignorance about AIDS by community*	• *Expect ASO to deliver on proposals (results)—hear good things in community, but ability to document results has only been fair* • *Expect ASO to be well managed—fair* • *Expect ASO to look for new funding source—good* • *Re competitors: Would be inappropriate to comment specifically. Concerned about limited resources and unnecessary duplication of services; wants more coordination*
Community Leader Joe Schmo	• Strength: *Only organization of its kind* • Strength: *Good reputation for services* • Weakness: *Not high enough public profile/not well known* • Weakness: *Not offer help to families* • Opportunity: *There must be more government funds available* • Threat: *Increase of HIV in our community* • Threat: *Not accessible HIV testing in community*	• *Expect to give input into planning process—fair in the past, currently good* • *Expect ASO to forge relationships with other providers in community—good* • *Expect ASO to continue leadership role—good* • *Re competitors: Don't know of competitors (said: "There shouldn't be any competitors, money is too tight to have competition."*
Client focus group	• Strength: *Caring, nonjudgmental staff* • Strength: *Help in navigating through the system* • Weakness: *Have to wait too long for some direct services* • Weakness: *Found out about ASO/USA from word of mouth* • Weakness: *ASO staff seem really overwhelmed* • Weakness: *We don't do HIV testing* • Opportunity: *Do more case management* • Threat: *Fear that city is going to cut back on services*	• *Need availability of services—generally feel it is good* • *ASO staff are caring providers (compassion, respectful)—excellent* • *Culturally specific help—excellent* • *Women-specific assistance—fair* • *Housing—poor* • *Re competitors: Have generally received good help from ABC group, not very responsive staff at DEF group. Frustration that everyone has different procedures*

Animal Rights Now Responds to Its Stakeholders

Animal Rights Now had outgrown its old facility. The board and staff convinced themselves that a large new building was the answer to their facility problems. As the visions of the new building became grander, extensions of the program were planned. The Board President, Jon, was particularly enthusiastic. "In addition to our advocacy work and our work with stray animals, if we build a theater/conference center we can expand our education work. And we can generate extra income by renting out the space when we're not using it!"

A site was located, preliminary designs were invited, and the train seemed ready to go. As part of their planning process, the Board and staff sought input from the external stakeholders whose support they would need: funders, individual donors, other organizations in the community, and neighbors. To their shock and ultimate benefit, the organization learned that three other organizations in the area had recently expanded their educational activities and that the theater/convention space would sink the building.

"It was tough," says Jon now. "We were so excited about the possibilities for growth and expansion. We even had a donation for lights in the theater. But in the end, our plan is much more realistic and I am glad we didn't find out *after* we had put down a lot of money that our original vision just wasn't going to fly."

With a scaled-down facilities plan and a mission focused on needed services where there was no unnecessary duplication, the organization completed its strategic planning process and built a smaller building with extensive community support behind them.

External stakeholders (in particular current and past clients, but also funders, community leaders, and potential collaborators) can give the Planning Committee insight into community opinions of what the organization does well, where it can improve, unmet community needs it might address, and other opportunities or potential threats. This information might be gathered through telephone or in-person interviews, questionnaires and client surveys, or focus groups. In addition to their general perceptions of the organization's strengths, weaknesses, opportunities, and threats, external stakeholders might also be asked some questions specific to their outsider perspective:[5]

- What does the stakeholder need or expect (criteria for performance) from the organization?
- How well does the organization perform against those criteria (excellent, good, fair, or poor) and why such a rating?
- How well does the organization perform relative to its competitors?
- Assuming sufficient resources, what might the organization do more or less of?

[5] Questions adapted from John Bryson. *Strategic Planning for Public and Nonprofit Organizations* (San Francisco: Jossey-Bass, 1993), pp. 73–74.

Step 3.4: Gather Information about the Effectiveness of Programs

Beyond the general input from external stakeholders collected in the previous step, the Planning Committee should make sure that current programs are assessed in some detail as a part of the strategic planning process.

Which of our programs or services makes the most difference to the community? Which are responding to growing needs? Which are the most cost-effective? Which will face funding cutbacks in the future? Which will face influxes of funding in the future? Program planning needs to look both to the past—to learn whether our programs have had the impact we want—and to the future—to assess future needs, funding opportunities, and emerging new ways to meet the needs.

Ideally, program evaluation is an ongoing process for an organization. Client feedback mechanisms should be built into programs so that client satisfaction and progress is monitored continuously. On a regular basis, formal evaluations should be done by outside evaluators or by staff or volunteers to help an agency consider how to improve a program, the degree to which a program is making a difference, and whether the program is cost-effective.

More practically speaking, in many organizations, the strategic planning process provides an opportunity to step back and decide what to do with existing programs: which to grow aggressively, which to discontinue, which to change dramatically, which to spin off to independent status or to another organization. For many organizations, the single most important decision about programs in the strategic plan may simply be deciding to develop an ongoing feedback and evaluation plan in the future.

Program evaluations can be based on quantitative and/or qualitative data. Quantitative data consists of fact-based information such as a review of records, descriptive statistics, and the like; it is more easily collected and less easily disputed because it translates experience into quantifiable data that can be counted, compared, measured, and manipulated statistically. Qualitative data consists of what people say about the programs based on interviews, focus groups or other meetings, direct or field observation, reviews of written materials, informal feedback, satisfaction surveys, and questionnaires.

Involving Staff in Assessing Programs and Client Needs. One of the places to start program evaluation may very well be with the program staff themselves. (See Exhibit 3-7.) Because program staff are usually the closest of the internal stakeholders to the clients themselves, staff will have a definite perspective on client needs, strengths and weaknesses of the program, and the quality of the program vis-à-vis the competition. Asking staff to evaluate their own programs, as well as the agency as a whole and its ability to serve or not serve specific populations, will not only allow program staff to have meaningful input into the planning process,

How the Program Is Doing Depends on Who You Ask!

The board of an established tutoring organization that worked with children whose native language was not English had great confidence that their program was doing a splendid job. Many of the board members had previously volunteered as tutors and a local newspaper article printed a few years ago had lauded the program. The part-time program director collected reports regularly from the tutors and it appeared that the number of children served was gradually increasing. The tutors consistently provided anecdotes of success stories they heard from parents and teachers.

As part of a strategic planning process, the board decided to gather more extensive feedback from their clients. They hired an outside evaluator to assess the effectiveness of the program and customer satisfaction. The evaluator put together a simple survey for the parents of each of the children enrolled and telephoned all the teachers who referred children to the program for feedback. The evaluator, along with two board members, attended a few tutoring sessions to observe the program in action and to casually ask some of the children what they thought. The evaluator also talked to the principals of all three elementary school program sites.

What the board found out from the evaluator's report surprised them greatly. In the first place, new tutoring programs had begun recently at two of the schools. In each case, the new group was serving many more children than was the established tutoring program. In the second place, many of the parents *and* teachers reported that some volunteers from the established program rarely showed up for appointments with the children and that the use of the program's materials was inconsistent at best. It seemed that a few of the volunteers saw their role more as a "big brother/big sister" than that of an educator/tutor. The teachers and parents had been reluctant to complain because, "after all, they weren't paying for the program."

The program evaluation information, collected easily and over a period of only weeks, allowed the board and the director to identify these critical issues and to respond. The program director immediately began much more active training, coaching, and monitoring of the volunteer tutors. A few tutors were informed that their services were no longer necessary. The group also quickly moved to develop closer relationships with the two new local programs, sharing materials and referrals, and helping the new groups find out about other resources available to tutoring programs. Twice-yearly surveys of parents, teachers, children *and* volunteers were instituted.

The dark cloud of the news about the program had another silver lining: a year after the strategic plan was completed, the tutoring program had developed such a positive word-of-mouth reputation for it's tutor training program that it was repeatedly asked to provide training to other tutoring programs and was expanding, carefully, its training services into a new program.

Exhibit 3-7 Worksheet 11: More Detailed Staff Assessment of Programs

Note: This worksheet expands on the work done with Worksheet 9. It asks staff to assess individual programs in detail, as well as to look at implications for the entire organization. This worksheet serves as a bridge between Phase 3 and Phase 4. The combined content of Worksheet 9 and Worksheet 12 overlaps with the content Worksheet 11. A planning process may make use of all three, or choose one set of worksheet pages or another.

Process Notes

How to do this activity	Have each program's staff meet and discuss the questions on the Staff Assessment of Programs worksheet. The program manager should summarize the discussions and complete Worksheet 11.
Why do this activity	Information about the needs and perceived effectiveness of your programs is necessary, and program staff are some of the most informed regarding client needs and how their programs actually operate. Especially if there is a need to reallocate resources or cut costs for particular programs, it is helpful to involve staff in suggesting new and different ways of doing things and making suggestions for the future.
Who to involve in the process	Appropriate program staff. Summary of findings presented to Planning Committee.

but provide useful data and perspectives to make future decisions. ASO/USA put this into practice when they completed Worksheet 11.

How Else Might We Evaluate Our Programs?

Many organizations find it useful to develop a document that evaluates each program on a single page using the following basic evaluation questions:

- *Assessment of inputs.* What is the cost of the program? What resources are required to operate the program? Are there special site licenses or staff qualifications required or desired? What physical elements, such as square footage, location, facility, or equipment are essential to the program's success?
- *Assessment of implementation (evaluation of the process).* How successful have we been in conducting the *activities* we planned (number of workshops delivered, number of meals served, research completed, performances held)?

♦ Worksheet 11

Staff Assessment of Programs and Organization in Relation to Client Needs and Competitive Position

☐ Evaluate your programs and organization in terms of client needs, results, competitive position, and potential for increased efficiency.

Program/Service Name: *Case Management* (Note: *only one program assessment is presented as an illustration*)

Description of program service: *Case management for people with HIV disease is a service that links and coordinates assistance from multiple agencies and caregivers who provide psychosocial, medical, and practical support. The purpose of case management is to enable clients to obtain the highest levels of independence and quality of life consistent with their functional capacity and preferences for care.*

Units of service and cost unit of service (if applicable): *1 hour of service provided to or on behalf of clients (in a range of approved activities = 1 unit of service. The contracted cost is $55 per hour.*

Prepared by: *Delores Molina*

Analysis of Competitive Position

Name of organization	Ability to provide service				Quality of service				Why did you rate ability to provide service the way you did? Why did you give the rating on quality of service?
Our program	4 Excellent	(3) Good	2 Fair	1 Poor	4 Excellent	(3) Good	2 Fair	1 Poor	*Both our ability to provide the service and the quality of our services in our monitoring reports from the federal program have been rated "good." Our client satisfaction data are consistent with this rating.*
Competitor: *City Clinic*	4 Excellent	(3) Good	2 Fair	1 Poor	4 Excellent	3 Good	(2) Fair	1 Poor	*Our information about the quality of their services is anecdotal from clients and staff conversations. We have no hard evidence about the quality of care.*
Competitor: *Ourtown Hospital*	4 Excellent	3 Good	(2) Fair	1 Poor	4 Excellent	(3) Good	2 Fair	1 Poor	*We know that their resources are stretched very thin. However, in general, what we hear from clients and staff indicates that their quality of services is good.*
Competitor:	4 Excellent	3 Good	2 Fair	1 Poor	4 Excellent	3 Good	2 Fair	1 Poor	

(Continued)

Worksheet 11 *(Continued)*

List Other Competitors Not Assessed:

Growth Strategy for this Program: _X_Increase __Maintain __Decrease __Eliminate

Why this strategy? Implications if we were to ignore this strategy. What impact would this growth strategy have on our resources (staff time and other expenditures) and revenues. Is there potential for collaboration? In what ways? With whom? Additional comments.
We think we can compete on quality and cost and that what we have to offer will better serve many clients now being served at City Clinic or not being served. This requires getting an increase in service contracts.

What are the greatest strengths of this program?
- *Our staff*
- *Our reputation*
- *Our training process*
- *Our access to clients*

What are the greatest weaknesses of this program?
- *Inadequate facilities for case managers*
- *Insufficient internal record-keeping systems*

How could we improve the cost-effectiveness of this program?
- *Make better use of computers?*
- *Assist case managers with certain clerical tasks and appointment scheduling?*

How could we improve the quality of this program?
- *Update information on all available resources more frequently (monthly vs. every six months)*
- *Arrange for more consistent intake procedures with the services we refer our clients to*

How could we improve our ability to provide this service?
- *Not sure*

If the budget for this program were suddenly *halved,* what would you recommend we do?
- *Serve only the clients on the north side of town; they are the people who have absolutely no other options*

If the budget for this program were suddenly doubled, what would you recommend we do?
- *Expand our services city wide!*

How should we measure results/impact/outcomes of this program in improving the quality of our clients' lives? What are the indicators of success (benchmarks upon which we should measure our success)? How do we know we are making a difference?
- *The measures of activity include the number of referrals and frequency of contact with clients, etc.*
- *The measures of impact with clients include their reports about the ways we have helped them, clients gaining access to services they previously did not know about or could not get to, and ultimately in an improvement (or maintenance) of their health status*

List client group(s) currently being served by our organization	How well is this client group being served by us?	Why did you rate our services to this client group the way you did? How could we ensure that this client group receives the best possible services available delivered either by our organization or from another organization?
Youth	(4) Excellent 3 Good 2 Fair 1 Poor	*We are acknowledged to be the most effective youth-serving agency in the state and have been asked to conduct workshops on our services for many other organizations.*
Women	4 Excellent (3) Good 2 Fair 1 Poor	*Our case management services are seen to be quite effective, however, they could be improved by expanding our capacity.*
Intravenous Drug Users	4 Excellent (3) Good 2 Fair 1 Poor	*Our prevention outreach has shown a reduction in unsafe sex and in sharing of intravenous needles. However, our staff are stretched to the max and we could use more resources in this area.*
Gay men	(4) Excellent 3 Good 2 Fair 1 Poor	*Initially, AIDS was predominantly a white, gay man's disease. We began serving this group and continue to have strong backing and quality of services even as the demographics have changed to include many more people of color and women.*
	4 Excellent 3 Good 2 Fair 1 Poor	
	4 Excellent 3 Good 2 Fair 1 Poor	

(Continued)

Worksheet 11 *(Continued)*

List client group(s) not currently being served (or severely underserved) by our organization	Why needs of this client group are not being met? Why are we currently not serving this client group? Should we allocate organizational resources to meeting the needs of this client group? How could we ensure that this client group receives the best possible services available delivered either by our organization or from another organization?
Middle-income men with insurance-covered case management programs	*There are some needs not met with this group, but it would be prohibitively expensive to try to meet them. This is not our primary mission.*
People living in Center City	*Because of the poverty in Center City, there is also a high concentration of intravenous drug users. We could better meet the needs of this group if we expanded our outreach program to serve more people. There are also many homeless people we think are at high risk.*

Assessment of Entire Organization:

How could we improve the cost-effectiveness of our organization?
By focusing our program efforts on the areas where we make the most impact and by eliminating our services where there is duplication in the city, we can improve the overall cost-effectiveness of our organization.

What do our customers/clients consider value? How could we improve the quality of services we provide as an organization to our customers/clients?
See individual client comments.

If the budget for this organization were suddenly *halved,* what would you recommend we do?
Cut both case management and prevention, focus efforts on the most vulnerable segments of our community.

If the budget for this organization were suddenly *doubled,* what would you recommend we do?
Expand both programs and cover the entire city thoroughly.

Summary: Suggested Overall Program Priorities

Short-Term Priorities	**Long-Term Priorities**
• *Expand case management* • *Cut support groups* • •	• *Develop subcontracts for additional case management* • *Increase the evaluation of behavioral change prevention efforts* • •

Summary: Suggested Overall Management/Operations Priorities

Short-Term Priorities	**Long-Term Priorities**
• *Get financial systems fixed; this is really a bigger issue, our overall infrastructure needs to adjust to the fact that our staff has doubled in the last three years but our systems haven't* • *Even out compensation of staff* • •	• *Invest in ongoing quality improvement effort* • *Centralize facilities* • •

- *Assessment of outcomes (evaluation of the program).* Are the goals of the program being met? Have the activities conducted led to the *outcomes* we sought (improvement in skills of workshop attendees, improved health of people receiving meals, influence of public opinion through research, cultural enrichment of performance goals)?
- *Assessment of impact.* What is the broader impact of the program? What unexpected or unintended impacts are occurring as a result of our program?

See Exhibit 3-8 and the case study for guidance.

Techniques Used in Program Evaluation. Included in Appendix E is a set of nine techniques used in program evaluation, such as surveys of client satisfaction and outcomes, focus groups, interviews, and tests. These techniques can easily be adapted to help any organization answer the basic program evaluation questions noted above.

Step 3.5: Identify Any Additional Issues or Questions That Surfaced during the Information-Gathering and Assessment Steps

By the completion of Phase 3: Assessing the Environment, the Planning Committee should have sufficient data collected so that its members can have informed discussions during the next phase of the strategic planning process—Agreeing on Priorities. Before leaving the Assessing the Environment phase, the Planning Committee should review all the data collected and see whether any additions or

Exhibit 3-8 Worksheet 12: Program Evaluation

Process Notes	
How to do this activity	Program staff meets to discuss questions. Program Manager summarizes findings on Program Evaluation Worksheet.
Why do this activity	A key component of the assessing the environment phase is the evaluation of program's effectiveness and efficiency. The information from this worksheet will help inform decisions about whether to continue or discontinue a program, maintain it at its existing level, expand or change its direction, etc.
Who to involve in the process	Appropriate program staff completes worksheet. Summary of findings presented to Planning Committee.

Case Study—ASO/USA

♦ **Worksheet 12** **Program Evaluation**	☐ Assess your program in relationship to inputs, implementation, outcomes, and impact.

Name of Program: *Case Management* (Note: *Only one program is evaluated here as an illustration.*)

Prepared by: *Delores Molina*

Date: *3/1/97*

Assessment of inputs: What resources are required to operate the program? Are there special site licenses or staff qualifications required or desired? What physical elements, such as square footage, location, facility, or equipment are essential to the program's success?

- *$170,000 program budget*
- *5 staff*
- *Meeting space for all staff (up to three conference rooms needed at the same time)*
- *Dedicated training program*

Assessment of implementation (evaluation of the process): How many units of service are we delivering?

- *300 cases, an average of 10 hours per client per month. Total of 3,000 hours of service*

Assessment of outcomes (evaluation of the program): Are the goals of the program being met?

- *93% of clients report that they are getting most or all of their needs met through the case manager*
- *91% of clients report that they are satisfied or very satisfied with the service they receive*
- *We have just begun to track health outcomes as a measure of success*

Assessment of impact: What unexpected or unintended impacts are occurring as a result of our program?

- *We are finding that people other than those with HIV want our help. At first it was just other family members or friends, but now word of mouth is leading to an increasing demand for the services*
- *A happy unintended outcome is that many of our clients become well-versed in the "system" and are able to serve as volunteer leaders to people new to the system*

Program Evaluation in Human Services and Arts Programs

Sample Evaluation	Human Services Program Assistance to families of children with disabilities (part of larger multi-service agency)	Arts Program Contemporary Latino-American art gallery
1. *Assessment of inputs:* What resources are required to operate the program? Are there special site licenses or staff qualifications required or desired? What physical elements, such as square footage, location, facility, or equipment are essential to the program's success?	Key requirements: • Strong, positive relationship with school district • Strong connections to referral agencies • Access to support group meeting space fully accessible	Key factors in success: • Good location with high foot traffic • Adequate working capital • Strong connections to artist community
2. *Assessment of implementation* (evaluation of the process): How many units of service are we delivering?	This year: • 24 support groups attended by 134 individuals from 61 families • Advocacy for 30 students with school and/or district • 435 informational calls from families	This year: • Eight "Meet the Artist" events • Four show openings • 45 artists exhibited • Open six days a week, average 41 walk-ins per day • Four visits by elementary school classes
3. *Assessment of outcomes* (evaluation of the program): Are the goals of the program being met?	*Primary goal:* To provide information, practical advice, and emotional support to families in order to help all members of the family achieve their goals. • A written survey of all parents participating in support groups showed that 91% felt the family was better able to function successfully as a result of the support groups. • Interviews done with 25% of the children with disabilities showed that 100% felt their families had been helped by the program.	*Primary goal:* To provide access to retail markets and to galleries for local Latino artists • This year two artists exhibited at major galleries in New York; both of these artists had their first gallery shows at our location more than four years ago. • Income to local artists through direct and catalog sales was $357,000 this year. • One exhibit received significant publicity from the major daily newspaper, sparking additional interest in the featured artists as well as in the gallery as a whole.
Assessment of impact: What unexpected or unintended impacts are occurring as a result of our program?	Interviews with parents and children with disabilities brought forward more emphasis than we expected on the children in the families who do not have disabilities. In some cases, resentment towards the disabled child was mitigated as a result of the support groups; in other cases it appears to have been aggravated. We need to look into this aspect of our work further.	Local elementary and middle schools are increasingly calling to arrange class visits to the gallery or to request that Latino artists visit their classrooms. We cannot meet the increasing number of requests in a quality, professional way without additional staff, and we need to decide how much importance to place on this educational work.

revisions need to be made to the list of critical or strategic issues as a result of the information gathering and analysis process. For example, it may not be until after all external stakeholders have been interviewed that the Planning Committee comes to the realization that the organization has a serious public image problem.

A private school had been working hard to diversify the student body for years. Many resources, both time and money, had been spent over recent years to recruit an economically and culturally diverse student body and faculty. Yet, during an extensive series of focus groups and interviews, the school came to find out that the perception of the general population, and especially of parents of potential enrollees, was that the school catered to white, upper-class families. The issue, "how can we change the image of our school to more accurately reflect who we really are," was not initially listed as a strategic issue on Worksheet 1, but was added to the list of key questions that needed to be answered by the end of the strategic planning process.

CHAPTER FOUR

Setting Your Course

Phase 4: Agreeing on Priorities

- Step 4.1: Determine the Interplay of Strengths, Weaknesses, Opportunities, and Threats
- Step 4.2: More Detailed Analysis: Choose Criteria to Guide Setting Priorities
- Step 4.3: Select Core Strategies
- Step 4.4: Decide on Priorities
- Step 4.5: Summarize the Scope and Scale of Programs
- Step 4.6: Write Goals and Objectives
- Step 4.7: Develop Long-Range Financial Projections

Phase 5: Writing the Strategic Plan

- Step 5.1: Identify the Writer of the Plan
- Step 5.2: Develop a Review Process for the Document
- Step 5.3: Choose a Format for the Strategic Plan
- Step 5.4: Write the Strategic Plan
- Step 5.5: Adopt the Strategic Plan and Celebrate!

PHASE 4: AGREEING ON PRIORITIES

This is where the planning process makes an important turn. The first three phases encourage expansive, exploratory thinking. Getting Ready, Articulating Mission and Vision, and Assessing the Environment all have to do with considering possibilities, gathering new information, and dreaming big dreams. The discussions undertaken during Phase 4: Agreeing on Priorities are frequently the most challenging and time consuming—and the most rewarding—part of the strategic planning process. It is now time to stop exploring and to start deciding. Choices have been clarified; it is time to choose.

Participants often experience the steps in this phase as confusing and frustrating as the group attempts to make sense of all the information and achieve consensus about the implications. The reason the phase can be so rewarding, though, is that insight is gained here, and from new insight new inspiration is often born!

Review of the Language

- *Strategic planning* is a systematic process through which an organization agrees—and builds commitment among key stakeholders—to priorities which are essential to its mission and responsive to the environment;
- *A strategy* is a coordinated, broad approach or direction adopted by an organization in response to the environment so that the organization can achieve its purpose;
- *A goal* is an outcome statement that guides a program or management function; and
- *An objective* is a precise, measurable, time-phased result that supports the achievement of a goal.

During this decision-making phase, a lot of data gathered from the previous phase must be absorbed and a lot of hard choices must be made. The strategic planning process suggests that an organization should be ready to establish its overall core strategies at this point since it has officially gone through the previous phases of developing a mission statement and assessing the environment. In reality, of course, the discussion of program and strategic choices began long before the planning process did and continues long after the strategic plan has been adopted! Nonetheless, it is productive to formally discuss possible strategies at this stage because:

- The mission statement has defined the purpose and should serve as a compass for setting the direction and identifying which programmatic and organizational strategies will best move the organization forward.
- The assessment of the organization's strengths and weaknesses, the evaluation of client needs and programs, and the external market data have produced information and analysis that will help align strategic choices with the most significant forces in the environment.

Do not be surprised if at this point the planning process becomes somewhat confusing and refuses to follow a simple, linear path. During the Agreeing on Priorities Phase, the Planning Committee may decide to circle back and revisit previous phases. For example, the Planning Committee might recognize that additional research is needed regarding a new target market, or alternative program design. If the Planning Committee starts to consider changing current program priorities, they might want to convene some focus groups to respond to new or changing program priorities. Sometimes the Planning Committee, as a result of such a shift in priorities, may even need to revisit the organization's mission statement.

The strategic planning process at this time involves in-depth discussions about the strategic issues or choices facing the organization and the appropriate long- and short-term priorities. The Planning Committee must devote sufficient time to these discussions. If an organization is looking for a shortcut to the strategic planning process, this is not the place to do it. The organization that hasn't sufficiently thought things out or hasn't tested the feasibility of certain ideas may likely make the wrong choices. Benjamin Tregoe and John Zimmerman, two highly respected strategic planning experts, once wrote, "If an organization is headed in the wrong direction, the last thing it needs is to get there more efficiently. And if an organization is headed in the right direction, it surely does not need to have that direction unwittingly taken in a strategic void." Sound strategic thinking requires sufficient data and adequate time for reflection and refinement.

If we do not change our direction, we are likely to end up where we are headed.

—Ancient Chinese proverb

While the prospect of discussing all possible program and organizational options might seem overwhelming at first, it can prove fun and invigorating to hash out the answers to "what do we need to do to best meet our clients needs and achieve our purpose?" Members of the Planning Committee will need to devote sufficient time to combine logical reasoning and intuitive best guesses by:

- Discussing each critical issue that has been identified
- Determining how the organization's strengths and weaknesses relate to its opportunities and threats and how that interplay affects the critical issues
- Developing and evaluating the various possible strategic approaches to each critical issue
- Narrowing down that array of options to arrive at the organization's primary strategies and related program, management, and operational priorities

Step 4.1: Determine the Interplay of Strengths, Weaknesses, Opportunities, and Threats

One aid to assessing and agreeing on program, management, and operational priorities is the SWOT grid, building on the SWOT analysis done in Phase 3. The SWOT grid analysis[1] can help make visible some important dynamics that influence an organization's strategic choices: the intersection of strengths, weaknesses, opportunities, and threats, and can offer suggestions about action the organization should consider undertaking. (See Exhibit 4-1.) In an article, "From Comparative Advantage to Damage Control: Clarifying Strategic Issues Using SWOT Analysis," Professor Keven Kearns states that if an organization simply brain-

[1] Adapted from Kevin P. Kearns. "Comparative Advantage to Damage Control: Clarifying Strategic Issues Using SWOT Analysis," *Nonprofit Management and Leadership.* Vol. 3, No. 1, Fall 1992, pp. 3–22. The SWOT grid is a widely used approach. Modifications of the grid have been attributed to R. Charistensen et al., *Business Policy: Text and Cases* (Homewood, Ill.: Irwin, 1983) and J. Freedman and K. Van Ham, "Strategic Planning in Philips." In B. Taylor and D. Hussey (eds.), *The Realities of Planning* (Elmsford, N.Y.: Pergamon Press, 1982).

storms strengths, weaknesses, opportunities, and threats, "SWOT analysis can degenerate into a superficial list-generating exercise that produces four unconnected lists: strengths, weaknesses, opportunities, and threats. Without a systematic effort to relate the lists to each other, they are of limited utility, especially in clarifying fundamental policy choices facing the agency . . . SWOT analysis requires nonlinear and iterative thinking, which assumes that goals and strategies emerge from the juxtaposition of opportunities and threats in the external environment and strengths and weaknesses in the internal environment." (See Exhibit 4-1.)

Dimensions of a critical issue and related responses may emerge which otherwise might not surface. For example, one small community-based counseling center faced two significant threats: a major loss of public support due to rumors of embezzlement and increasing demands from funders for more complex financial reporting. These threats intersected with weaknesses in financial management in the "damage control/divest" cell of the SWOT Grid. Because the organization felt that its programs were valuable, the initial response was to quell the rumors and build financial management capacity. However, the grid highlighted the fact that these threats were compounded by organizational weaknesses. Thus, instead the organization developed a new strategy which was, in effect, to divest its financial management function through collaborating with a larger organization as its fiscal agent.

In discussing the interplay of strengths, opportunities, weaknesses, and threats, the Planning Committee may find a much more advantageous way to frame the question. Case in point: Public Broadcasting Service (PBS) during the mid-1990s increasingly needed to look at their loss of government funding, a major threat to its survival. PBS's strength was a loyal and relatively affluent audience. A recognized strength from the past (and a lesson from its history) was the use of innovative programming (e.g., Sesame Street). Rather than simply ask, "How can we replace our government funding?", the question was reframed as, "How can PBS leverage or mobilize its strengths to avert or respond to the loss of government moneys?" This led to redoubling efforts to provide greater visibility to funders willing to sponsor specific programming.

Step 4.2: More Detailed Analysis: Choose Criteria to Guide Setting Priorities

The discussions regarding the SWOT grid has started to provide some guidance as to how the organization's resources should be allocated. At this point, the Planning Committee should start to work closely with staff to discuss the criteria that will be used to prioritize programs and agree on what services or products should be offered now and for the next three to five years.

Exhibit 4-1 SWOT Grid

	Opportunities	Threats
Strengths	INVEST Clear matches of strengths and opportunities lead to comparative advantage.	DEFEND Areas of threat matched by areas of strength indicate a need to mobilize resources either alone or with others.
Weaknesses	DECIDE Areas of opportunity matched by areas of weakness require a judgement call: invest or divest; collaborate	DAMAGE CONTROL/DIVEST Areas of threat matched by areas of weakness indicate need for damage control

(*Source:* Adapted from Kevin P. Kearns, "Comparative Advantage to Damage Control: Clarifying Strategic Issues Using SWOT Analysis." *Nonprofit Management and Leadership.* San Francisco: Jossey-Bass, Vol. 3, No. 1, Fall 1992, pp. 3–22. All rights reserved.)

Exhibit 4-2 Worksheet 13: SWOT Grid and Suggested Responses

Process Notes	
How to do this activity	Using Worksheet 9, brainstorm how you can leverage your strengths to capitalize on a perceived opportunity; mobilize your strengths to avert a perceived threat; invest or divest resources in weak programs or your infrastructure in order to respond to a perceived opportunity; or respond to a weakness that makes you vulnerable given an impending threat.
Why do this activity	Helps to stimulate creative thinking and develop appropriate short-term and long-term organizational responses to the environment.
Who to involve in the process	Planning Committee members. Alternatively, this exercise can be done in a planning retreat where four groups, made up of a mix of Board and staff members, can look at each of the four quadrants in the grid.

Case Study—ASO/USA

♦ Worksheet 13

Interplay of SWOT

☐ SWOT grid: Using Worksheet 9, look at the interrelationship of your organization's external opportunities and threats and its internal strengths and weaknesses and assess possible short-term and long-term organizational responses.

	Major Opportunities • *New AIDS treatments could help our clients* • *Still many people needing services* • *Case management could serve other types of cases*	**Major Threats** • *New AIDS treatments could make our services obsolete* • *Outreach program threatens our credibility in the community* • *Dependence on federal funding* • *Funders requiring better record-keeping, increased accountability*
Primary Strengths • *Strong track record* • *Excellent staff and ED* • *Solid volunteer program* • *Good relationships with funders*	*Invest:* Clear matches of strengths and opportunities lead to comparative advantage. • *Position ASO/USA to be the lead case management agency dealing with new treatments across the city; seek support for staff training and additional service contracts (perhaps subcontract with the hospital for our specialty case management with persons with HIV)*	*Defend:* Areas of threat matched by areas of strength indicate a need to mobilize resources either alone or with others. • *Respond to new AIDS treatments as "Invest"* • *Finish Outreach contract and don't renew it; end the relationship on good terms if possible, but seek separate funding for next round*
Primary Weaknesses • *Financial management* • *Board not as active as it could be* • *Program record-keeping* • *Staff overwhelmed*	*Decide:* Areas of opportunity matched by areas of weakness require a judgment call: invest or divest; collaborate. • *We have to improve our financial management and program record-keeping ASAP; no other option* • *Engage board in a rebuilding, re-energizing campaign* • *Actively deal with staff burnout*	*Damage Control:* Areas of threat matched by areas of weakness indicate need for damage control. • *Need to compensate for our current weakness in financial management and program record-keeping to make sure that we don't have the Outreach program blow up in our faces!* • *Need to take steps to assure funders that we are "getting our house in order" regarding financial management, board affairs, and program record-keeping*

(*Source:* Adapted from Kevin P. Kearns: "From Comparative Advantage to Damage Control: Clarifying Strategic Issues Using SWOT Analysis," *Nonprofit Management and Leadership*, Vol. 3, No. 1, Fall 1992.)

Using the SWOT Grid in a Large Health Care Organization

The University of Texas Medical Branch at Galveston (UTMB) is an academic health science center focusing on research, education, and patient care. Because of this triple focus, planning at a department level can be a complex task. All parts of the mission are interdependent, but resource allocation is not equal. The SWOT grid was used by UTMB for identifying the important issues on which the organization needed to focus. In addition, the experience in using it in a multi-mission healthcare organization offered an opportunity to refine the organization's usage and outcomes.

In developing a strategic focus for the Obstetrics and Gynecology (OB/GYN) Department, the SWOT grid was used to develop the overall department strategies and priorities. The Grid was used as part of a three-day planning retreat. Key agenda items for the three-day retreat were:

- Environmental Scan: National, state, regional, local presentation and discussion
- Internal Situation Analysis: Presentation and discussion on what is going on internally—financial situation, funding, patient mix, research grants, leadership changes
- Identifying Strengths, Weaknesses, Opportunities, and Threats (SWOT)
- SWOT grid, Identification of key issues
- Identification of key strategies and goals
- Development of objectives

The Grid was used after the department had completed a thorough environmental scan, which was the basis for SWOT analysis. This helped to ensure that the ultimate outcome of the SWOT grid was based upon data and fact, not on intuition or individual agendas alone.

The 30 individuals involved in the planning retreat included physicians and other clinical care staff, researchers, academicians, and administrators. Comments from these individuals indicated that it was the SWOT grid that brought it all together and helped SWOT itself make sense. This same comment was heard from three other UTMB groups as well. In the past, using SWOT alone left people hanging, wondering where to go next.

(One challenge was noted in using the grid in a multi-mission organization: the outcome can tend to focus on a single part of the mission, depending upon the results of the environmental scan. On the other hand, this is the grid's strengths—to provide focus.)

However, the results of the OB/GYN Department focused heavily on patient care, which left researchers and educators feeling disconnected and their needs and issues unaddressed, in spite of the fact that they were involved in the development of the SWOT grid. Because of massive changes in healthcare itself, all academic health science centers are facing challenges in meeting the demands of a managed care market while still supporting education and research. This issue dominated the SWOT grid results. Since the Obstetrics and Gynecology (OB/GYN) Department needed to continue to provide for research and education, it was necessary for individuals involved in the planning to go back and develop strategies for those two issues. The results were influenced by issues identified in the environmental scan, SWOT, and the SWOT grid.

This step provides additional opportunities for analyzing information collected in Phase 3. Two additional analytical tools are included as aids to this work if needed. The next steps in this process are where the decisions about priorities and strategies get made. Is more analysis needed at this point? In which areas? Each of the following tools can be used for specific purposes to go beyond the level of the interplay of strengths, weaknesses, opportunities, and threats.

Analyze the Competitive Strength of Programs in Developing a Program Portfolio. Nonprofits have not traditionally been thought of as organizations that need to be competitively oriented. Unlike for-profit businesses, which compete for customers and whose very survival depends on providing services or products to satisfied paying clients, many nonprofit organizations have operated in a *non-market,* or *grants,* economy—one in which services were not commercially viable. In other words, the marketplace did not supply sufficient resources to support an adequate, ongoing provider base. Moreover, the customer (client) did not decide which provider got adequate, ongoing funding (in fact, many nonprofits were considered sole-source—the only place to get the service—so there wasn't any choice in which provider would get funding). There were few incentives for nonprofit organizations to limit rather than expand their services, to define or even consider narrowing their niche, or provide quality services, as long as traditional funders were willing to pay the bills.

As a result, nonprofit organizations have traditionally lacked an incentive to question the status quo, to assess whether client needs were being met, or to examine the cost-effectiveness or quality of available services. But while many nonprofit organization's goods and services are still not commercially viable, the competitive environment has changed. In the 1990s it is harder to decide whether competition is or isn't good for clients, especially if that competition, along with increased demand by funders for proven effectiveness, motivates organizations to do a better job. Funders and clients alike are beginning to demand more quality products and accountability; sole-source nonprofits are finding that their very success is encouraging others to enter the field and compete for grants; and grant money and contributions are getting harder to come by, even as need and demand increase. This last trend—increasing demand for a smaller pool of resources—requires today's nonprofits to rethink how they do business, to assess the implications of duplication of services, to better define or narrow their niche, and to increase collaboration when possible.

As part of the process of deciding what services (or programs) to maintain, cut, eliminate, expand, or start, an organization should ask some of the following pragmatic questions:

- Why is this service needed? What is the current and future market demand for this service?

- For current services: Is this the most effective way for us to meet the needs of our clients? Could we meet those needs by providing the service in a different format?
- Are we the best organization to provide this service? Why? What makes us the best? Do we have the necessary organizational capabilities to provide quality service?
- Is competition good for our clients? By offering this service ourselves are we meeting a need that is not being effectively done by anyone else?
- Are we spreading ourselves too thin without the capacity to sustain ourselves? Does this current program (or future program) fit well within our organization's niche? Does this program build on our distinct competency? Are we trying to be all things to all people? Can we be all things to all people?
- Should we work cooperatively with another organization to provide some of our services? Could our clients be better served and resources used more effectively if we were to work with another agency?

In 1983, Professor I.C. MacMillan of Columbia University's Graduate School of Business wrote one of the first articles that specifically addressed the issue of competition in the nonprofit sector. In "Competitive Strategies for Not-for-Profit Agencies," Professor MacMillan developed a matrix to help nonprofits assess their programs within the context of a nonmarket economy and within the reality of decreasing funds to support needs of clients. The matrix was based on the assumption that duplication of existing comparable services (unnecessary competition) among nonprofit organizations can fragment the limited resources available and leave all providers too weak to increase the quality and cost-effectiveness of client services. The matrix also assumed that trying to be all things to all people resulted in mediocre or low-quality service and that nonprofits should focus on delivering higher-quality service in a more focused (and perhaps limited) way.

The MacMillan Matrix assesses each current (or prospective) program according to four criteria: fit with mission, potential to attract resources, competitive position, and alternative coverage. The intersection of these four criteria creates a ten cell matrix. Each of the criteria, as well as the strategic implications of each cell are discussed in detail in Exhibit 4-3.

Fit. The degree to which a program belongs or fits within an organization. Criteria for "good fit" include:

- Congruence with the purpose and mission of the organization
- Ability to draw on existing skills in the organization
- Ability to share resources and coordinate activities with other programs

Exhibit 4-3 MacMillan Matrix

		Potential to Attract Resources and Enhance Existing Programs: Yes		**Potential to Attract Resources and Enhance Existing Programs: No**	
		Alternative Coverage		Alternative Coverage	
		High	Low	High	Low
Good Fit	Strong competitive position	1. Aggressive competition	2. Aggressive growth	5. Build up the best competitor	6. "Soul of the Agency"
	Weak competitive position	3. Aggressive divestment	4. Build strength or get out"	7. Orderly divestment	8. "Foreign aid or joint venture
	Poor Fit	9. Aggressive Divestment		10. Orderly Divestment	

(Adapted from: I. C. MacMillan, "Competitive Strategies for Not-For-Profit Agencies." In *Advances in Strategic Management,* (London: JAI Press Inc., 1983.) Vol. 1, pp. 61–82.)

Potential to Attract Resources and Enhance Existing Programs.[2] The degree to which a program is attractive to the organization from an economic perspective, as an investment of current and future resources—which primarily has to do with whether the program easily attracts resources or enhances existing resources. Programs that can attract resources are more likely to be economically viable. Conversely, programs that cannot attract resources or have limited resources may not be economically viable. No program should be classified as "Yes: Attract Resources" unless it is ranked as attractive on a substantial majority of the criteria as follows:

- Complements or enhances existing programs
- Market demand from a large client base
- High appeal to groups capable of providing current and future support
- Stable funding
- Appeal to volunteers
- Measurable, reportable program results
- Able to discontinue with relative ease if necessary (low exit barriers/ability to discontinue program or abandon past commitment)

[2] The original matrix described this variable as attractive. Program attractiveness was defined as the degree to which a program was attractive to the agency as a basis for current and future resource deployment. For many organizations, this term was confusing and it usually gets interpreted as "it's something that we want to do." Therefore, the authors of this Workbook have changed the wording to "Potential to Attract Resources."

Alternative Coverage. The extent to which similar services are provided. If there are no other large, or very few small, comparable programs being provided in the same region, the program is classified as "low coverage." Otherwise, the coverage is "high."

Competitive Position. The degree to which the organization has a stronger capability and potential to deliver the program than other such agencies—a combination of the organization's effectiveness, quality, credibility, and market share/dominance. Probably no program should be classified as being in a strong competitive position unless it has some clear basis for declaring superiority over all competitors in that program category. Criteria for a strong competitive position include:

- Good location and logistical delivery system
- Large reservoir of client, community, or support group loyalty
- Past success securing funding; strong potential to raise funds for this program
- Superior track record (or image) of service delivery
- Large market share or the target clientele currently served
- Better quality service and/or service delivery than competitors
- Superior organizational, management, and technical skills needed for the program
- Most cost-effective delivery of service

The MacMillan matrix is used by assessing existing and potential new programs in relation to each of the four criteria: fit, potential to attract resources and enhance existing programs, alternative coverage, and competitive position, and placed within the matrix. For example, a private art school, based on numerous requests from parents, was considering offering classes for elementary school children. While the new service was ascertained to be a good fit (within the school's mission), it was deemed not to be able to attract sufficient resources to pay for itself, or enhance existing services; the school was in a strong competitive position because it was well respected as the place to get formal art training in the county, but they were also aware that there were many other agencies in the city who catered to elementary school children. The children's art classes were assessed as fitting in cell #5. The suggested growth strategy was "build up the best competitor." The art school worked with a small children's museum located in a nearby city to offer art classes at the museum, with faculty from the art school teaching the classes with the assistance of the children's museum's education director.

Each of the cells in the matrix has a suggested growth strategy—compete, divest, grow the program, cooperate—except for cell #6 "soul of the agency." "This is one of the key concepts of the MacMillan matrix. Soul of the Agency programs are unable to attract sufficient resources to pay for themselves, have low alternative coverage, but offer services that make a special and important contribution in society. The clients who depend on "soul of the agency" programs have no other place to turn to for help and are therefore reliant on the organization to continue to provide that service. The challenge for organizations who provide "soul of the agency" services is either to use their scarce, unrestricted resources to subsidize the services or subsidize it from other programs. An organization, however, usually cannot afford to fund unlimited "souls," and as such might have to face some difficult decisions about how to develop a mix of programs that ensure viability of the agency as well as high-quality service to clients. The MacMillan matrix offers some guidance as to how to choose what programs an organization should offer.

Market forces and position may or may not be the appropriate criteria for your nonprofit organization to use in selecting which products or services to offer, but the Planning Committee should come up with a list of criteria to making that selection. Some of the criteria might include (but would certainly not be limited to):

- Congruence with purpose (effective use of resources to support the achievement of our purpose)
- Supports analysis from the SWOT grid (leverages strengths to capitalize on an opportunity, mobilizes strengths to avert a perceived threat, prevents a weakness from compounding a threat, or supports the ability of the organization to take advantage of an opportunity that it couldn't do if it continued to demonstrate a specific weakness)
- Program self-sufficiency (program can pay for itself either through fees for service or contributions or grants)
- Documented need (current and future demands for product or service)
- Increases organization's visibility (improves its public image)
- Increases networking potential (supports collaborative efforts with other organizations)
- Enhances existing programs (complements current programs)
- Fills a need not being met in the community (not duplicating services that are effectively being done by others; we can do it better than others)
- Proven track record (credible service, demonstrated results)
- Supports or is part of a core strategy
- Benefits outweigh or at the very least equal costs (cost-benefit analysis)

Should We Continue to Support the Children's Theater Program?

In their strategic planning process, the small but successful City Theater Company had an important strategic decision to make about their new multicultural children's theater program. As a pilot program, it was well received by communities of color. The foundation which funded the pilot stipulated that in the second year the funding be matched. The new program was also partially competitive with a long established and extremely popular Children's Theater, located in the same city but not targeting a multicultural approach. There were intense pro and con feelings about the program from both Board and staff members. Continuing the funding of the children's program could potentially drain resources from the other theater's programming. The SWOT analysis proceeded as follows:

- *Strengths:* Successful first year pilot with staffing established; actors from adult theater programming intricately involved in the multicultural children's theater program; and good reviews in the local paper.
- *Weaknesses:* Funding not readily available; would need to fund second year with funds from adult theater, creating a moderate risk to an agreed expansion; and revenues from ticket sales not sufficient to cover direct costs.
- *Opportunities:* Well received by communities of color, and increased demand for arts programs that specifically address them; remote possibility of funding from a private foundation for funding the program as a national model.
- *Threats:* Competitive relationship with established Children's Theater; decreased funding on both a national and state level for the arts.

In the SWOT grid, the multicultural children's program fell into two boxes: if the strengths of the successful first year were juxtaposed with the opportunities of client demand, loyalty, and the possibility of alternative funding, then the suggested strategy was to invest resources. If, however, the weakness of the lack of confirmed resources was judged as more significant than the perceived strength and was juxtaposed with the same opportunities, then the suggested strategy was "Decide: Invest or divest; collaborate." The Board and staff were split on the invest/divest decision.

When using the MacMillan matrix, the proposed solution became clearer. Although the children's program was successful, it did not seem like it was going to be able to attract resources to cover its costs. The Children's Theater was clearly in the stronger competitive position, even though it did not have a multicultural focus. The Planning Committee made a recommendation to the Board of Directors that the Children's Theater be approached as a collaborative partner in the continued development and expansion of multicultural programming for children. The Children's Theater accepted their proposal. This decision helped the Board to look at increased partnership as a core strategy in their strategic plan.

Using Cost-Benefit Analysis to Assist in Defining a Program Portfolio. As part of the discussion regarding prioritization and selection of programs, the Planning Committee might recommend that the staff prepare some cost-benefit analyses for both current and future programs. As the name indicates, a cost-benefit analysis entails comparing the costs of providing a service or product with the benefit to be gained. Some of the questions that would be normally included in a cost-benefit analysis are as follows:

- Describe the product or service:
  - Who is the client or customer?
  - What product or service would we offer them?
  - How would the product or service be provided?
  - What are the short-term and long-term objections for the product or service?
- What costs would go into the activity?
  - How much staff and volunteer time would be required to provide this service?
  - How much money would we have to spend on paid staff, additional supplies, advertising, additional rent, other expenses?
- What benefits would you get out of the activity?
  - What are the revenue benefits to be gained: earned revenue, contracts, individual, foundation, or corporate contributions?
  - What are the direct benefits to the client or customer, or to the organization? What are the direct benefits to society if this product or service is offered?
  - What would it cost to purchase the service or product on the open market? Could we do it for less than what it would cost on the open market?
  - What intangible benefits are gained by either the organization (e.g., building a base with potential donors or increasing the organization's image), the client or customer (e.g., providing a support system that would not be readily available in the private sector), or society?

Profitability

"Profitability in nonprofit work can be defined as 'measurable increases in human values, security, equity, or dollars available.' When we improve services, increase the number of clients served, conserve operating dollars, and find new contributions, we are operating profitably."

Source: *Larry Kennedy.* Quality Management in the Nonprofit World (San Francisco: Jossey-Bass, Inc., 1991), p. 19.

Unfortunately, doing a cost-benefit analysis on a particular service often proves difficult for nonprofit organizations. Unlike the for-profit sector, which uses the measurement of profit gained by owners and stockholders as its primary benchmarks for benefits, nonprofits do not usually have an explicit indicator of benefits. Moreover, there may not be comparable services or products with clearly defined prices available on the open market. Finally, some benefits may be difficult to quantify because they are intangible, or literally unmeasurable. How, for example, could an organization measure the "benefit" gained by providing one woman and her child shelter and support for two weeks? Yes, the cost of temporary housing could be calculated (assuming that such alternatives were available), but that would not begin to measure the intangible benefits.

Consider the Following when Doing Cost-Benefit Analysis

1. Before using cost-benefit analysis, make sure your goals are clearly specified and that your strategies are aimed at achieving your goals . . .
2. Do not compare cost-benefit figures for two programs or strategies that are really aimed at different objectives . . .
3. Be skeptical of benefit calculations that are highly quantitative. Nonprofit organizations often provide services whose benefits are not highly visible or very immediate. It makes little sense to try to quantify them. On the other hand, be sure that you have a good grasp of what these intangible benefits are, even when they do not make it into the cost-benefit equation.
4. Allow for a good margin of error in any cost-benefit result obtained. Benefits will almost always be imprecisely estimated. Costs can often be determined more accurately; therefore, if two proposals with similar benefits have significantly different costs, it may be safe to go with the cheaper one. Even so, do not decide solely on the basis of the analysis.

Source: *Richard S. Wasch. "Budgeting in Nonprofit Organizations," in* Handbook of Budgeting, Third Edition, *Robert Rachlin and H. W. Allen Sweeny (eds.) (New York: John Wiley and Sons, Inc., 1993), p. 31.18. Reprinted by permission of John Wiley & Sons, Inc.*

If an organization offers a service for which no comparable alternative exists, or if the organization cannot define what the cost would be to society if the service were not provided, a cost-benefit analysis will be difficult to do. If, however, similar products or services exist whose benefits can be readily measured, then an organization can calculate and compare its costs and benefits to those of the competing product. In any case, cost-benefit analysis should not be the sole criterion for accepting or rejecting a program, but it could prove a helpful tool when it comes time to make difficult choices about how to use scarce resources to support the achievement of the organization's purpose. (See Exhibit 4-4.)

Exhibit 4-4 Worksheet 14: Selection Grid for Prioritizing Programs

Process Notes

How to do this activity	• On the left side of the worksheet is a list of criteria for use in choosing program priorities. Cross out any that would not be applicable to your organization and add any additional priorities that you feel are important. You may wish to weigh the criteria; to do so, star the five that you think are more important. • On the top of the worksheet, write down all the programs and services you are offering or would like to offer in the future. Place a check mark beside all the criteria that apply to the specific program being assessed.
Why do this activity	• If any organization had unlimited resources, it could choose to do everything that it wanted to do. Since most organizations have limited resources, there should be some agreement as to the criteria that might be used to choose which programs are most important. Programs that meet the majority of criteria, or meet the most important criteria, might be selected as being a higher priority, or worth a greater investment, if resources were not available. • This activity emphasises that not every service or program is equally important.
Who to involve in the process	• The Planning Committee should devote some time at a meeting to list criteria. Staff input should also be sought regarding what they think are important criteria. Management staff or the Planning Committee would then assess each program against the criteria agreed upon.

Step 4.3: Select Core Strategies

At this point in the process, the organization has been considering the strategic choices facing the organization and needs to start making decisions regarding the organization's overall core strategies.

William Rothschild defines a strategy as "a statement of an organization's investment priorities, the management thrust, and the ways that it will use its

Case Study—ASO/USA

♦ Worksheet 14

Selection Grid for Prioritizing Programs

- ☐ Review the list of criteria to use in choosing program priorities, add additional priorities specific for your organization.
- ☐ List all programs (services) you wish to assess in relation to the listed criteria. Place a check (√) beside all criteria that apply to the program.

(*Note:* Only select programs done as illustration)

Criteria to Use in Choosing Program Priorities	Program: Case management	Program: Outreach program	Program: Transportation	Program: Research and policy	Program:
Congruence with mission	√	√	√	√	
Measurable results	√	√	√	Indirectly	
Needed to support core strategies	√	Yes, but doesn't have to be a collaboration	√	√	
Fills a need not being met in the community (either does not duplicate services that are effectively being done by others, or the competition is good for our clients)	√	√	No	√	
Organization is capable of providing quality services or products relative to other providers	√	√	No	√	
Demonstrated need (documented current demands or predicted future demands for product or service; market share growth potential)	√	√	√	√	
Increases organization's visibility	No	√	√	√	
Funding is available to cover costs (through fees or third party funding)	√	Not as currently structured	√	√	
Shares resources (complements) existing programs		Too much!	Not really	Yes, much so	
Support collaborative efforts with other organizations	√	Yes, but ...	No	√	
Benefits outweigh or at the very least equal costs	√	Barely	No	√	
Produces surplus revenue to support other programs (after paying its share of indirect costs)	No	No	No	No	
Other					
Other					

strengths and correct its limitations to pursue the opportunities and avoid the threats facing it."[3]

These core strategies represent the primary focus of the organization's scarce resources, the overarching priorities that will help the organization move toward the achievement of its purpose. For each strategic issue, the Planning Committee should look at a proposed future strategy (or strategies) to respond to the issue. As part of the discussion, the Planning Committee should also consider:

- The assumptions, facts, and values which support the proposed strategy
- The possible obstacles that the organization may face in implementing the strategy
- What triggers (warning signs) might encourage the organization to reevaluate the suggested new strategy

For example, in response to the critical issue of increased competition from Health Maintenance Organizations, a drug treatment center decided to implement a Total Quality Management (TQM) process as one of their core strategies:

- Suggested core strategy:
  - Implement a Total Quality Management (TQM) process
- Assumptions, facts, and values to support the strategy
  - In the face of new competition and funding cuts, we need to look at increased efficiency and increased effectiveness
  - Our customers/clients deserve quality service
  - Our customers are both external (clients) and internal (staff and Board)
  - A successful TQM program can improve staff morale, foster cooperation, improve communication, and foster teamwork among our departments
  - Paying attention to quality can provide a point of leverage for convincing funders that the goodness of the agency's mission is being accomplished
- Possible obstacles and/or triggers for re-evaluating the suggested new strategy
  - *Obstacles.* Resistance on the part of staff to change; difficulty of establishing benchmarks or other measures of success; availability and

[3] William E. Rothschild. *Putting It All Together. A Guide to Strategic Thinking* (New York: American Management Associations, 1976), p. 53.

TQM as a Core Strategy

Many of the questions that are part of a TQM process (Total Quality Management) are the same questions an organization should be asking during the planning process: How can we provide quality services to our clients? Is quality service a high priority? What are the quality requirements of our clients? Do we treat each other like customers? Who are our customers? How should we define quality? How can we provide quality service to our clients within the limits of our resources? Are we willing to change our organization, and in what ways, to better satisfy the needs of our customers (clients, patrons, students, etc.)?

TQM should be viewed as more than just a program. The institutionalization (or implementation) of TQM is a core strategy (overarching theme) that can help an organization to achieve increased effectiveness and efficiency; improve program marketability; improve morale; renew commitment and energy; and improve organizational competitiveness.

commitment of resources (staff and Board time, consultant costs, etc.) to support a Total Quality Management program

- *Triggers.* None identified at present. However, we need to make sure that the implementation of this strategy includes action steps to deal with the above obstacles.

Since strategies represent the major agreement as to where the organization is going to invest its resources in the future, the Planning Committee should be sure to get the buy-in of those who will be called upon to implement the strategies. To get buy-in, the Executive Director or designated representative(s) of the Planning Committee should discuss proposed strategies with staff and Board. Staff

Sample Strategies

Example of a Financial Strategy	*Full cost recovery:* manage programs and services in order to break even financially, providing as much service as finances will allow
Example of a Program Service Strategy	*Usage targeting:* provide services in a manner that encourages serving a specific number or type of constituents.
Example of a Fund-Raising Strategy	*Retrenchment:* reduce internal costs to reduce impact of decrease in funding; increase staff work load, make use of volunteers, reduce administrative support staff, institute salary freezes, etc.

Source: *Adapted from Philip Kotler and Alan Andreasen,* Strategic Marketing for Nonprofit Organizations, *Fourth Edition (Englewood Cliffs, NJ: Prentice Hall, 1979), pp. 115–117. Reprinted with permission from Prentice-Hall, Inc.*

Where Do Program Strategies Come From?

The Legion of Goodwill, a Catholic religious and social service organization in São Paulo, Brazil, decided to develop a five-year strategic plan. The primary strategic issues on the table were: what should their primary future goals be and how should they maximize their resources. In the initial discussions, participants found it easy to describe major goals and objectives, such as increasing membership, expanding the number of churches in Brazil and foreign countries, and building greater awareness of the religion's teachings, both nationally and internationally.

However, it was difficult for the participants to define the overall core strategy or strategies through which these goals should be accomplished. Members of the planning group were clear about what they wanted; they simply were unable to describe how best this could be accomplished.

In order to overcome this hurdle, the consultant working with the group suggested a simple visioning exercise. The participants were asked to break into small work groups, and to draw upon large sheets of paper what the ideal organization would look like at the end of the five-year planning period.

The exercise provided an unexpected, yet critical, revelation: each of the groups included a drawing of telecommunications innovation in some form or another, from satellites to uplink stations to television broadcast stations. Through the visioning process, the participants came to realize that the use of broadcast media and telecommunications technology in order to promote awareness and grow their membership was a pivotal strategy which would support the overall goals and objectives they desired.

Exhibit 4-5 Worksheet 15: Core Future Strategies

Process Notes

How to do this activity	Review all of the strategic issues, making sure to reframe them in the form of a question rather than a statement. Look at the pros and cons of all strategic approaches and select the strategy or strategies that make most sense. After selecting the best strategy, respond to the rest of the questions on the worksheet: what assumptions, facts, and values ? what possible obstacles may the organization face in implementing the strategy? and what triggers might encourage the organization to reevaluate the suggested new strategy?
Why do this activity	After all this thinking and brainstorming, it's time to make some decisions!
Who to involve in the process	Planning Committee members and selected others develop core strategies to review with Board and staff. Board and staff should have some involvement (the level of which will depend on the organization) in the development of the short-term and long-term programmatic and management/operations strategic priorities.

♦ Worksheet 15

Core Future Strategies

☐ Identify and assess your core future strategies.

Strategic issue (stated as a question)	Proposed strategy	Assumptions, facts, and values which support this proposed strategy?	What possible obstacles do we face in implementing this strategy?	What triggers might encourage us to re-evaluate this strategy?
How do we respond to the issue of new AIDS treatment?	*Develop our case management as the experts in dealing with new treatments. Look for opportunities to subcontract our services to others such as the local hospital*	• *Our case management services are among the best in town* • *We can acquire the additional expertise we need* • *Our reputation will support our strategy to subcontract for additional case management service delivery*	• *Cost and time involved in becoming expert and in staying on top of the new treatments* • *Resistance and competition from other providers* • *Resistance to contract with us for a specialized service*	• *Inability to quickly get on top of new treatments* • *Poor response from our funders/potential partners*
How do we deal with our heavy dependence on federal funding?	1. *Take all possible steps to protect our current competitiveness for federal funding* 2. *Take immediate steps to expand our fund-raising program*	• *Federal funding may go away, but it won't go away in the next two years* • *There are opportunities for private funding we have not yet tapped*	• *Our internal management could get in the way of protecting our reputation with federal funders* • *Federal funding might not disappear, but priorities of office could change* • *Where is the time going to come from to explore new funding opportunities?*	• *Any hints of changes at the federal funding level* • *Lack of progress in first six months at finding promising new funding sources*
What should we do about the Outreach program?	*Finish the contract with City Clinic, take pains to preserve a good relationship, but don't renew the contract*	• *We have already tried to improve our collaboration with City Clinic and we've lost hope of improving the situation sufficiently* • *It is possible to end the contract without ruining our relationship with City Clinic or the funder* • *Doing a good job is more important than maintaining a surface-level collaboration*	• *City Clinic might be unhappy with our decision* • *We could have difficulty replacing the funding we are getting through the collaborative contract* • *The program could still cause us big problems in its final year*	• *If the situation got dramatically better in the next three months, we might change our minds*

(Continued)

Worksheet 15 *(Continued)*

Strategic issue (stated as a question)	Proposed strategy	Assumptions, facts, and values which support this proposed strategy?	What possible obstacles do we face in implementing this strategy?	What triggers might encourage us to re-evaluate this strategy?
Should we keep all our current programs? (This was not listed as an issue at the beginning, but it has become clear we need to address it.)	*Divest any programs which are not central to our mission* if *there is another provider available*	• *Transportation and English classes are not central to our mission* and *there are other providers* • *It is distracting from our overall work to have programs that don't fit well with the other programs*	• *Some of our clients and staff will be unhappy, because they have become used to our services* • *We need to take extra care to prevent unneeded disruption to our clients*	• *Very little. If it turns out that the quality of the other services is not as good as we thought, we will deal with this by advocating for the creation of better services in these areas*
What changes are necessary to adjust to the growth we have experienced in the past few years? (This issue was originally listed as "financial management problems" but it has become clear that while our program has grown, our management and governing systems haven't kept pace	*In addition to the upgrade of financial management systems, we will undertake a thorough review of management and governance systems by the end of the year: Changes will be made as soon as is reasonable after the assessment is completed*	• *Our budget and staff have doubled in the past few years* • *We have not changed our financial management systems or adjusted in other important ways* • *Staff are feeling burned out by inadequate communication and confusion over lines of responsibility, etc.* • *Many of these issues require restructuring, and will require some investment in our infrastructure to catch up to the work load we have created*	• *We won't get around to it because other crises surface* • *Cost* • *Resistance by board to accept need for investment in infrastructure*	• *Only if our funding got cut severely and permanently would we need to rethink this strategy*

and Board should be given an opportunity to voice either support or concerns for these strategies, and make suggestions regarding the long-term and short-term programmatic and management/operations strategic priorities that support the implementation of the core strategies. (See Exhibit 4-5.)

Step 4.4: Decide on Priorities

Once the overall core strategies have been defined and agreed upon, then the organization is ready to discuss and agree on the long-term and short-term programmatic and management/operations priorities that support the criteria agreed upon in Step 4.2 and core strategies that have been defined in Step 4.3. These priorities should be those that are responsive to the environment and move the organization forward in the achievement of its purpose. For all programs/services, there will need to be consensus as to what is most important in the long term and short term and where resources should be directed. Once overall program priorities have been agreed upon, then discussions need to take place as to which management/operations priorities that will support the program priorities. (See Exhibit 4-6.)

Develop Contingency Plans

Because nonprofit organizations are operating in turbulent and constantly changing environments, it is useful to devote some of the setting priorities discussions to the "what ifs" of the organization's future. Some of these conversations may already have been started during the above future strategy discussion when the

Exhibit 4-6 Worksheet 16: Long–Term and Short–Term Priorities

Process Notes	
How to do this activity	Brainstorm and then agree on the long-term and short-term program and management/operations strategic priorities that support the implementation of the core strategies and help the organization achieve its purpose.
Why do this activity	After all this thinking, it's time to make some more decisions!
Who to involve in the process	Board and staff members should have some involvement (the level of involvement will depend on the organization) in the development of the short-term and long-term programmatic and management/operations strategic priorities.

Case Study—ASO/USA

♦ Worksheet 16

Long-Term and Short-Term Priorities

☐ What are your long-term and short-term strategic priorities?

Suggested Overall Program Priorities

Short-Term Program Priorities	Long-Term Program Priorities
• *Improve staff training for case management services to accommodate new treatments and to prepare to subcontract* • *Settle the issue with City Clinic over our Outreach program* • *Divest two programs where our services are now duplicative* • *Remain active in the city-wide HIV prevention network*	• *The leading, comprehensive case management service in the city for people with HIV* • *A successful, independent outreach program operating city-wide* • *A spectrum of support services for people living with HIV* • *An aggressive and highly successful prevention program*

Suggested Overall Management/Operations Priorities

Short-Term Management/Operations Priorities	Long-Term Management/Operations Priorities
• *Begin organizational restructuring process to include a complete assessment of staff compensation and development of new policy* • *Create a new board development committee to lead the effort of assessment and rebuilding on our Board* • *Support the development director in investigating new funding opportunities* • *Conduct quarterly assessment meetings with the Planning Committee in the first year to see if this is the best way to conduct ongoing planning*	• *Increase our staff to 35 full-time equivalent positions* • *Strong, active board of 15 members* • *Image in the community of a well-run, aggressive, and effective community organization* • *No more than 60% of our funding from government in 3 years, with steady renewable funding sources making up the remaining 40%* • *Sufficient internal resources, including space, computers, etc. to do our jobs well* • *A vital, ongoing planning process which incorporates quality assessment on a frequent basis*

Planning Committee considered possible triggers for reevaluating a suggested new strategy.

If many of the assumptions upon which the organization's newly developed strategies are based are tentative, then it may be useful for the organization to imagine possible alternative scenarios and prepare contingency plans. For example, an organization might ask the following question, "Based on the experience of the last two years, we expect service demand to increase by x percent in the next three years." What if it is significantly more? Or less?

Not too long ago, arts organizations might have stated the following: "We *think* we will be receiving more funding from the National Endowment for the Arts. And, if we do receive that money, here's what will do. But what if it doesn't happen? What could and should we do?" The answers to such questions can prepare the organization for several different futures and allow the organization to be more prepared when such alternative futures become a reality. In *The Art of the Long View: Planning for the Future in an Uncertain World,* Peter Schwartz describes how alternative scenarios can help an organization to "take a long view in a world of great uncertainty." He defines scenarios as "stories about the way the world might turn out tomorrow," and makes the case that such stories help us "recognize and adapt to changing aspects of our present environment. They form a method for articulating the different pathways that might exist for you tomorrow, and finding your appropriate movements down each of those possible paths. Scenario planning is about making choices *today* with an understanding of how they might turn out."[4] Such scenarios, therefore, allow an organization to be better prepared for whatever happens by addressing any of the array of possibilities. "Scenarios are not about predicting the future, rather they are about perceiving futures in the present."[5]

Schwartz says that scenarios often seem to fall into three groups: more of the same, but better; worse; and different but better. In fact, reality may turn out to be a combination of all three scenarios. Making the case that scenario-thinking is an art, not a science, he encourages his readers to develop an array of scenarios and rehearse possible responses.[6] After developing these scenarios, an organization would identify the possible factors that would influence the scenario, the degree of uncertainty, and the implications if the scenario were to get played out in real life.

Healthcare organizations that have been better able to respond to the changes in healthcare delivery are in all likelihood those organizations who were asking the "what if" questions early on. Those organizations who started to think about Medicare and health reform movements long before their competitors did, and

[4] Peter Schwartz. *The Art of the Long View: Planning for the Future in an Uncertain World* (New York: Doubleday, 1991), pp. 3–4.
[5] *Ibid.*, p. 38.
[6] *Ibid.*, pp. 20–29.

"What If . . . ?"

The Asian Immigrant Organization had a close and collaborative relationship with the Pacific Islander Immigrants Association. The two organizations often gave referrals back and forth, but had a tacit agreement not to approach each others' donors, board members, and volunteers for support.

AIO had proposed a merger for the past three years, to no avail. PIIA, while continuing to talk about collaboration, had also continued to insist on maintaining the gentleman's agreement about turf. AIO felt that it is being held back unfairly, and yet was reluctant to give up the possibility of a merger, which they felt would be in the best interest of the community.

Rather than wait for PIIA to make a move, AIO decided to pursue a dual strategy, which allowed the organization to take advantage of *either* possible scenario (PIIA chooses to merge or chooses not to merge with AIO). AIO announced unilaterally to PIIA that a) it remained committed to a merger and was prepared to begin discussions at any time *and* b) it would no longer refrain from contacting any potential supporters in the community.

While running the risk of alienating PIIA, AIO had chosen a proactive strategy and was prepared to deal with the range of possible consequences.

who as a result outlined a series of future scenarios, are now probably at a competitive advantage.

It is not usually necessary to include formal contingency plans in the strategic plan, but it is a good idea to discuss "what ifs," and generate ideas about possible alternative responses—in the hope that they *won't* be needed in the future!

"Formal strategic planning is based on events that have a high probability of occurring—the most likely happenings. However, there are less likely conditions that could create serious difficulties for a company if they actually occurred. . . . Contingency plans are preparations to take specific actions when an event or conditions not planned for in the formal planning process actually does take place."[7]

Step 4.5: Summarize the Scope and Scale of Programs

The next step in the Agreeing on Priorities phase is to agree on the scope and scale of anticipated future program activities (see Exhibit 4-7). To do so, a program portfolio needs to be developed. The program portfolio (a term borrowed from the financial investment world to describe an investor's holdings) outlines all programs in terms of current and proposed scope and scale. Developing this program portfolio is a matter of answering the following questions about each current program or prospective program:

[7] George Steiner. *Strategic Planning* (New York: Free Press, 1979), pp. 229–230.

- What is the program's current level of activity? (This question, of course, applies only to existing programs; new programs will not yet have a current level of activity.)
- What is its proposed growth strategy (expand, maintain, decrease, eliminate, start new program)? Why the proposed growth strategy? What are the consequences of ignoring the strategy?
- What is the program's projected future level of activity?
- Are there any modifications in the way the current services are being provided that should be considered? If yes, what are they?

Remember, during this step we are not looking at the infrastructure needed to support the programs, but rather a description of all the programs (products and services) that an organization intends to offer over the next three to five years. The program portfolio will be the basis for developing specific objectives for each program goal and will be used to define the management and support goals and objectives needed to support all products and services. See the ASO/USA Case Study for an example of this process.

Time for a Reality Check. After completing the desired scope and scale of programs, collectively step back and take a deep breath for a reality check. It will be

Exhibit 4-7 Worksheet 17: Summarize Scope and Scale of Programs

Process Notes	
How to do this activity	Use Worksheet 17 to identify the current and planned scale and scope of activity. As part of this exercise, you should affirm the proposed growth strategy and the reasons for that strategy. You should also discuss the reasons for the proposed growth strategy and the consequences of ignoring it, as well as any modification to existing services that should be considered.
Why do this activity	To quantify the amount of change in the level of anticipated activity. This sets the context for objective setting. Also, to present a simple, visual summary of the scope and scale of programs and services that will be offered in the future.
Who to involve in the process	Staff should take the lead in developing the program portfolio and presenting it to the Planning Committee for their comments.

Case Study—ASO/USA

◆ Worksheet 17

Summary of Program Scope and Scale

☐ Develop a detailed program portfolio for current and future programs.

Program or Service	Current level of activity (if applicable; new programs will not have a current level of activity)	Proposed growth strategy: • Expand • Maintain at existing level • Decrease • Eliminate • New program	Proposed future level of activity for this program or service
Case Management	*300 individuals*	*Expand*	*400 next year, 600 in 2 years*
Outreach Program	*Weekly outreach to bars* *Street outreach in Central City* *2 staff, 3 times weekly outreach*	*Maintain*	*Same*
Transportation Program	*25 round trip rides per week*	*Eliminate*	*Zero by next year*
Research and Policy	*1 full-time staff position involved in two longitudinal studies, producing monthly update pieces for the community*	*Maintain*	*Same staffing, focus of work may change*

tempting to develop an ambitious wish list that is not realistic within the constraints of expected resources. Either pare back the plans as necessary or prioritize the areas of growth to ensure that the organization does not fail by spreading itself too thin.

There is another problem to guard against. Individuals charged with implementing what they consider to be unrealistic plans will refuse to be held accountable for falling short of the goals and objectives outlined to support the program growth. The plan may be viewed as exciting, ambitious, and challenging, but it cannot be seen as patently unrealistic: if it is, the plan will be ignored.

Step 4.6: Write Goals and Objectives

As with strategies, the discussions about goals and objectives will in actuality be occurring throughout the planning process—but the conclusion of these discussions signals the final stage of the strategic planning process. All that is left is to put the decisions into writing by developing a strategic planning document, creating an annual implementation plan, and then making it all happen!

By this time, most of the big decisions have been made and the big picture should have become relatively clear. The organization knows what problems it needs to address, what services it will provide to address the problems, the critical issues that will affect its ability to deliver those services, and its core strategies for responding to those critical issues. It is time to develop concrete measures of how much of the problem the organization will try to solve and by when; this is the most detailed aspect of the strategic planning process and also the aspect that most people have experience with. If an organization chooses not to translate its priorities into formal goal and objective language, that doesn't mean that it has not completed its strategic plan. A Planning Committee may choose to simply summarize the short-term program and management/operations priorities (for example, using the format suggested in Worksheet 16) and have that summary be the guidepost for helping the organization develop a detailed annual operating plan.

If the Planning Committee chooses to have a more formal and traditional strategic plan that articulates specific goals and objectives, then at this point in the process someone needs to take all the decisions that have been made regarding program services and translate those decisions into goals and objective language. The writing goals and objectives should not be a group project. One or two individuals should take responsibility for drafting the initial statements. The drafts of these goals and objectives statements might go through two or three versions before everyone's feedback has been incorporated and a final document is agreed upon. The Planning Committee should not shortchange this process of gathering feedback on the outcomes delineated in the goals and objectives. Often in the

Goals and Objectives Must Be Written to Support Accountability!

Goals and objectives must be written so that they can be monitored. "Improve the well-being of the community" is a laudable goal, but it would be very hard to determine whether such a broad goal had been attained. In developing the precision of language that will allow goals and objectives to be monitored, important areas of potential ambiguity are likely to arise. Work hard to eliminate ambiguity at this stage. Work done now to ensure clearly articulated goals and objectives which can be actively monitored will save hours of frustration later, during the implementation of the plan.

course of the these discussions, important questions arise and insights emerge which substantially improve the quality and viability of the entire strategic plan.

Program Goals. Goals are outcome (ends) statements that guide the organization's programs and management/operations functions. For the organization as a whole, for example, the ultimate goal is the purpose spelled out in the mission statement; similarly, the organization's programs, program groups, and management/operations functions need to be guided by their own "mini-purposes," that is, their own goals.

A good place to start the development of program goals is to go back to the Organizational Profile developed earlier with Worksheet 4, that worksheet identified programs or services and placed them into relevant program groupings (goals). The planning process thus far may have generated information or decisions that warrant taking another look at, and perhaps modifying, certain aspects of the profile—for example, altering some programs, grouping them differently, or adding a new program. If so, the Planning Committee must draft a new outline of program goals. For example, a children's museum initially had grouped all of their programs into two major goal categories: programs offered at the museum and programs offered off-site. As a result of the planning process, the museum reframed their programs to more accurately reflect the broadening of their activities: environmental education; geography and history; celebrating diversity; and art and culture.

Once the appropriate program groupings have been agreed upon, revised or new goal statements must then be drafted for each program grouping (goal). A program grouping is an umbrella or collection of related programs. Larger organizations with many programs may have sub-goals. For example, if a new program, Case Management, is added to the Direct Services program group, the program sub-goal for Case Management might be "to ensure better coordination of the delivery of direct services to our clients"; whereas the overall goal for the Direct Services program group might be more global—"to deliver a continuum of services which improve the quality of life for our clients."

Setting Goals and Objectives in Large Organizations

The basic sequence of phases in this planning process (mission/vision, assess the environment, agree on priorities) is applicable to any level of organizational planning. For a small program or even an individual, up to planning for a multi-million dollar corporation, this approach to planning works.

If you are the manager of a program which is part of a department in a large organization, what is different in this planning process is that part of the environmental assessment will include input from department and organizational leaders.

Conversely, if you are the Executive Director of a large organization, what is different in the planning process you will undertake is that there are subordinate levels of operational planning which will be done by others using the strategies and priorities established at the corporate level as guidelines.

Thus, a strategy at the corporate level to "emphasize education in everything we do" will cascade down through the organization as the strategy is translated into both goals and objectives at the department and subordinate program levels.

Program Objectives. Each goal usually carries with it two or more specific objectives. An objective is a precise, measurable, and time-phased result that supports the achievement of the goal.

The program portfolio should contain all the guiding information necessary to develop specific program objectives for each program. These objectives should typically cover a time frame of one to three years; if the organization's environment is particularly turbulent, the time frame may be shorter. In any case, the objectives must identify the measurable numbers that will support the fulfillment of the organization's strategies, goals, and purpose.

Drafting Objectives

Area of change	Unemployment status
Direction of change	To reduce
Target population	1996 trainees
Degree of change	75 percent gain full-time employment
Time frame	Within six months of graduation
Method for collecting data	Pre-post training questionnaires
Objective	To reduce the unemployment status of our 1996 trainees, so that 75 percent are fully employed within six months of graduation.

The standard form for an objective is:

(verb noting direction of change) + (area of change) + (target population) + (degree of change) + time frame.

All objectives should be precise, measurable, and time-phased. However, in developing objectives to support program goals, it is important to distinguish between activities and outcome objectives.

- Activities, also known as *process objectives,* typically begin with phrases such as "to develop, to implement, to establish, to conduct, etc." These phrases all describe activities which will be undertaken by the *organization.*
- On the other hand, *outcome objectives* describe changes which will be made by the organization's *clients* as a result of these process activities. Outcome objectives typically begin with phrases such as "to increase, to decrease, improve, etc."

The chart on the language of strategic planning on page 16 makes it clear that the distinction between activities and outcomes is exactly the same as between business and purpose in the mission statement. It is the difference between means and ends. Activities (or process objectives) and business statements are means selected to achieve the ends of outcome objectives and the purpose statement.

Remember if the objective describes something a staff person or volunteer is going to do, it is almost certainly an activity or process objective. If the objective describes a change in behavior, skills, awareness, health status, etc., by a client, it is almost certainly an outcome objective.

See the following sidebar/exhibit for examples of both process and outcome objectives in support of program goals.

Management/Operations Goals and Objectives. After program goals have been identified, the Planning Committee should turn its attention to the management/operations functions (internal management activities) required to support the programs, such as:

- Staffing and benefits (paid and volunteer staff)
- Board of directors
- Marketing and public relations
- Resource development

Sample Goals, Objectives, and Tasks

Examples of Program Goals	Examples of Related Program Objectives (Process/Outcome)
Family Workshop Program	
To increase coping skills of families in stress (Martha's Shelter offers workshops to family members who need to acquire healthy coping skills.)	• Present two workshops for 20 families in July (process objective) • Increase performance on self-administered test in coping strategies by 50% on average for all participants as a result of the two workshops (outcome objective)
Volunteer/Victim Advocate Program	
To decrease the immediate trauma of victims of crime (This program of the Victim's Assistance Fund provides victims of crime with volunteers who will accompany them and speak for them at police and legal proceedings.)	• To match 200 victims of crime with 200 volunteers to provide support during police interviews in 1997 (process objective) • Using provider-administered surveys, achieve a significant decrease in the immediate trauma reported by victims as a result of this program; "significant" to be defined once a baseline is established in 1997 (outcome objective)
Traveling Exhibition Program	
To increase the public's awareness of neon art (This program of the Museum of Neon Art makes the collection of world-class neon art pieces available to the finest museums in the world.)	• To sponsor one showing per quarter in 1997 (process objective) • Using attendance as a measure of cultural awareness, double the number of people attending the exhibit in 1997 compared to previous year (outcome objective)

- Systems—financial, management information, and infrastructure
- Facilities and equipment/technology
- Planning and evaluation

Just like the programs and program groups, each management/operations function is a focus of activity that should have its own goal statement to guide it. For example, a goal statement for Staffing and Benefits might read, "To attract and retain qualified, competent staff, volunteers, and interns to carry out programs of the Community Counseling Center." A long-range objective for the above mentioned staffing goal might then read, "Community Counseling Center anticipates a staff of 13 full-time employees in the next three to five years to fully staff the program and its projects as outlined in the organizational chart attached to this plan."

It is important that the objectives be as specific and measurable as possible. For example, "increase board involvement in fund-raising this year" is too vague; a more effective objective would be "to achieve 100 percent board contributions to our agency in each fiscal year of the strategic plan" or "the board will lead a major donor fund drive to raise $25,000 by the end of Year Two" is both measurable and specific.

The selection of the management/operations goals will depend on the complexity of the organization. (See Exhibit 4-8.) Small organizations may only have two management goals: fund-raising and administration. Larger organizations may have many more goals. If the Planning Committee's discussions regarding

Exhibit 4-8 Worksheet 18: Setting Goals and Objectives

Process Notes

How to do this activity	For each program grouping and management/operations function, identify and write goals—the broad result(s) to be accomplished during the period of the strategic plan. Develop related objectives for each goal.
Why do this activity	To define, in detail, the specific results that will support the organization achieving its purpose. The litmus test for objective setting is to ask "if these objectives are achieved, will we successfully accomplish the goal?" The litmus test for goal setting is to ask "if these goals are achieved, will we successfully accomplish our purpose?"
Who to involve in the process	Program managers should take the lead in developing goals and objectives for their programs; in a smaller organization, the executive director or designated writer might take on that responsibility. Usually the executive director or designated writer will figure out the right language to use and write the management/operations goals and objectives. The board of directors should, however, take the lead in developing its own objectives; the fund-raising committee and the fund-raising staff likewise might take the lead in developing fundraising goals, etc.

Case Study—ASO/USA

◆ Worksheet 18

Setting Goals and Objectives

☐ Write your program and management/operations goals and objectives.

Program Goals*	Program Objectives
Transition support groups to the Neighborhood Network	1. *Finalize arrangements with the Neighborhood Network to accept our ongoing support group clients; develop smooth transition plan* 2. *Ensure that ongoing referral mechanisms are in place*
Support Services Division *Goal: Improve the quality of life and health for people living with HIV and AIDS.* <u>Case Management Program</u> *Goal: Increase access to primary health care for people living with HIV and AIDS*	Process Objectives 1. *Increase the number of referrals we receive from other providers in the city:* • *Meet with all potential referral sources at least once every six months* • *Ensure materials on our program are current at each provider at least every six months* 2. *Explore additional subcontract relationships with the two hospitals in the city regarding clients who need case management help* 3. *Develop and implement new quality control procedures to ensure that our case management services remain of highest quality* 4. *Provide on-going training for case management services to accommodate new treatments* Outcome Objectives 1. *Survey all clients regarding access to primary health care. After baseline is established, set objective for level of increase in access to be sought over the next three years* 2. *Expand our case management services to serve 600 clients*

**Note:* Sample goals and objectives are written for each area of service as illustration, but not all programs are included.

Program Goals*	**Program Objectives**
Public Education Division *Goal:Prevent new HIV infections.* <u>Outreach Program</u> *Goal: Increase awareness of risk behaviors associated with HIV, and decrease rate of transmission.*	Process Objectives 1. *Reorganize our volunteer peer-educators by district* 2. *Recruit ten more volunteers willing to support our effort in Central City district* 3. *Meet with all potential partners in conducting outreach program within first six months* 4. *Increase overall prevention outreach effort in Central City from less than ten contacts per week to 15 per week by year end. Maintain this level of outreach over the next three years* Outcome Objectives 1. *Of the 50% of individuals contacted with whom we expect to develop an ongoing relationship (approximately 500 individuals), test their awareness of risk behaviors associated with HIV at six-month intervals with a random sample of at least 100 individuals. Objective is to achieve and maintain close to 100% accurate awareness within one year of primary risk behaviors* 2. *With the same population, decrease rate of transmission from estimated 8 new infections per 100 people per year to less than 3 new infections per year*
Public Policy Division *Goal: Improve public policy as it affects HIV and AIDS issues.* <u>Research and Policy Program</u> *Goal: Increase quality of information available to support policy development for ASO/USA and local public agencies.*	Process Objectives 1. *Continue epidemiological study support to Department of Public Health AIDS Office* 2. *Design and conduct client surveys for both the Outreach Program and the Case Management Program over next three years* Outcome Objectives 1. *Improve the understanding of policy makers and local activists about the actual HIV transmission rate in homeless and intravenous drug user populations, as measured by feedback about the quality of the study from both policy makers and activists* 2. *Increase understanding of program managers and others interested in effectiveness of the Outreach Program and the Case Management Program by producing studies which are accepted as valid and reliable reports about the outcome achievement of these two programs over the next three years*

**Note:* Sample goals and objectives are written for each area of service as illustration, but not all programs are included.

(Continued)

Worksheet 18 *(Continued)*

Management/Operations Goals	Management/Operations Objectives
Staffing and benefits *To attract and retain qualified paid and volunteer staff for all services and activities*	1. *Staffing* • *Increase the number of paid staff from 20 full-time employees to 35 to support our ability to provide needed services and increase the number of volunteer hours per year from 5,750 to 9,000* • *Assess whether more complex and differing needs of clients require certain jobs that were done by volunteers to be done by paid staff* 2. *Salaries and benefits* • *Assess overall salary structure and benefits package; develop and implement a plan to increase staff salaries and offer a competitive benefit package* • *Analyze fringe benefits package on an ongoing basis and identify ways of meeting employees' needs (such as a pension plan, cafeteria approach to benefits, etc.)* • *Review personnel policies annually to make sure they are in legal compliance* 3. *Training, evaluation, and other support* • *Establish and maintain a more formalized, ongoing training program for all staff and volunteers* • *Implement and maintain a new staff evaluation system that establishes overall objectives for positions and specific objectives for all employees* • *Expand our volunteer and paid staff appreciation program* • *Develop and coordinate an agency-wide management training program to help staff build skills needed to perform their duties and interface with other departments, including a cross-training program* 4. *Volunteers* • *Increase number of volunteers from 50 to 75* • *Assess current volunteer recruitment, orientation, and training program; make modifications as necessary*
Resource development *To acquire stable, broad-based, financial and non-financial resources to support the programs and growth envisioned in this strategic plan*	1. *Diversification of funding* • *Within the next three years, at least 40 percent of ASO/USA's annual operating budget will be raised through private sector philanthropy; the development of this subsidy is critical for the maintenance and growth of our programs* • *Explore donations in kind such as printing, equipment, etc. to help support our services. Within the next three years, have similar donations to support all educational brochures and our annual report* • *Increase the money the organization receives from private individuals a minimum of 10 percent each year* • *Raise a minimum of $50,000 annually from special events* 2. *Infrastructure support for resource development function* • *Establish a development department within the management structure of the organization, staffed by a full-time professional development officer to supervise overall fundraising functions and work closely with board and management staff to develop and implement a successful development program* • *Establish and maintain a computerized donor history file and increase the personal contacts made with donors* 3. *Board of Directors role in fund-raising* • *Maintain a Board giving policy that requires all Board members to contribute financially to the organization* • *Increase the Board's participation in all aspects of fund-raising*

Management/Operations Goals	Management/Operations Objectives
Board of directors *To develop and maintain an effective, active, and informed Board of Directors whose governance and support roles help the achievement of ASO/USA's mission*	*1. Board membership* *• Increase board to approximately 15 individuals* *• Diversify the Board so it more accurately reflects who we serve* *• Develop and maintain an advisory board to help supplement the board's expertise and contribution* *2. Board training* *• Increase the capability of the Board to assist with the following functions: marketing, fund-raising, legal matters, public relations, and evaluation* *• Develop and maintain an effective Board orientation and ongoing training program* *3. Board effectiveness* *• Increase effectiveness of the board by redefining Committees and each Committee's mandate, and assessing ongoing mandates yearly; holding an annual board retreat to set overall objectives for the board as a whole and each Committee; requiring each Committee to submit detailed workplans to support accomplishing agreed goals and objectives* *• Continue yearly evaluation of all aspects of the Board* *• Continue 100 percent contribution from all Board members* *• Increase the Board's participation in all aspects of fund-raising*
Planning and evaluation *To guarantee that we meet the needs of our constituencies and that all programs provide the highest level of service to our clients*	*1. Establish an ongoing evaluation process for all programs to assess program results, quality of services, and our ability to address the (changing) needs of the community* *2. Annually, hold a Board/staff retreat(s) to plan for future needs and assess current capabilities* *• Review strategic plan and make changes as needed* *• Assess changing environment* *• Make modifications to strategic plan as necessary* *• Ensure that detailed annual operating plans are developed for all programs and internal management functions* *3. Establish and maintain protocols for data collection, data entry, and outcome evaluation*
Public relations/marketing *To increase the visibility and community awareness of ASO/USA and to make sure that ASO/USA is properly recognized for its achievements and closely identified as a premier provider to people with AIDS and those affected by HIV*	*1. Build public awareness of ASO/USA in the community through increased media coverage and public service announcements* *2. Produce and distribute a newsletter on a regular basis* *3. Update our brochures regularly, and make sure they are available in English, Spanish, and Cantonese*

(Continued)

Worksheet 18 *(Continued)*

Management/Operations Goals	Management/Operations Objectives
Infrastructure *To increase the operational/ management efficiency and effectiveness of ASO/USA*	Subgoals *1. Conduct thorough overall review of infrastructure to assess ways in which our program growth needs accommodating* *• Senior management will review all systems and investigate hiring an external consultant* *• Assessment will be shared with executive of Board, and an action plan will be implemented* *2. Ensure timely, accurate, useful information is available and consistently applied in sound decision-making throughout the agency* *• Improve and maintain a fully computerized accounting system which is able to produce timely, accurate financial reports for the organization as a whole and for all departments* *• Provide executive management and the Board with required financial reports, budget comparisons, and cash flow projections* *• Annually assess organization's internal controls to ensure adequate safeguard of all resources* *• Develop a system for tracking all necessary management information and train all staff to use the MIS systems and proper documentation of services* *3. To have available the most technology and equipment necessary to be able to provide quality, efficient, and effective service* *• Continually assess technology needs and update computers and other technology as needed* *4. To provide adequate and accessible space in a pleasant, comfortable environment for all ASO/USA clients and paid and volunteer staff* *• Develop and implement a facilities master plan to locate programs and services in facilities which provide comfort and ease of access to clients and staff* *• Explore option of getting a building donated* *• Consider opening a satellite office in the southwest part of the city* *• Maintain facilities which are attractive to clients*
Networking and collaboration *To maximize closer communication with other agencies in order to maximize community involvement and ensure increased coordination and collaboration among AIDS service providers and organizations doing related work*	*1. Support the development of regular meetings of other agencies' staff in order to share information, increase advocacy efforts, and maximize networking among all service providers* *2. Continue to investigate forming or expanding partnerships with other AIDS service providers to make sure that our clients' needs are met and resources are used effectively*

strategic issues and program priorities have not yet provided sufficient guidance to the setting of management/operations priorities, then some questions the Planning Committee may want to consider include:

Staffing and Benefits

- What is our current ability to provide services to our clients/customers/consumers?
- What additional staff are needed to meet increased levels of service? (Or, if staff cuts are anticipated, how will these cuts be managed?)
- How can we remain competitive with regard to salary and benefits?
- How do we recruit and retain quality staff?
- How do we orient and provide continuing education for our paid and volunteer staff?
- What other reward and recognition systems can we implement to support staff?
- How do we improve our performance appraisal systems?

Board of Directors

- Given the future vision of the organization, does the role of the board need to change, and, if so, how?
- Does our board composition need to change to effectively govern and support our preferred future and, if so, why and how?
- How do we provide continuing education, support, and recognition for our board?

Process Note: The board should devote at least one or two meetings to respond to these board-related questions and develop its own short-term and long-term priorities.

Marketing/Public Relations

- How strong is our ability to communicate with intended clients/customers/consumers?
- What strategies should we put in place to communicate program/service changes?
- Are there additional marketing materials that should be prepared or alternative methods for communicating our mission to be developed?
- What are our short-term and long-term priorities for increasing our visibility in the community?

Process Note: If there is no one connected to the organization who has a strong marketing and public relations background, the Planning Committee might consider asking a public relations firm to donate some time to assist with the responses to marketing related questions.

Resource Development

- What resources do we need to support our future vision? Can we invest in this future?
- If we have to raise more money, how much? What is our plan for how to do this?
- Do we have sufficient development staff to succeed in meeting our financial goals?
- What should be our future funding mix?

Process Note: These questions are best answered by staff with fund-raising responsibilities and the board Fund-raising Committee.

Systems—Financial, Management Information, and Infrastructure

- What kinds of systems or processes do we need to support (or develop) up-to-date, accurate, and useful financial management and reporting?
- What information do we need on an ongoing basis to assess efficiency and effectiveness of our services/programs?
- What management information systems (MIS) do we need to improve or change in order to produce reports to assess our efficiency and effectiveness?
- What other processes need to be developed to support the overall operations of the organization (such as file maintenance systems; materials acquisition and management; equipment maintenance, etc.)?

Process Note: Staff should probably take the lead in answering these questions.

Facilities and Equipment/Technology

- What are our short-term and long-term technologic needs regarding phones and other communication systems, computers, etc.?
- Are our current facilities adequate for current and future service delivery models? What changes are anticipated and how do we go about financing them?
- What capital improvements are necessary to maintain our existing facilities?

Process Note: Larger institutions may have facilities and equipment/technology as separate goals. Smaller organizations may combine facilities and equipment/technology with the above

"Systems" goal and simply call it "infrastructure." Staff should probably take the lead in answering questions regarding facilities and equipment/technology.

Planning and Evaluation

- How should we formalize our strategic and operational planning processes so as to be better able to monitor our results and to respond in a timely way to changes in our environment?
- What processes do we need to put in place so that we can, on an ongoing basis, assess customer satisfaction, constituent needs, and our ability to meet those needs in a quality, cost effective way?

Process Note: Hopefully, one of the major by-products of a strategic planning process is the institutionalization of strategic thinking by both the Board and the staff. Formalizing the strategic and operational planning processes can lead to a more strategically managed organization and strategic management is what keeps an organization adaptive, relevant, and more effective.

Step 4.7: Develop Long-Range Financial Projections

Now that the scope and scale of programs and services have been decided upon and the organization is clear on which management and operations objectives will be needed to support those programs and services, the Planning Committee is ready to work with staff to develop long-range financial projections. The Planning Committee will need to involve the finance department in estimating the overall costs of implementing the plan and ask those involved in fund-raising to develop a strategic fund-raising plan. (Obviously, revenue and cost considerations have been involved from the beginning. Now is the time to finalize projections.)

The long-range financial projections are not precise forecasts. But the Planning Committee does need to know whether the staffing needed to support the strategic plan will cost $600,000 or $1,000,000, or whether the total budget to support the preferred future is $1,500,000 or $3,000,000. This general sense of the scale of the program is necessary for developing a strategic fund-raising plan; staff members will need to have to have some sense of the size of the organization for which they are developing a fund-raising plan. The projected financial plan provides a reality check about the cost of implementing the strategic plan and where that money will come from.

How Much Is All This Going to Cost: Strategic Budgeting. Just as strategic planning is different from planning, strategic budgeting is different from regular, year-to-year budgeting. For example, one decision in a strategic plan might be to open a new clinic in a neighboring town. The strategic plan may not include details such as which specific services to offer at the new clinic and probably will not discuss how much space will be needed, which section of town is preferable, how to publicize the new location, etc. But such a decision reflects a strategic choice to expand geographically; more detailed operational planning will take place later. The strategic plan recognizes that geographic expansion may take a different turn than expected: in the course of the more detailed planning an opportunity may unexpectedly present itself to move the current clinic to a location that would be accessible to both areas.

In a similar way, strategic budgeting focuses on a broad-stroke plan that reflects the programmatic and organizational strategic plan. Strategic budgeting focuses on the anticipated scale of each of the programs, the organization, and on how the organization will be supported. Strategic budgeting draws elements from program planning, financial analysis and projections, assessment of opportunities and threats for funding and fees, and discussion of values and priorities within the organization.

Forecasting Future Expenses. A budget, simply stated, is a plan expressed in dollars. To estimate future expenditures, therefore, an organization's financial staff will have to review the goals and objectives with an eye to identifying what major resources are going to be needed to achieve those end results. This can be an extremely difficult task. The authors of the premier text on accounting, *Financial and Accounting Guide for Not-for-Profit Organizations,* aptly summed it up when they wrote: "[Estimating the costs involved in reaching each of these goals] can be difficult because there are always many unknowns and uncertainties as to the details of how each goal will be accomplished. . . . "[8]

The expense side of the strategic budget is most easily derived by looking at the big ticket items that make up the organization's budget, for example, staffing and benefits, overhead expenses, supplies, and capital improvements, etc. Since much of the nonprofit sector is service-oriented, these expenses will typically make up the majority of the expense items.

Program managers or department managers who have responsibility for the development of annual operating budgets should be involved in the development of projected expenditures to support any long-range goals and objectives that have been articulated in the strategic plan. The Planning Committee is not looking for detailed expense projections but rather an overall sense of the costs associated with implementing the strategies and achieving the objectives outlined in the three to five year period.

How big an organization are you projecting to have? Fund-raising challenges for an organization that chooses a no or slow growth strategy ("our environment suggests that we should continue to operate as we currently are") differs from the fund-raising challenges for an organization that has a major growth strategy ("we

[8] Malvern J. Gross, Jr., Richard F. Larkin, Rogers S. Bruttomesso, and John J. McNally. *Financial and Accounting Guide for Not-for-Profit Organizations, 5th Edition,* (New York: John Wiley & Sons, Inc., 1995), p. 375.

need to expand our services to better meet the needs of the entire county, and we need to invest in our staff as well.") A broad-stroke estimate of the revenues needed to support the strategic plan may serve as a reality check: "The plan sounds great, but can we raise the revenues to support our vision? Perhaps we need to develop some contingency strategies as well!" Or, perhaps we have to just be more optimistic: "If the objectives are good ones which the membership or public will agree should be accomplished, the financial support should follow. An organization gets into difficulty when it does not periodically reevaluate its direction and thus finds itself out of step with those who support the organization financially and in other ways. The procedure is first to define the objectives and goals, then to associate dollar amounts with each, and finally to determine how to raise the necessary income."[9]

Developing Overall Revenue Strategies. The principles of how the programs and organization will be supported are important subjects for discussion throughout the organization. Some examples of broad strategic budgeting principles could include:

- *Each program will pay for itself.* Each program must pay for itself in restricted funding and, to a lesser degree, fees. Unrestricted grants and donations will be used for research and development of new programs. Planning for each program must include planning for funding and fee changes.
- *Some programs will subsidize others.* Begin an endowment fund. Our employment-related services to individuals must be kept affordable to low-income clients. To do so, we expect that this program will require subsidies of 20 percent over the next several years. The corporate services program must bring in a net surplus of at least 15 percent of customer fees which will be used to subsidize the employment program. Unrestricted grants and donations will be placed into the endowment fund.
- *Maintain government funding of programs. Grow donations for cash reserve.* With our current funding at 96 percent from government agencies, we will maintain current government funding, but hope to triple individual donations over the next four years. Individual donations and occasional grants will be used to build a cash reserve for cash flow smoothing and to make up for occasional over expenditures in funded programs.
- *Fees will cover costs.* We will set fees at what it takes to cover costs. At our school, one tuition covers full costs for that student. Fund-raising activities

[9] Malvern J. Gross, Jr., Richard F. Larkin, Roger S. Bruttomesso, and John J. McNally. *Financial and Accounting Guide for Not-for-Profit Organizations, 5th Edition.* (New York: John Wiley & Sons, Inc., 1995), p. 375.

go entirely to scholarship funds with the plan being to have 15 percent of students on full scholarship.

- *Fees will be kept below costs.* We will *never* charge what it takes to cover costs. At our school, individual contributions and endowment earnings currently subsidize 40 percent of costs and tuition covers the remaining 60 percent. Contributions need to increase with the rate of inflation.
- *All our funds will continue to be raised through direct mail donations.* Each year we project direct mail income to our environmental advocacy organization and base the budget on that. Our program will grow or shrink based on response.
- *We will spend only what we have already raised.* We will raise funds through special events, individual donations, and a few small business donations. As we raise funds, we will make grants on a quarterly basis to public schools in our county.

The principles above will probably have been discussed in the context of program planning and as part of the SWOT analysis. Where these questions are raised is less important than whether these questions are raised and discussed as part of the strategic planning process. Strategic budgeting is more than simple projections; it is a process through which the organization grounds the strategic plan in both business realities and the organization's shared values.

Strategic Fund-Raising Plan. An organization's strategic fund-raising plan consists of two parts: an overall plan that links several fundraising components together, and planning for each of the components. Most organizations undertaking strategic planning have already developed some fund-raising activities and have some sense of which areas have the most potential for growth. Furthermore, a comprehensive discussion of fund-raising planning is beyond the scope of this workbook. The strategic planning process provides the opportunity to consider the role of fund-raising in the organization's future and to plan for what will be needed to implement the plan. Usually a detailed strategic fund-raising plan is developed as a companion piece to the Strategic Plan.

Forecasting Revenues. When estimating revenues, many people simply use intuitive judgment and make an educated guess. Sometimes the educated guess is made by a group, or is based on the opinions of several informed people.

In the for-profit sector, forecasting techniques are used, for example, to predict sales income, costs of parts and materials, investment performance, and the effects of capital purchases. In the nonprofit sector, forecasting is usually used to project revenue, such as sales or fees. Forecasting techniques can also be used to predict the number of hospital admissions, enrollment in various college classes, etc.

For small or new organizations, and for simple decisions in all kinds of organizations, making an educated guess may be the best forecasting method. More formal forecasting involves applying statistical and mathematical techniques to historical data to make projections for the future.

All forecasting and predicting—from "seat of the pants" to highly complex modeling—is based on the premise that future events can be predicted based on patterns discovered through reviewing historical information. This might seem obvious, but future events may not follow the patterns of the past.

Steps in forecasting revenue include:

1. Graph results from previous years; note any trends
2. Make educated guesses about key factors that influence the revenue from a certain activity (i.e., advertising may influence ticket sales for a theater event)
3. Determine how these factors affected revenue (i.e., certain advertising dollars may be more effective than others)
4. Project what may happen to these factors during the next budget period
5. Return to the original graph and add your projections

An organization's overall fund-raising plan begins with broad goals for how many contributed dollars will be raised each year and with selection of major fund-raising vehicles. Here are some common vehicles to consider:

- Unrestricted foundation grants
- Restricted foundation grants
- Corporate contributions
- Individual memberships
- Annual luncheon
- Annual mail campaign
- Year-round direct mail
- Annual Walkathon
- Annual auction
- Major gifts
- Bequests
- Planned gifts: life income funds

For example, a community theater may identify contributed funds at the annual dinner as comprising about half the funds needed for each season, with box office funds making up the remainder of the budget. On the other hand, a public interest law firm which has relied predominantly on attorney fees from class action settlements may see fund-raising growth in major donor gifts supplanting attorney fees over time.

Once the anchor fund-raising vehicles have been selected, then the following questions should be applied against each of the vehicles:

- Which of the vehicles represent increasing opportunities? Declining opportunities?
- Which have the highest return on investment (including cash, staff time, volunteer time)?
- Which have the most nonfinancial benefits? What are those benefits?
- Which have the most positive impact on other fund-raising components?
- Which are the most popular among volunteers? Board members? Least popular?

Whoever is developing the strategic fund-raising plan might also link the vehicles in order to maximize the connections. For example, one homeless shelter

Exhibit 4-9 Worksheet 19: Long-Range Financial Projections

Process Notes

How to do this activity	Identify the expenses needed to achieve your long range goals and objectives. Consider the organization's current and projected sources of revenue to determine the organization's long-range revenue goals and objectives. Compare the projected total revenue budget to the current revenue and budget, and the projected revenue in relation to projected expenses. Determine if the projections are realistic and/or prudent, given the organization's experience.
Why do this activity	Building a projected financial plan will provide a reality check about the cost of the organization's goals: what will it cost to implement these goals and where will the money come from?
Who to involve in the process	Finance staff should take responsibility for the development of the expense estimates. Fund-raising staff and the Resource Development of the Board should take responsibility for the development of a long-range strategic fund-raising plan.

Case Study—ASO/USA

♦ Worksheet 19

Long-Range Financial Projections

☐ Estimate the financial resources required to support the strategic plan.

Revenue and Support

Current Revenue and Support

$645,000

Percentage Breakdown by Source of Funds

10% Other
90% Government

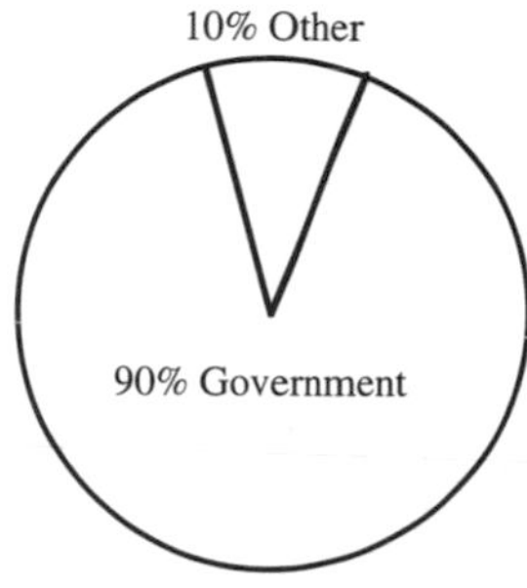

Future Revenue and Support

$1,000,000

Percentage Breakdown by Source of Funds

40% Other
60% Government

Expenses

10% Administrative
5% Fund-raising
20% Facility
60% Personnel

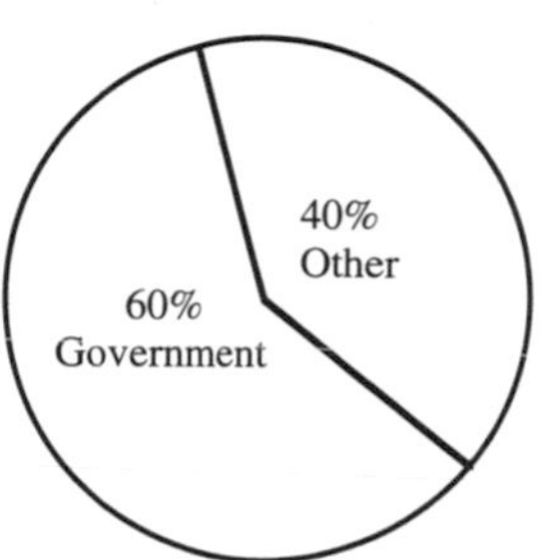

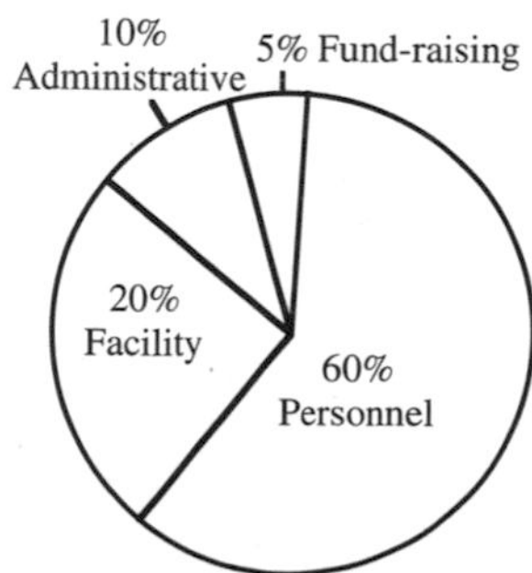

Current Expenses:

$645,000

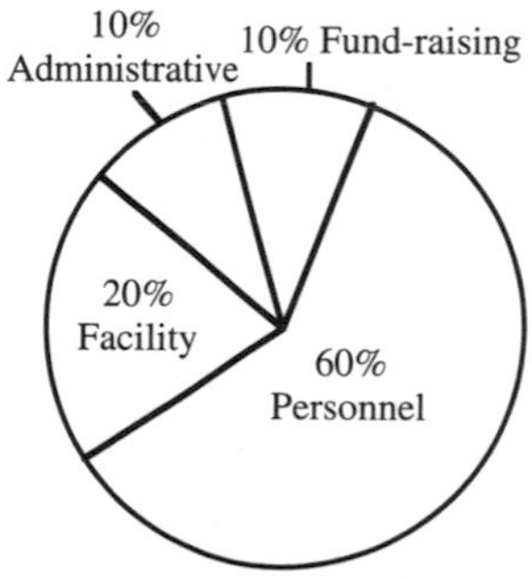

10% Administrative
10% Fund-raising
20% Facility
60% Personnel

Future Expenses:

$1,000,000

conducts an annual mail campaign for contributions, mailing to existing donors and volunteers, and tries to expand the list each year by about 10 percent. This mail campaign makes a modest amount of money, but its bigger purpose is to identify more significant donors who are then invited to an annual open house during the holiday season. Following the open house, volunteers make personal visits to all donors who attended the open house, seeking more substantial contributions. During those visits, names are solicited for next year's mailing as well. If any of these activities (mail campaign, open house, major donor visits) were considered in isolation of the others, each would be far less successful.

After the key components are selected and linked into a plan and calendar, the organization must identify what is needed to make the fund-raising plan work. For example, if major gifts are identified as key for fund-raising growth, such a decision will have an impact on board recruitment and composition. Board training in asking for contributions may also be appropriate. If corporate contributions are targeted for growth, more efforts may be invested in recruiting volunteers from selected corporations. If contributed funds have not been a significant factor up to now, but the organization wishes to grow in this area, a multi-year investment in a development officer may be appropriate.

Hank Rosso of the Fund-Raising School was famous for his maxim: "There are five parts to successful fund-raising: Planning, Planning, Planning, Planning, and Asking." Strategic planning for successful fund-raising is an important component for long-term success—the agencies with strategic fund-raising plans may not have more money next year or even the year after that, but they will be the ones that are successful ten years from now.

PHASE 5: WRITING THE STRATEGIC PLAN

The end is in sight! Now that everyone has had a chance to contribute their ideas, now that all the options have been wrestled with, now that the choices have been made and the details worked out, all that remains is to commit the ideas to paper and make it official.

Step 5.1: Identify the Writer of the Plan

First of all, who actually writes the plan? It is useful to remember that writing is done most efficiently by one or two individuals, not by a whole group—the writer simply crafts the presentation of the group's ideas. Often an executive director will draft the plan, or the task may be delegated to a staff person, board member, or a consultant who has been working with the Planning Committee. In the end, it really doesn't matter who writes the strategic plan; what matters is that it accurately documents the decisions made by the Planning Committee, that it represents a shared vision, and that it has the support of the those responsible for carrying it out. (In all likelihood, this decision will have been made early on. The designated writer will be able to begin work sooner if this is the case.)

Step 5.2: Develop a Review Process for the Document

The process of review and approval is the most important consideration in this phase. The Planning Committee should decide in advance who may review and respond to the draft plan—obviously committee members will participate in the review process, but should the full board and the full staff? The guiding principle of participation in the strategic planning process is that everyone who will help execute the plan should have some input in shaping it; whether or not this includes review of the final drafts of the plan is a judgment call that depends upon the particular circumstances of an organization.

Ideally, the big ideas have been debated and resolved, so that revisions only amount to small matters of adding detail, revising format, or changing wording in a particular section. Still, if reviewers get bogged down in crossing too many T's and dotting too many I's, the plan could linger in draft form forever. The Planning Committee must exercise leadership in setting a realistic time frame and in bringing the review process to a timely close. The Committee needs to choose the level of review appropriate for the organization, provide copies for review to the selected individuals, and set a deadline for submitting feedback (usually allowing one to two weeks is sufficient). Upon receiving all the feedback, the committee must agree on which suggested revisions to accept, incorporate these into the document, and submit the strategic plan to the full board of directors for approval.

Step 5.3: Choose a Format for the Strategic Plan

A strategic plan is simply a document that summarizes why an organization exists, what it is trying to accomplish, and how it will go about doing so. Its audience is anyone who wants to know the organization's most important ideas, issues, and priorities: board members, staff, volunteers, clients, funders, peers at other organizations, the press, and the public. It is a document that should offer edification and guidance—so the more concise and ordered the document, the greater the likelihood that it will be used, and that it will be helpful in guiding the operations of the organization.

Each of the three strategic planning processes—abbreviated, moderate, and extensive—will have slightly different formats containing various levels of specificity and length. The written plan should reflect the nature and extent of the planning discussions and the level of detail that needs to be communicated to the reader. Whatever the format, remember that the point of the document is to allow the best possible explanation of the organization's plan for the future—the format should serve the message!

For an abbreviated strategic planning process, the strategic planning document will probably be no more than three to eight pages in length and will include the mission statement, a summary of core strategies, and a list of long-term and short-term program and management/operations priorities. The edited notes from the retreat may serve as the appendix.

For a moderate planning process, the strategic planning document will probably be 8–12 pages and will include the following:

- Introduction by the president of the board (one page)
- Mission statement (one page)
- Summary of core strategies (one page)
- List of long-term and short-term program and management/operations priorities *or* program and management/operations goals and objectives (four to six pages)
- Optional appendices: summary of environmental assessment, summary of client surveys, summary of any other stakeholder surveys or interviews (one to three pages)

For an extensive strategic planning process and multi-department organizations, a document that is 12–40 pages will most likely be needed. Exhibit 4-10 is a sample table of contents for such a strategic planning document, as well as brief descriptions of each component listed. The table of contents should help writers as they begin to organize their thoughts and their material.

Step 5.4: Write the Strategic Plan

For an *abbreviated* strategic planning process, the writer(s) of the plan simply needs to use the notes from the planning retreat and summarize the key ideas on paper. Usually, two or three individuals who were at the retreat will have volunteered to draft or revise a mission statement using each participants' filled out Worksheet 6: Creating a Mission Statement and ideas generated during the retreat discussion. The newly drafted mission statement would be given to the strategic plan writer to include in the final document. The key to writing the plan is to keep it simple and short, circulate it among internal stakeholders for their comments, and then submit the final version to the board of directors for approval.

For a *moderate* planning process, the writer(s) of the plan should use the notes from the retreat and all Planning Committee meetings. These notes, plus copies of completed worksheets, would be the basis for creating a first draft of the strategic

Exhibit 4-10 Sample Strategic Planning Document

Sample Table of Contents:

I. Introduction by the President of the Board
II. Executive Summary
III. Mission Statement and Vision Statement
IV. Organization History and Profile
V. Strategic Issues and Core Strategies
VI. Program Goals and Objectives
VII. Management/Operations Goals and Objectives
VIII. [Possible] Appendices
   A. Summary of environmental assessment: strengths, weaknesses, opportunities, and threats
   B. Summary of client surveys, community interviews, etc.
   C. Membership of Board and Planning Committee
   D. Long-range budget projections

Exhibit 4-10 *(Continued)*

I. Introduction by the President of the Board

A one-page cover letter from the President of the organization's Board of Directors introduces the plan to readers; it gives a stamp of approval to the plan and demonstrates that the organization has achieved a critical level of internal agreement. (This introduction is often combined with the Executive Summary below.)

II. Executive Summary

In one to two pages, this section should summarize the strategic plan: it should reference the mission and vision, highlight the long-range goals (what the organization is seeking to accomplish), and perhaps note the process for developing the plan as well as thank participants in the process. From this summary, readers should understand what is most important about the organization.

III. Mission Statement and Vision Statement

The mission statement, not more than one page, can stand alone without any introductory text, because essentially it introduces and defines itself. An optional vision statement may also be included.

IV. Organization Profile and History

In one or two pages, the reader should learn the story of the organization—key events, triumphs, and changes over time—so that they can understand its historical context (just as the Planning Committee needed to at the beginning of the planning process). Major accomplishments for the past year should be highlighted here as well.

V. Strategic Issues and Core Strategies

Sometimes organizations omit this section, choosing instead to "cut to the chase" and simply present goals and objectives. The advantage of including this section is that it makes explicit the strategic thinking behind the plan. Board and staff leaders may refer to this document to check their assumptions, and external readers will better understand the organization's vantage point. The section might be presented as a brief outline of ideas or as a narrative that covers one or two pages.

VI. Program Goals and Objectives

In many ways the program goals and objectives are the heart of the strategic plan. The mission statement answers the big questions about why the organization exists and how it seeks to benefit society, but the goals and objectives are the plan of action—what the organization intends to do over the next few years. As such, the section should serve as a useful guide to operational planning and a reference for evaluation. Depending on the complexity of the organization this section may be three to fifteen

Exhibit 4-10 *(Continued)*

pages in length. Multi-departmental institutions and very large organizations often exceed that number of pages.

VII. Management/Operations Goals and Objectives

The management/operations functions are separated from the program functions here to emphasize the distinction between service goals and organization development goals; this gives the reader a clearer understanding both of the difference and the relationship between the two, and enhances the guiding function of the plan. Depending on the complexity of the organization, this section usually is three to twelve pages in length, but may be longer.

VIII. Appendices

The reason to include any appendices is to provide needed documentation for interested readers. Perhaps no appendices are truly necessary (many organizations opt for brevity); they should be included only if they will truly enhance readers' understanding of the plan, not just burden them with more data or complicating factors. Most organizations at the very least will summarize strengths, weaknesses, opportunities, and threats here, and results of any client/customer surveys. Appendices can be from one to five pages, but could be considerably longer.

plan. The following worksheets would probably be most helpful for developing the moderate strategic plan:

- Worksheet 6: Creating a Mission Statement
- Worksheet 7: Vision Statement (optional)
- Worksheet 15: Core Future Strategies
- Worksheet 16: Long-Term and Short-Term Priorities

If the Planning Committee wishes to have the strategic plan translate those long-term and short-term priorities into goal and objective language, then Worksheet 18: Setting Goals and Objectives should be used.

The appendices to the moderate strategic plan should include data from: Worksheet 9: Staff and Board Perceptions of SWOT; Worksheet 10: External Stakeholders' Perceptions and Expectations; and summary of any client or other stakeholder interviews and surveys.

After the board president has written the introduction to the strategic plan, the document should be circulated among key stakeholders for their input and then a final version submitted to the board of directors for their approval.

For an *extensive* strategic planning process and multi-department organizations, the strategic planning document has, for the most part, already been written if most of the worksheets have been completed. The writer(s) of the strategic plan could simply cut and paste the supporting worksheet data into the strategic planning document. For example, the mission statement and vision statement data will be found on Worksheets 6 and 7; the strategic issues and core strategies were reviewed in Worksheet 15; an outline of the goals and objectives has already been created with Worksheet 18, etc. And even if organizations have not completed every worksheet (most organizations probably will have not!), the worksheets would have framed the discussions, and therefore the notes from the meetings simply need to be summarized in the strategic plan. See Exhibit 4-11 for a Case Study of ASO/USA strategic plan.

The rule of thumb for writing the extensive strategic plan is the same rule for writing the abbreviated strategic plan: keep it simple and keep it short (or as short as you can so that it provides enough guidance to develop annual operating plans, but not so long or complex that no one reads or uses it)! The heart of the strategic planning document is the core strategies and goals and objectives sections. The supporting data should all be contained in the strategic plan's appendices.

For multi-department organizations, overall strategies and overarching program and management/support goals and objectives should be developed first. Then, each department manager or director would be responsible for developing goals and objectives for his or her department. The prime writer or writers of the extensive strategic plan would then incorporate those department plans into the overall strategic planning document.

Exhibit 4-11 ASO/USA Strategic Plan

CASE STUDY: AIDS SERVICE ORGANIZATION/U.S.A.

Table of Contents

Exhibit 4-11 *(Continued)*

I. Introduction by the President of the Board

On behalf of the board, staff, and volunteers of AIDS Service Organization, U.S.A., it is my honor to introduce the strategic planning document which is enclosed in the following pages.

This plan is the culmination of six months of intensive work by staff, Board members, and volunteers. During that period, we have conducted focus groups, one-on-one interviews, held management and staff meetings and retreats, made numerous presentations to our board of directors, and poured over research and statistical data. Our board/staff strategic planning committee, charged by our board of directors to conduct this plan, has devoted a great deal of time and effort to this process. Our discussions have been at times serious, comical, frustrating, contentious, and engaging, but have always centered upon one critical focus: how best to reduce the impact of HIV and AIDS in our community.

We have evaluated our strengths and learned from our experience. As a result, over the next three years, we have decided to focus our efforts on three areas of organizational competence: providing comprehensive case management services for people living with HIV/AIDS and conducting HIV Prevention and Education programs. As part of our prevention efforts we will conduct community organizing efforts, but we will no longer conduct services such as transportation and English classes. We will support our clients in taking advantage of such services offered by other agencies.

We remain committed to a vision of eliminating HIV as a danger in our community and will work with leading researchers and other colleagues to stay at the forefront of the fight against AIDS.

Thank you for your interest in ASO/USA.

Sincerely,

Sam Green
President of the Board, ASO/USA

2

Exhibit 4-11 *(Continued)*

II. Mission and Vision Statements

Mission statement

AIDS Services Organization/USA (ASO/USA) is dedicated to reducing the impact of HIV in our community. We do this by providing services to improve the quality of life for people with HIV, advocating for responsible public policies, and striving to prevent the spread of HIV in our communities. We believe that AIDS education programs and services to people with AIDS must be culturally sensitive and linguistically appropriate. ASO/USA is committed to the value of indigenous leadership, the value of all human life, and the possibility of success in achieving our mission.

Vision statement

Our vision is that all people with HIV get the appropriate care they need in a comfortable, accessible setting and that we see the day soon when HIV is no longer a killer in our community.

3

Exhibit 4-11 *(Continued)*

III. Organizational History and Profile

AIDS Service Organization/USA was founded in 1988 to meet the needs of the growing number of people becoming infected and affected by AIDS. Ken Brown, our founding executive director, has led the organization through a period of sustained growth. The organization started out doing prevention work and won a federal grant to continue the work in their second year.

In subsequent years, the organization expanded its programs to include case management services for persons with AIDS and support groups for people with AIDS and caregivers of people with AIDS. ASO/USA has become known as a reliable community agency and serves men and women of all races, with most clients in the low to moderate income range. ASO/USA does a limited amount of advocacy and public education, supported by local foundations.

The organization's budget in 1996 was $645,000 with twenty full- and part-time staff and a core of fifty volunteers. $280,000 per year is from the federal Centers for Disease Control, $190,000 is from the city, approximately $140,000 is from foundations, and $35,000 is raised through special events, mailers, and other fund-raising.

4

Exhibit 4-11 *(Continued)*

IV. Critical Issues

Medical advances in AIDS treatment are both exciting and challenging. A critical issue that our organization had to examine was whether our current services were the most appropriate match for our community over the next few years. Strategies selected to deal with this issue:

- Focus on case management services to help our clients understand and access the latest, most appropriate treatments available
- Invest in ongoing staff and volunteer education to keep ourselves current with the fast-changing landscape of treatment options
- Participate actively in the city-wide network of AIDS treatment providers and community activists

Dependence on federal funding has helped the organization grow to a substantial size over the past six years. However, federal funding is uncertain in the future, and ensuring that we will be here for the people in our community if federal funding priorities change is a critical issue for us. Strategies selected to deal with this issue:

- Ensure our relationship with our federal funding sources is as strong as it can be
- Increase support from individuals, foundations, and corporations

We have had to examine our collaborative relationships to decide how we can best work to serve our community. Strategies selected to deal with this issue:

- Develop a set of criteria which will help guide our decision-making about how and when to collaborate on programs and projects
- Keep all informal collaborative efforts going, terminate the collaboration with City Clinic for outreach services, and explore alternative collaborative relationships which better fit our mission and organizational strengths

Our internal management systems have been outstripped by the growth of the organization. A critical issue is how to bring our systems up to speed with the current pace and scale of our program work. Strategies selected to deal with this issue:

- Hire our auditor to develop recommendations on staffing and updating our computerization of financial management
- Finance Committee of the Board of Directors will meet with the Executive Director and Finance Manager monthly to discuss implementation of recommendations during the next year

Not all programs fit equally with our mission and organizational abilities. Strategies selected to deal with this issue:

- Divest transportation program and English classes
- Support delivery of these services to our clients by others

5

Exhibit 4-11 *(Continued)*

V. Goals and Objectives

Program Goals and Objectives*
Support Services Division
Goal: To deliver a continuum of services which improve the quality of life and health for people living with HIV and AIDS

Case Management Program
Subgoal: To ensure better coordination of the delivery of direct services to our clients

Case Management Program Objectives:

1. Expand our case management services to serve 600 clients within the next two years
2. Increase number of referrals we receive from other providers in the city
3. Explore additional subcontract relationships with the two hospitals in the city regarding clients who need case management help
4. Develop and implement new quality control procedures to ensure that our case management services remain of highest quality
5. Survey all clients regarding access to primary health care. After baseline is established, set objective for level of increase in access to be sought over the next three years
6. Provide on going training for case management services to accommodate new treatments

Support Groups Program
Subgoal: To improve the mental well-being of individuals impacted by HIV disease while decrease their feeling of isolation

Support Group Objectives:

1. Transition all current support groups to the Neighborhood Network
2. Ensure that ongoing referral mechanisms are in place for placing all clients with appropriate support groups
3. Work with Neighborhood Network staff to provide on-going training to support group leaders so as to increase their ability to work with clients whose needs are changing (and more complex) as the epidemic changes

AIDS Hotline
Subgoal: To ensure that individuals with questions regarding AIDS and HIV have a safe place to have their questions answered and made aware of the full spectrum of resources available to them

AIDS Hotline Objectives:

1. Increase coverage for our AIDS Hotline from 18 hours a day to 24 hours a day coverage within the next year
2. In addition to having full coverage from volunteer and paid staff who speak Spanish, be able to provide translation services in Chinese

Translation Services
Subgoal: To ensure that all individuals, regardless of what language they speak, have access to information and full range of services provided by this agency

Translation Services Objectives:

1. Increase the number of volunteers and staff who are able to provide assistance in languages other than English
2. Eliminate the waiting list for non-English speaking clients seeking case management assistance in Spanish and Chinese
3. Develop a cooperative arrangement with the Hearing Society to provide sign language assistance when needed
4. Within the next three years, ensure that all essential educational materials are available in Spanish and Chinese

---

**Note:* For the sake of brevity, for this case study example only Support Services Division's goals and objectives have been outlined. In actuality, the other divisions (public education and public policy) would also have goals, subgoals, and objectives described.

Exhibit 4-11 *(Continued)*

Management/Operations Goals and Objectives

Staffing and Benefits: To attract and retain qualified paid and volunteer staff for all services and activities

Staffing

- Increase number of paid staff from 20 full-time employees to 35 full-time employees to support our ability to provide needed services, and increase the number of volunteer hours per year from 5,750 to 9,000
- Assess whether more complex and differing needs of clients require certain jobs that were done by volunteers to be done by paid staff

Salaries and benefits

- Assess overall salary structure and benefits package; develop and implement a plan to increase staff salaries and offer a competitive benefit package
- Analyze fringe benefits package on an ongoing basis and identify ways of meeting employees needs (such as pension plan, cafeteria approach to benefits, etc.)
- Review personnel policies annually to make sure they are in legal compliance

Training , evaluation, and other support

- Establish and maintain a more formalized ongoing training program for all staff and volunteers
- Implement and maintain a new staff evaluation system that establishes overall objectives for positions and specific objectives for all employees
- Expand our volunteer and paid staff appreciation program
- Develop and coordinate an agency-wide management training program to help staff build skills needs to perform their duties and interface with other departments, including a cross-training program

Volunteers

- Increase number of volunteers from 50 to 75
- Assess current volunteer recruitment, orientation, training program, and make modifications as necessary

7

Exhibit 4-11 *(Continued)*

Resource Development: To acquire stable, broad-based, financial and non-financial resources to support the programs and growth envisioned in this strategic plan

Diversification of funding

- Within the next three years, at least 40 percent of ASO/USA's annual operating budget will be raised through private sector philanthropy. The development of this subsidy is critical for the maintenance and growth of our programs.
- Explore donations in kind such as printing, equipment, etc., to help support our services. Within the next three years, to have similar donations to support all educational brochures and our annual report.
- Increase the money the organization receives from private individuals a minimum of 10 percent each year.
- Raise a minimum of $50,000 annually from special events

Infrastructure support for resource development function

- Establish a development department within the management structure of the organization, staffed by a full-time professional development officer to supervise overall fund-raising functions and work closely with Board and management staff to develop and implement a successful development program
- Establish and maintain a computerized donor history file and increase the personal contacts made with donors

Board of Directors role in fund-raising

- Maintain a board giving policy that requires all Board members to contribute financially to the organization
- Increase the board's participation in all aspects of fund-raising

8

Exhibit 4-11 *(Continued)*

Board of Directors: To develop and maintain an effective, active, and informed Board of Directors whose governance and support roles help the achievement of ASO/USA's mission	Board membership • Increase board to approximately 15 individuals • Diversify the board so it more accurately reflects who we serve • Develop and maintain an advisory board to help supplement the board's expertise and contribution Board training • Increase the capability of the Board to assist with the following functions: marketing, fund-raising, legal matters, public relations, and evaluation. • Develop and maintain an effective board orientation and ongoing training program Board effectiveness • Increase effectiveness of the board by redefining Committees and each Committee's mandate, and assessing on-going mandates yearly; holding an annual board retreat to set overall objectives for the board as a whole and each Committee requiring each Committee to submit detailed workplans to support accomplishing agreed upon goals and objectives • Continue yearly evaluation of all aspects of the board • Continue 100 percent contribution from all board members • Increase the board's participation in all aspects of fund-raising

9

Exhibit 4-11 *(Continued)*

Planning and Evaluation: To guarantee that we meet the needs of our constituencies and that all programs provide the highest level of service to our clients

1. Establish an ongoing evaluation process for all programs to assess program results, quality of services, and our ability to address the (changing) needs of the community
2. Annually, hold a Board/staff retreat(s) to plan for future needs and assess current capabilities
   - review strategic plan and make changes as needed
   - assess changing environment
   - make modifications to strategic plan as necessary
   - ensure that detailed annual operating plans are developed for all programs and internal management functions
3. Establish and maintain protocols for data collection, data entry, and outcome evaluation

Public Relations/ Marketing: To increase the visibility and community awareness of ASO/USA, and to make sure that ASO/USA is properly recognized for its achievements and closely identified as a premier provider to people with AIDS and those affected by HIV

1. Build public awareness of ASO/USA in the community through increased media coverage and public service announcements
2. Produce and distribute a newsletter on a regular basis
3. Update our brochures regularly and make sure they are available in English, Spanish, and Cantonese

10

Exhibit 4-11 *(Continued)*

Infrastructure: To increase the operational and management efficiency and effectiveness of ASO/USA	1. Ensure timely, accurate, useful information is available and consistently applied in sound decision-making throughout the agency • Improve and maintain a fully computerized accounting system which is able to produce timely, accurate financial reports for the organization as a whole, and for all departments • Provide executive management and the Board with required financial reports, budget comparisons, and cash flow projections • Annually assess organization's internal controls to ensure adequate safeguard of all resources • Develop a system for tracking all necessary management information and train all staff to use the MIS systems and proper documentation of services 2. To have available the most technology and equipment necessary to be able to provide quality, efficient, and effective service • Continually assess technology needs and update computers and other technology as needed 3. To provide adequate and accessible space in a pleasant, comfortable environment for all ASO/USA clients and paid and volunteer staff. • Develop and implement a facilities master plan to locate programs and services in facilities which provide comfort and ease of access to clients and staff • Explore option of getting a building donated • Consider opening a satellite office in the southwest part of he city • Maintain facilities which are attractive to clients
Networking and Collaboration: To maximize closer communication with other agencies in order to maximize community involvement and ensure increased coordination and collaboration among AIDS service providers and organizations doing related work	1. Support the development of regular meetings of other agencys' staff in order to share information, increase advocacy efforts, and maximize networking among all service providers 2. Continue to investigate forming or expanding partnerships with other AIDS service providers to make sure that our clients needs are met and resources are used effectively

11

Suggested Format for Presenting Goals and Objectives

Goal	Commentary	Subgoals	Objectives
To ensure that parents are an integral and respected part of the child care delivery system and that the system is responsive to their needs	Parents are the core of what we are and what we do. During the next five years, the Network will make an all-out effort to strengthen our connection to parents. During the past ten years, we have made progress addressing the supply and quality of child care by developing and implementing a variety of successful programs and initiatives, and working effectively as advocates for an expanded, improved child care delivery system. As we assess the overall state of child care in the mid-1990s, we are faced with overwhelming needs and a continually inadequate supply of quality, affordable child care. Our frustration with the slowness of real public policy change for quality, affordable child care propels parents to the top of our agenda for the next five years. We are convinced that meaningful change in child care policy will only come when the parents who need and depend on child care are more present and respected in the policy debate. The Network and its member agencies are committed to supporting this expanded parental voice for child care.	A. Help parents better understand the intricacies of the child care delivery system and articulate their child care needs and preferences	A1. Develop and implement a plan to identify, encourage, and support parents from diverse backgrounds in the assumption of leadership roles A2. Assist member agencies in their expanded efforts to organize grass roots parents' coalitions and to implement the principles of community organizing
		B. Ensure that all parents have easy access to information about affordable child care options and available financial assistance	B1. Intensify efforts to create a more user-friendly child care system B2. Help direct parents to local resource and referral agencies and child care subsidy programs B3. Expand and improve the availability of information and services to diverse parent populations
		C. Ensure that all parents are well-informed child care consumers	C1. Continue to develop consumer education resources and strategies accessible to diverse populations C2. Distribute new consumer education materials throughout the state C3. Expand public knowledge and utilization of consumer protections in California including child care licensing standards and Trustline registry for license-exempt care C4. Expand media coverage for child care consumer issues C5. Increase business commitment in California to provide child care referral services to working parents

Note: *The columnar format allows the reader of the plan to easily see the connection between goals, subgoals, and objectives. The inclusion of the commentary column allows the reader of the strategic plan to have a greater understanding of why the goal is important. The inclusion of either background, historical data, or a summary of the future emphasis or focus of the goal helps the reader to put the goal in some context.*

(Source: *California Child Care Resource and Referral Network: 1995–2000 Strategic Plan*)

Like the abbreviated strategic plan and the moderate strategic plan, the draft strategic plan would be reviewed by members of the Planning Committee and other individuals whose input is needed. The final strategic plan would be presented to the board of directors for its approval. Once the plan has been approved, an executive summary should be prepared and sent out to the members, funders, and other individuals and organizations who have been identified as key stakeholders—those individuals whose knowledge of the organization's future is key to their support.

Step 5.5: Adopt the Strategic Plan and Celebrate!

At last! The planning process is completed and a document has been produced. Make certain to have the plan formally adopted by the board of directors as the official strategic plan of the organization. This is a moment of closure on the process, and for getting energized to put the plan in action.

Have a party, write the planning committee notes of thanks, publish the document in condensed version for distribution, give copies to all board and staff members: in short, celebrate the accomplishment and choose an appropriate way to convey the message that this plan represents an important consensus about where we are going together!

CHAPTER FIVE

Keeping the Plan Relevant

PHASE 6: IMPLEMENTING YOUR STRATEGIC PLAN

"A vision without a plan is a hallucination."—Anonymous

Congratulations! You have completed your strategic plan. Long-term direction is clear and priorities have been set. This work by itself, shared among all the people who have a role in implementing the plan, will go a long way toward aligning the efforts of the team with the strategic direction.

To ensure that the strategic plan is implemented in a coordinated and effective manner, it must be translated into specifics; the strategic plan must be converted into *both* an annual operating plan and an annual budget. These two plans describe the same work over the same period of time; they are simply written in different languages. Clearly, they need to be telling the same story.

The annual operating plan provides a detailed plan in the language of objectives, action steps, and responsibilities. The budget provides a detailed plan in the language of dollars, organized by types of revenue and types of expenses. The operating plan describes what services will be provided, what types of action will be conducted to provide these services and who is responsible. The budget describes how much it will cost to carry out the plan.

What Level of Detail Is Necessary in an Operating Plan?

Imagine you are driving a car going on vacation. It is important to have a destination in mind, your "long-range goal." The destination alone, however, is not enough to get you there successfully—you need to have detailed information about which roads are most likely to get you there, estimates about the distance to be covered and the time it will take, estimates of how much money will be needed for meals and gas for the car, and warning systems to tell you if the engine gets overheated.

Now imagine that you aren't driving the car alone. Instead you have twenty people doing different jobs simultaneously: your organization's executive director is at the steering wheel with a couple of board members looking over her shoulder, staff are stationed at each wheel making them spin, other people are pooling their money, and someone else is in the back making sandwiches. It is going to take an impressive plan to move this crew in the same direction efficiently!

This is the stuff of annual operating plans and annual budgets: which programs and management/operations functions are going to do what, by when, and how much "gas" (money and person power) will they require? This level of detail is unnecessary in a strategic plan itself—in fact, it would clutter up the presentation of the long-range vision. The strategic plan focuses on the beach you are going to, not which gas station to stop at along the way. The annual operating plan needs to provide enough guidance for the travelers to move ahead at full speed—so there is no need at *every* rest stop to discuss where to go next or why the driver took the last turn!

What if You Don't Have All the Information You Think You Need?

Organizations typically have more developed routines around annual budgeting than they do around annual program planning. It is a rare and foolish board that would approve a budget including vague information about planned expenses and little detail about projected revenue. (For this reason, and because there are many useful resources already available, this workbook does not go into detail about the mechanics of the annual budgeting process.)

However, the language of operating plans is much less precise than the language of dollars and cents. Perhaps for this reason, nonprofits have tended to have less well-developed program planning routines and often the program planning is not coordinated agency wide as the budgeting process nearly always is. The potential for staff to waste effort, or worse, work at cross purposes, is much greater when program planning is not as well-coordinated as the budgeting process.

The purpose of the operating plan is to provide enough detail to keep everyone moving in the same direction with a common understanding of how far and how fast to move. This does not mean every detail. To go back to the vacation metaphor above, the operating plan probably does not need to include instructions on how to make sandwiches, but it does need to mention that someone is in charge of feeding the travelers.

What if you do not know who is going to be in charge of feeding the travelers, or what route to take, or where the gas stations will be located, or how fast the car will go? The operating plan makes mention of the fact that these jobs will have to be done or the information gathered, and assigns responsibility for figuring them out.

For example, organizations doing strategic planning for the first time may never have conducted in-depth program evaluation. If there isn't time to do this work before the strategic plan is to be completed (and often there isn't), doing program evaluation work can become an *objective* of the operating plan. "We think our programs are doing a good job but we do not know as much as we'd like, so our objective this year is to conduct a thorough program evaluation. When we get new information we will adjust our strategic plans accordingly."

What if We Already Have Program Operating Plans Written for Specific Grants?

No problem. In an organization with more than one program, it may well make sense to have two levels of operating plans.

The level of detail required in a program plan by many funders is often quite specific. It may not be practical or useful to compile several of these plans into one large operating plan. In the first place, they are usually too long to be useful to individuals not directly involved with the particular program. In the second place, the funding cycles are often different from the organization's fiscal year.

For both of these reasons, the answer is to create a less detailed organization-wide annual operating plan which serves as the one-year implementation version of the strategic plan and as the umbrella plan for more detailed program plans. The organization-wide plan is useful to the board and to all staff interested in better understanding the work of a program in the context of the work of the entire organization. This concept is illustrated in Exhibit 5-1.

Exhibit 5-1 The Levels of the Operating Plan

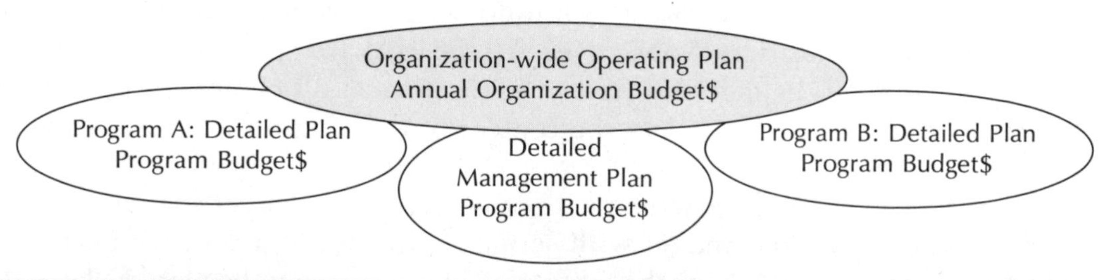

Characteristics of a Useful Annual Operating Plan

There are three important characteristics of a useful annual operating plan:

1. An appropriate level of detail—enough to guide the work, but not so much detail that it becomes overwhelming, confusing, or unnecessarily constrains flexibility
2. A format that allows for periodic reports on progress toward the specific goals and objectives
3. A structure that allows a user to easily see that it is consistent with the priorities in the strategic plan

The appropriate level of detail depends on how much authority or latitude staff have to use their judgment in pursuing objectives. Jack Welch, CEO at General Electric, says he doesn't even want to know about any decisions which cost less than $25 million to implement. Below this expenditure level, his staff have the authority to use their own judgment in pursuing corporate objectives. Few nonprofit staff will have quite this much authority! Typically, more detail is useful when a program is new, staff are inexperienced, or actions in one program area have extensive implications for the operation of other programs. In general, the more concise the operating plan, the easier it is to implement and the easier it is to monitor. So, provide only as much detail as is appropriate!

The format of an annual operating plan is important. A confusing format belies confused thought, and inevitably leads to confused implementation. There are two questions to ask yourself about your annual operating plan format:

1. Can everyone who needs to use the plan make sense of what it says?
2. Are the objectives and action steps written and organized in a way that makes it easy to monitor?

Develop a User-Friendly Annual Workplan

The operating plan is the beginning of the implementation of the strategic plan. Thus, the structure of the operating plan must be congruent with the priorities outlined in the strategic plan. As the year unfolds, choices will arise about whether and how to modify the original objectives. All the work that goes into the strategic planning process will be more useful to decision makers if choices in the middle of the year can be easily placed in the context of the long-term priorities of the organization.

Just as monthly financial statements often present a budget for revenue and expenses and compare the budget with actual figures for a given time period, so should operating plans allow for the same type of comparison: the plan declares the budgeted work in terms of goals and objectives for each program area and management/operations function and reports the actual progress on a monthly or perhaps quarterly basis. This operating plan "budget-to-actual" report, along with the financial "budget-to-actual" report, gives a clear reading of how the year is going.

Two sample operating plans are shown below. The first is for a government agency, the second is for a fictional development effort at a nonprofit agency.

Exhibit 5-2 provides a good example of an annual operating plan that meets all three characteristics of an effective operating plan: it states the strategic goal to be addressed, clearly breaks out the activities or action steps required to accomplish the goal, establishes time frames and who is responsible, and then notes the progress thus far (obviously, the information in this last column would change with each report). These are the requisites for the operating plan—many organizations already have some tracking system in place that might be adapted for the purposes of the operating plan, or perhaps will want to customize the suggested format to best suit their purposes—the point is to develop a format that keeps the organization on the right track! A blank Annual Operating Plan template is included in Appendix G.

Annual Operating Plan for a Government Agency

Overall Commerce Agency Goal 1: Increase economic development capacity to foster job creation and business investment at the local level by facilitating statewide development of local and regional organizations.

Enterprise Zone Unit Goal 1.2: Enhance the application of the tax incentive programs by (1) completing the designation process for approval of new zones and by (2) offering suggestions for the improvement of the programs of those previously approved.

Task	Measure	Staff	Date	Status as of 9/96
1. Select and train scoring team for final Enterprise Zone application	Select two sets of five scorers	AB/PM	Dec 96	Done
2. Print and distribute scoring materials and final applications	Distribute materials to scorers	AB/PM	Sept 96–Dec 96	Done
3. Conduct technical review	Complete six technical reviews	AB/PM	Sept 96–Jan 97	Done
4. Conduct substantive review	Complete six substantive reviews	PGN and scorers	Oct 96–Feb 97	Done
5. Tabulate results of scoring team	Compile two sets of results	PGN	Oct 96–Feb 97	
6. Announce winners of competition	Two press releases and two e-mails	JW and PM	Feb. 97	

Exhibit 5-2 Example of Successful Action Plan

Annual Goal: (same as strategic plan goal): *Acquire a stable, broad base of financial and non financial resources to support our museums' programs.*

Strategic Objective: (same as strategic plan objective): *Increase the number of new funders who are aware of and support our program.*

Annual Operating Plan Objective: (what needs to be accomplished this year): *Gain three new funders for our new children's programs, with total new contributions of $25,000.*

Feedback Mechanisms: (check-in mechanisms to ensure that the work is being accomplished): *Director of development will provide a monthly status report of all proposals pending and resulting decisions.*

Detailed Action Plan: (What activities need to happen, who is responsible for making sure they happen, and by when; status report updated quarterly).

Action steps	Responsible personnel	Time frame or by when	Status as of 3/31/96
1. Develop annual report to describe program	Selena Garcia, Program Director	January 1–February 1	Done: It looks beautiful!
2. Research possible funders and develop list of at least ten prospective funders	Susan Seeker and Pam Proposal* (= designated prime mover)	February 1	Completed 1/25/96
3. Arrange interviews with each prospect	Pam Proposal	February 15	3/1/96
4. Submit at least eight proposals	Pam Proposal	April 15	Three proposals submitted as of 3/31
5. Follow up on proposals	Pam Proposal	Two weeks after submission	
6. Cash the checks!	Pam Proposal	As soon as the money arrives!	

PHASE 7: MONITORING AND EVALUATING YOUR STRATEGIC PLAN

Aren't we finished? Well, yes and no. A strategic plan is written and annual operating plans are in place. However, it is also now time to assess the job the Planning Committee and staff have done, and develop systems and processes to monitor and evaluate the strategic plan as it is implemented.

Evaluation of the Strategic Plan and the Strategic Planning Process

The Planning Committee should plan a meeting to celebrate its accomplishments and evaluate its work. This meeting is an opportunity to reflect on the process so as to set the stage for future successful plans. Therefore, at this celebration, the Committee should evaluate both the planning process and the planning documents that have been developed. The Committee might simply ask the questions: What worked about the planning process? What did we learn that can help improve future planning endeavors?

In a slightly more formal evaluation process, the Planning Committee might evaluate both the planning documents and the planning process. The strategic plan should be assessed in terms of whether it:

- Provides guidance to both short-term and long-term priorities
- Helps the organization to allocate resources
- Is understandable by people who have not participated in the development of the plan
- Is responsive to the organization's best understanding of its internal and external environments
- Is the product of a consensus and commitment building process
- Has been formally adopted by the board of directors

The annual operational plan(s) meets these measures of success:

- Has been developed by staff who are responsible for the implementation of the goals and objectives
- Provides an easy implementation, monitoring, and reference tool
- Operationalizes the strategic plan
- Is realistic

See Exhibit 5-3 and the ASO/USA Case Study Worksheet for an illustration. This celebration and evaluating meeting should represent the formal ending of the present cycle of the strategic planning process.

Exhibit 5-3 Worksheet 20: Evaluating the Strategic Planning Process

Process Notes	
How to do this activity	Use the Evaluation of Plans and the Strategic Planning Process Worksheet to: • evaluate the strategic plan • evaluate the annual operational plan(s) • make suggestions for how future planning endeavors may be improved
Why do this activity	You want to build on your successes and ensure successful future planning efforts.
Who to involve in the process	The Planning Committee. Feedback may be sought from other stakeholders regarding how they felt about the process and the products of the Strategic Planning Process.

Case Study—ASO/USA

◆ Worksheet 20 **Evaluation of Plans and the Strategic Planning Process**	☐ Evaluate your strategic plan, your annual operating plans, and the strategic planning process. ☐ Make any suggestions for improving future planning endeavors.

The Strategic Plan:	**Yes**	**No**
• Provides guidance to both short-term and long-term priorities:	√	
• Helps the organization to allocate resources?	√	
• Is understandable by people who have not participated in the development of the plan?	?	
• Responds to the organization's best understanding of its internal and external environments?	√	
• Develops from a consensus and commitment-building process?	√	
• Has been formally adopted by the board of directors?	√	
Comments and suggestions for future strategic plans:		

The Annual Operational Plan(s):	**Yes**	**No**
• Has both process and outcome objectives specified?	√	
• Has been developed by staff who are responsible for the implementation of the goals and objectives?	√	
• Provides an easy implementation, monitoring, and reference tool?	√	
• Operationalizes the strategic plan?	√	
• Is realistic?	√	
Comments and suggestions for future annual operational plans: *These plans are in a different format from the ones we are used to, so we will have to see if they work better.*		

The Planning Process Met the Following Criteria:	**Yes**	**No**
• The process itself was consensus building: It offered a way to surface the needs and interests of all stakeholders and allowed sufficient time to reach agreement on what is best for the long-term and short-term interests of the client/customer;	√	
• The process allowed sufficient time to assess programs, and the strengths, weaknesses, opportunities, and threats; and	√	
• The process supported the achievement of the outcomes that were initially identified at the Getting Ready Phase, Worksheet 1	√	
Comments and suggestions for future planning processes: *We could easily have taken more time, but we are glad we moved the process right along.*		

Establish Intermediate Checkpoints

At this last meeting, the Planning Committee should establish intermediate checkpoints that will be used to measure progress toward the achievement of the strategic plan. For example, in its strategic plan, a museum may want to increase its membership from 500 fee-paying members to 1000 members. The Planning Committee might set two targets or milestones to assess progress: the first checkpoint might be an increase in membership to 750; the second milestone might be 850. The final, or ideal, target would be to reach 1000.

Develop an Appropriate Planning Cycle to Monitor and Evaluate Progress

Are we now finally finished? No! Since strategic planning is designed to help the organization do a better job, the organization will need to put processes into practice to find out if it is doing a better job! Therefore, the organization will need to monitor and evaluate the plan on a regular basis once it is implemented.

Strategic planning is a dynamic process, therefore it is really never completed. However, there is a rhythm that needs to be established, for by necessity the intensity of information gathering, analysis, and decision-making has ebbs and flows. Each organization needs to decide the rhythm of their planning efforts. For every organization there should be time set aside to do strategic planning, develop annual operational plans and budget, and then to implement these plans. Implementation is going on all the time. The development of annual operational plans happens once a year. A formal strategic planning process should happen every three to five years, but the strategic plan should be monitored at least yearly, to assess progress toward the achievement of the goals, and to modify if necessary to reflect the usually ever changing environment. A typical three-year planning cycle might follow a pattern similar to the one in Exhibit 5-4.

Many organizations already gather information necessary to assess implementation. Once a planning cycle has been agreed on, the parties responsible for implementation need to know how to track and report on the objectives included in the plans, and to make adjustments as necessary.

Monitoring the Strategic Plan

On a regular basis, no less than once a year, the Planning Committee should monitor the progress that has or has not been made toward the completion of the strategic plan, and assess whether any major or minor adjustments should be made to

Exhibit 5-4 Three-Year Planning Cycle

January 1	April 1	July 1	October 1	December 31
Year 0			Develop Three-Year Strategic Plan and Annual Operating Plan and Budget	
Launch plan Year 1	√	√	√	Monitor Strategic Plan, adjust if necessary, and develop Annual Operating Plan and Budget
Continue plan Year 2	√	√	√	Monitor Strategic Plan, adjust if necessary, and develop Annual Operating Plan and Budget
Finish plan Year 3	√	√	Develop NEW Three-Year Strategic Plan and Annual Operating Plan and Budget	

√ = Quarterly check-in on annual operational plan and budget

Monitor Strategic Plan = assess progress toward achievement of goals in three-year strategic plan

the strategic plan. As part of this monitoring process, the Planning Committee should organize and plan a retreat that will focus on these questions:

- Is the current strategic plan on target? What has or has not been accomplished?
- Are the assumptions of the internal and external environment still valid?
- What are the current issues that are facing the organization, and, after discussing these issues, are there any changing or new priorities that have to be added to the strategic plan?
- Are there new performance targets, and/or modified intermediate checkpoints that need to be looked at?

If the organization is relatively small, all staff and board might be invited. If the number of board and staff members represents more than forty or fifty people, then smaller meetings of all internal stakeholders should be held prior to the annual retreat. The board would then meet with senior managers and program directors to discuss the above questions, and agree on overall priorities. The Planning Committee may also choose to gather information in advance of the retreat from external stakeholders (client surveys, etc.) and present that information at the retreat.

As a result of the retreat, the executive director would work with senior managers and program directors to develop the next year's annual operating plan.

A written record of the decisions made at the planning retreat should be summarized on the Worksheet 21: Monitoring the Strategic Plan.

Worksheet 21 (see Exhibit 5-5 for process notes) summarizes the discussions that the organization has at the end of the fiscal year regarding the implementation of the strategic plan, and sets the stage for either major or minor change to the strategic plan.

Exhibit 5-5 Worksheet 21 Monitoring and Updating the Strategic Plan

Process Notes

How to do this activity	The worksheet should be filled out after a series of meetings that assess the current strategic plan and set new priorities for the upcoming year and beyond. The worksheet should: • Summarize overall accomplishments and the status of the implementation of the core strategies as articulated in the strategic plan; • Summarize status of the implementation of long-term and short-term objectives/priorities; • Briefly explain the reasons for not implementing the core strategies or non-accomplishment of objectives/priorities; • List the changes in the environment since last meeting; • Record any changes in core strategies and long-term and short-term priorities.
Why do this activity	Plans are roadmaps from which you should consciously choose to deviate.
Who to involve in the process	Planning Committee has responsibility to coordinate the monitoring efforts and plan the necessary retreat(s) that involve board, staff, and other key stakeholders in revisiting the strategic plan and either affirming or modifying the overall direction and priorities.

Case Study—ASO/USA

Note: This worksheet not completed because it is to be completed after one year of implementation.

♦ **Worksheet 21** **Monitoring the Strategic Plan**	☐ Review your strategic plan, noting accomplishments and disappointments. ☐ Assess any changes in the environment since the last strategic planning meeting. ☐ If necessary, make changes in core strategies and long-term and short-term priorities.

Date: ________________

Overall accomplishments and status of implementation of Core Strategies:

Overall accomplishments and status of implementation of long-term and short-term Objectives/Priorities:

Reasons for nonaccomplishments:

Worksheet 21 *(Continued)*

Change in the Environment Since Last Meeting:

Previous strengths • • • • • • •	Current strengths • • • • • • •
Previous weaknesses • • • • • • •	Current weaknesses • • • • • • •
Previous opportunities • • • • • • •	Current opportunities • • • • • • •
Previous threats • • • • • • •	Current threats • • • • • • •

(Continued)

Worksheet 21 *(Continued)*

Recommended Changes in Core Strategies:

Recommended Changes in:

Long-Term Priorities (Program and Management/Operations Goals and Objectives)	**Short-Term Priorities (Program and Management/Operations Goals and Objectives)**

CONCLUSION: A WORD TO LEADERS

If we had reliable crystal balls, strategic planning would be a snap. Because there is uncertainty about the future, strategic plans are more like roadmaps to a new land drawn up before the journey has been made. No one has been to where we want to go; it is in the future. We can ask many people their advice about how best to make the journey. We can do extensive analysis to forecast the conditions we will encounter and to assess our capabilities to handle various situations. We can dream about how we would like the journey to go. All of this work can be discussed and written down in the form of a strategic plan. Once the journey begins, a strategic plan will remind us where we want to go as well as where we don't want to go.

The Cheshire Cat says to Alice, "If you don't know where you are going, any road will take you there." The strategic planning process helps the leaders of an organization to articulate their vision about where they are going and to choose the best road to take the organization there.

Still, things change.

In the external environment, the economy is better, or worse, than expected and this has a ripple effect on your clients or your environment. Science finds a new way to deal with an issue you have long worked on. A new organization begins offering services which compete with one of your programs. A long-time funder changes its priorities. Any of the many assumptions you have made as part of the planning process turns out to be wrong. Internally, the executive director might move or become ill, a case of embezzlement might surface, or staff members either do much more or much less than they thought possible.

There is no way, of course, to foresee these changes. They must be responded to as they arise. Ultimately, the end sought is to be effective in pursuing your mission, not to correctly predict the future. The strategic planning process is a means to that end. As the future unfolds, because the organization knows where it wants to go, it will be much easier to see if the road is taking you there, and if not, to select a better road.

It is the responsibility of the leadership of every organization to ensure a strategic plan is in place and to ensure that appropriate adjustments are made in the implementation of that plan as circumstances change. The strategic plan is a reference document, a map to assist with these responsibilities.

We hope this workbook will make it a little easier to put the process of strategic planning to good use in your organization. Good luck. We are counting on you to succeed, for our world will be better for it.

Appendix A: Blank Worksheets

♦ Worksheet 1

Planning Process Outcomes and Issues

- ☐ What does your organization wish to achieve from a planning process?
- ☐ What issues or choices do you think need to be addressed?
- ☐ Are there any non-negotiables or constraints that need to be articulated up front?

What would success look like at the completion of the planning process? What does your organization wish to achieve from a planning process?

What are the issues facing your organization? What questions need to be answered during the planning process?

Issue	Why is it an issue? What are the consequences of not responding?	Check (√) whether the issue is strategic or operational Strategic	 Operational

Are there any issues which are non-negotiable (not open for discussion)?

◆ **Worksheet 2** **Check Your Readiness to Plan**	☐ Assess your organizational readiness: • What criteria for successful planning are in place? • Which pitfalls can be avoided? • What can you learn from your prior experience with planning? ☐ Answer the question: • Are you ready to plan? Go or No Go

The Following Criteria for Successful Planning Are in Place

Yes	No	Criteria
		1. Commitment and support from top leadership, especially the executive director and board president, throughout the entire process
		2. Commitment to clarifying roles and expectations for all participants in the planning process, including clarity as to who will contribute to the plan and who will be the decision makers
		3. Willingness to understand and respond to the organization's internal and external environment (strengths, weaknesses, opportunities, and threats); a commitment to gathering relevant information for assessing current programs and evaluating how to meet current and future client needs—sufficient market research
		4. At least one strategic thinker and at least one actionary (someone to make sure the projected goals and objectives are realistic) who are willing to be active participants on the Planning Committee
		5. Willingness to be inclusive and encourage broad participation, so that people feel "ownership" of and are energized by the process
		6. An adequate commitment of organizational resources to complete the planning process as designed, for example, staff time, board time, dollars spent on the process (for market research, consultants, etc.), and so on
		7. A board and staff that understands the purpose of planning, realizes what it is and is not able to accomplish, and has consensus about the desired outcomes of the planning process
		8. A willingness to question the status quo, to look at new ways of doing things; a willingness to ask the hard questions, face difficult choices, and make decisions that are best for the clients
		9. Good working relationships and no serious conflicts between key players

Comments to explain and respond to "No" or "Questions" answered:

(Continued)

Worksheet 2 *(Continued)*

The Following Pitfalls Can Be Avoided:

Yes	No	Pitfalls that Can Be Avoided
		10. Top management's assumption that it can completely delegate the planning function to a planner and not remain actively involved
		11. Executive Director and Board President so engrossed in current problems (such as a financial crisis or other extreme circumstance) that they have neither the time, nor the leeway, to look far enough ahead, to plan for the future
		12. Top management's tendency to reject the decisions made during the planning process in favor of its own intuitive decisions
		13. Board or Executive Director's unwillingness to involve line staff, management staff, and Board in the planning process
		14. Failure of the Board and top management to articulate constraints and non-negotiables up front
		15. Reluctance to create a realistic strategic plan that will provide guidance to current operational decisions
		16. Lack of an organizational climate that inspires forward thinking and rewards creativity

Comments to explain and respond to "No" (pitfalls cannot be avoided) or "Questions" answered:

Prior Experience Doing Planning: What Has Worked? What Hasn't Worked? Why?

Other Issues:

Organizational Readiness: **Go** or **No Go**?

♦ **Worksheet 3** **Participation in the Planning Process**	☐ Create a Planning Committee and clarify its mandates. ☐ Identify who to involve in the planning process.

Planning Committee Responsibilities:

Milestones and Deadlines:

Planning Principles and Values (e.g., the planning process is as important as the plan itself):

Chair of the Planning Committee:

Who Will Write the Plan:

Planning Committee Membership:

Name	Representing what key stakeholder

Who Should Be Involved in the Planning Process? (Circle all those who should have some involvement)

Board of Directors   Executive Director   Management Team   Line Staff

Volunteers   Current Clients   Past Clients   Donors   Funders

Other: ______________________   Other: ______________________

♦ Worksheet 4

Organizational History and Profile

- ☐ Summarize your organization's history and identify lessons from your history.
- ☐ Describe your programs and related infrastructure.

Presentation of Organization's History

Timeline	19__	19__	19__	19__	19__	19__	19__	19__	19__	19__	19__	19__	19__
List Key Organizational Events and Shifts in Priorities (use the timeline to place in chronological order)													
List External Events Impacting the Organization (use the timeline to place in chronological order)													

Lessons from History: Keys to Stability and Growth	Lessons from History: Recurring Themes that Show Causes for Instability

Organizational Profile

List all programs, projects, and services (and note their current scope and scale of service)	Group the activities into categories (sort by common outcome, write program goal for each grouping)	Note any related management and operations data (infrastructure data such as number of staff, number of board members, breakdown of revenue and expenses, etc.)

♦ Worksheet 5

Information-Gathering Plan

☐ Identify which strategic issues need to have information gathered.
- What information do we need?
- Who will collect it?
- How will it be collected?

☐ List key external stockholders.
- What questions can they help answer?
- How should we collect this information?

What are the strategic issues that we need to gather information about (refer to Worksheet 1)	What information do we need?	Who will collect it?	Format for collecting this information; time

Worksheet 5 *(Continued)*

List external stakeholders	**What questions can they help answer?**	**How should we collect stakeholder feedback? Who should collect this information and by when?**
Current clients		
Past clients		
Funders		
Community leaders		
Potential collaborators/competitors (both competitors for clients and competitors for funding)		
Other		
Other		
Other		

◆ Worksheet 6

Creating a Mission Statement

☐ Draft Your Mission Statement
(Note: Please write legibly. Use only the space provided.)

What is the *focus problem(s)* that our organization exists to solve? What need or opportunity does our organization exist to resolve? (In considering the focus problem or need, you might want to consider the following questions: Who is affected by the problem? How are they affected?) Describe how the world would be improved, changed, or different if our organization was successful in solving the problem or responding to the need.

What is the *purpose* of our organization (answers the question of why we exist, does not describe what we do)? This should be a short succinct statement that describes the ultimate result we are hoping to achieve; make sure to indicate outcomes and results (e.g., to eliminate homelessness), not the methods of achieving those results which is your mission (e.g., by constructing houses).

What is our business? Describe the business or businesses we are in—our primary services or activities.

Worksheet 6 *(Continued)*

What are the *fundamental values and beliefs* that should guide us in our day-to-day interactions with each other and our constituencies? What are the *major assumptions* upon which our organization provides its services?

We believe:

•
•
•
•

We assume:

•
•
•
•

Our Mission Statement

(Combine the information above to create a compelling mission statement about *who* the organization is, what the organization does, and why the organization does it.)

◆ Worksheet 7

Vision Statement

☐ Dare to dream the possible. What is your organization's realistic but challenging guiding vision of success?

External vision: Describe how the world would be improved, changed, or different if our organization was successful in achieving its purpose.

Internal vision: Envisioning our organization's future.

What is your programmatic vision for our organization for three to five years from today? (What would be our ideal program mix/service? List in order of priority—top priority services at the top of the list.)	**Describe your administrative vision for our organization for the next three to five years in terms of: staffing and benefits, board of directors, our image in the community, our funding, our infrastructure and use of technology, facilities, information systems, planning and evaluation, quality control, or other.**

◆ Worksheet 8

Previous and Current Strategies

☐ Identify and assess your organization's previous and current strategies.

Previous and current strategy	Was or is the strategy effective? Why or why not? Should it be considered as a strategy for the future? Why or why not?

♦ Worksheet 9

Staff and Board Perceptions of SWOT

- ☐ List our program and administrative strengths and weaknesses (star [*] the top three internal forces).
- ☐ List the external opportunities and threats (political, economic, social, technological, demographic, and legal trends) that may impact the organization (star [*] the top three external forces).

Internal Forces	External Forces
Strengths • • • • •	**Opportunities** • • • • •
Weaknesses • • • • •	**Threats** • • • • •

◆ Worksheet 10

External Stakeholders Perceptions and Expectations

☐ Summarize findings regarding stakeholders' perception and expectations of the organization

Constituency	• **What does this constituency say about our organization's strengths and weaknesses?** • **What trends do they perceive as either opportunities or threats?**	• **What does this constituency need or expect from our organization? (What is the criteria they use to judge our performance?)** • **How well does our organization perform against those criteria (excellent, good, fair, or poor)? Why such a rating?** • **What does this constituency want us to do more of or less of?** • **What additional or increased programs or services do they think we should be offering if resources were available?**

◆ Worksheet 11

Staff Assessment of Programs and Organization in Relation to Client Needs and Competitive Position

☐ Evaluate your programs and organization in terms of client needs, results, competitive position, and potential for increased efficiency.

Program/Service Name: ______________________________

Description of program service: ______________________________

Units of service and cost unit of service (if applicable): ______________________________

Prepared by: ______________________________

Analysis of Competitive Position

Name of organization	Ability to provide service	Quality of service	Why did you rate ability to provide service the way you did? Why did you give the rating on quality of service?
Our program	4 Excellent 3 Good 2 Fair 1 Poor	4 Excellent 3 Good 2 Fair 1 Poor	
Competitor:	4 Excellent 3 Good 2 Fair 1 Poor	4 Excellent 3 Good 2 Fair 1 Poor	
Competitor:	4 Excellent 3 Good 2 Fair 1 Poor	4 Excellent 3 Good 2 Fair 1 Poor	
Competitor:	4 Excellent 3 Good 2 Fair 1 Poor	4 Excellent 3 Good 2 Fair 1 Poor	

List Other Competitors Not Assessed:

Growth Strategy for this Program: ___Increase ___Maintain ___Decrease ___Eliminate

Why this strategy? Implications if we were to ignore this strategy. What impact would this growth strategy have on our resources (staff time and other expenditures) and revenues. Is there potential for collaboration? In what ways? With whom? Additional comments.

What are the greatest strengths of this program?

What are the greatest weaknesses of this program?

How could we improve the cost-effectiveness of this program?

How could we improve the quality of this program?

How could we improve our ability to provide this service?

If the budget for this program were suddenly halved, what would you recommend we do?

If the budget for this program were suddenly doubled, what would you recommend we do?

How should we measure results/impact/outcomes of this program in improving the quality of our clients' lives? What are the indicators of success (benchmarks upon which we should measure our success? How do we know we are making a difference?

(Continued)

Worksheet 11 *(Continued)*

Client Needs Assessment

List client group(s) currently being served by our organization	**How well is this client group being served by us?**	**Why did you rate our services to this client group the way you did? How could we ensure that this client group receives the best possible services available delivered either by our organization or from another organization?**
	4 Excellent 3 Good 2 Fair 1 Poor	
	4 Excellent 3 Good 2 Fair 1 Poor	
	4 Excellent 3 Good 2 Fair 1 Poor	
	4 Excellent 3 Good 2 Fair 1 Poor	
	4 Excellent 3 Good 2 Fair 1 Poor	
	4 Excellent 3 Good 2 Fair 1 Poor	

List client group(s) NOT currently being served (or severely underserved) by our organization:	**What needs of this client group are not being met? Why are we currently not serving this client group? Should we allocate organizational resources to meeting the needs of this client group? How could we ensure that this client group receives the best possible services available delivered either by our organization or from another organization?**

(Continued)

Worksheet 11 *(Continued)*

Assessment of Entire Organization:

How could we improve the cost-effectiveness of our organization?

What do our customers/clients consider value? How could we improve the quality of services we provide as an organization to our customers/clients?

If the budget for this organization were suddenly *halved,* what would you recommend we do?

If the budget for this organization were suddenly *doubled,* what would you recommend we do?

Summary: Suggested Overall Program Priorities

Short-Term Priorities	**Long-Term Priorities**
•	•
•	•
•	•
•	•

Summary: Suggested Overall Management/Operations Priorities

Short-Term Priorities	**Long-Term Priorities**
•	•
•	•
•	•
•	•

◆ Worksheet 12

Program Evaluation

☐ Assess your program in relationship to inputs, implementation, outcomes, and impact.

Name of Program: ______________________________________

Prepared by: ____________________

Date: ______________

Assessment of inputs: What resources are required to operate the program? Are there special site licenses or staff qualifications required or desired? What physical elements, such as square footage, location, facility, or equipment are essential to the program's success?

Assessment of implementation (evaluation of the process): How many units of service are we delivering?

Assessment of outcomes (evaluation of the program): Are the goals of the program being met?

Assessment of impact: What unexpected or unintended impacts are occurring as a result of our program?

◆ Worksheet 13

Interplay of SWOT

☐ SWOT grid: Using Worksheet 9, look at the interrelationship of your organization's external opportunities and threats and its internal strengths and weaknesses and assess possible short-term and long-term organizational responses.

	Major Opportunities • • • • •	**Major Threats** • • • • •
Primary Strengths • • • • •	Invest: Clear matches of strengths and opportunities lead to comparative advantage.	Defend: Areas of threat matched by areas of strength indicate a need to mobilize resources either alone or with others.
Primary Weaknesses • • • • •	Decide: Areas of opportunity matched by areas of weakness require a judgment call: invest or divest; collaborate.	Damage Control: Areas of threat matched by areas of weakness indicate need for damage control.

(*Source:* Adapted from Kevin P. Kearns: "From Comparative Advantage to Damage Control: Clarifying Strategic Issues Using SWOT Analysis," *Nonprofit Management and Leadership,* Vol. 3, No. 1, Fall 1992).

♦ Worksheet 14

Selection Grid for Prioritizing Programs

- ☐ Review the list of criteria to use in choosing program priorities, add additional priorities specific for your organization.
- ☐ List all programs (services) you wish to assess in relation to the listed criteria. Place a check (√) beside all criteria that apply to the program.

Criteria to Use in Choosing Program Priorities	Program: ______	Program: ______	Program: ______	Program: ______	Program: ______
Congruence with mission					
Measurable results					
Needed to support core strategies					
Fills a need not being met in the community (either does not duplicate services that are effectively being done by others, or the competition is good for our clients)					
Organization is capable of providing quality services or products relative to other providers					
Demonstrated need (documented current demands or predicted future demands for product or service; market share growth potential)					
Increases organization's visibility					
Funding is available to cover costs (through fees or third party funding)					
Shares resources (complements) existing programs					
Support collaborative efforts with other organizations					
Benefits outweigh or at the very least equal costs					
Produces surplus revenue to support other programs (after paying its share of indirect costs)					
Other					
Other					
Other					

◆ Worksheet 15

Core Future Strategies

☐ Identify and assess your core future strategies.

Strategic issue (stated as a question)	Proposed strategy	Assumptions, facts, and values which support this proposed strategy?	What possible obstacles do we face in implementing this strategy?	What triggers might encourage us to re-evaluate this strategy?

◆ Worksheet 16

Long-Term and Short-Term Priorities

☐ What are your long-term and short-term strategic priorities?

Suggested Overall Program Priorities

Short-Term Program Priorities	Long-Term Program Priorities

(Continued)

Worksheet 16 *(Continued)*

Suggested Overall Management/Operations Priorities

Short-Term Management/Operations Priorities	**Long-Term Management/Operations Priorities**

♦ Worksheet 17

Summary of Program Scope and Scale

☐ Develop a detailed program portfolio for current and future programs.

Program or Service	Current level of activity (if applicable; new programs will not have a current level of activity)	Proposed growth strategy: • Expand • Maintain at existing level • Decrease • Eliminate • New program	Proposed future level of activity for this program or service

◆ Worksheet 18

Setting Goals and Objectives

☐ Write your program and management/operations goals and objectives.

Program Goals	Program Objectives

Management/Operations Goals	**Management/Operations Objectives**
Staffing and benefits	
Resource development	

(Continued)

Worksheet 18 *(Continued)*

Management/Operations Goals	Management/Operations Objectives
Board of directors	
Planning and evaluation	
Public relations/marketing	

Management/Operations Goals	Management/Operations Objectives
Infrastructure	
Networking and collaboration	

♦ Worksheet 19

Long-Range Financial Projections

☐ Estimate the financial resources required to support the strategic plan.

Revenue and Support

Current Revenue and Support:

$____________________

Percentage Breakdown by Source of Funds

Future Revenue and Support:

$____________________

Percentage Breakdown by Source of Funds

Expenses

Current Expenses:

$____________________

Future Expenses:

$____________________

♦ Worksheet 20

Evaluation of Plans and the Strategic Planning Process

- [ ] Evaluate your strategic plan, your annual operating plans, and the strategic planning process.
- [ ] Make any suggestions for improving future planning endeavors.

The Strategic Plan:	**Yes**	**No**
• Provides guidance to both short-term and long-term priorities?		
• Helps the organization to allocate resources?		
• Is understandable by people who have not participated in the development of the plan?		
• Responds to the organization's best understanding of its internal and external environments?		
• Develops from a consensus and commitment-building process?		
• Has been formally adopted by the board of directors?		
Comments and suggestions for future strategic plans:		

The Annual Operational Plan(s):	**Yes**	**No**
• Has both process and outcome objectives specified?		
• Has been developed by staff who are responsible for the implementation of the goals and objectives?		
• Provides an easy implementation, monitoring, and reference tool?		
• Operationalizes the strategic plan?		
• Is realistic?		
Comments and suggestions for future annual operational plans:		

The Planning Process Met the Following Criteria:	**Yes**	**No**
• The process itself was consensus building: It offered a way to surface the needs and interests of all stakeholders and allowed sufficient time to reach agreement on what is best for the long-term and short-term interests of the client/customer;		
• The process allowed sufficient time to assess programs, and the strengths, weaknesses, opportunities, and threats; and		
• The process supported the achievement of the outcomes that were initially identified at the Getting Ready Phase, Worksheet 1.		
Comments and suggestions for future planning processes:		

♦ **Worksheet 21** **Monitoring the Strategic Plan**	☐ Review your strategic plan, noting accomplishments and disappointments. ☐ Assess any changes in the environment since the last strategic planning meeting. ☐ If necessary, make changes in core strategies and long-term and short-term priorities.

Date: ________________

Overall accomplishments and status of implementation of Core Strategies:

Overall accomplishments and status of implementation of long-term and short-term Objectives/Priorities:

Reasons for non-accomplishments:

Worksheet 21 *(Continued)*

Change in the Environment Since Last Meeting:

<table>
<tr><td>Previous strengths
•
•
•
•
•
•
•</td><td>Current strengths
•
•
•
•
•
•
•</td></tr>
<tr><td>Previous weaknesses
•
•
•
•
•
•
•</td><td>Current weaknesses
•
•
•
•
•
•
•</td></tr>
<tr><td>Previous opportunities
•
•
•
•
•
•
•</td><td>Current opportunities
•
•
•
•
•
•
•</td></tr>
<tr><td>Previous threats
•
•
•
•
•
•
•</td><td>Current threats
•
•
•
•
•
•
•</td></tr>
</table>

(Continued)

Worksheet 21 *(Continued)*

Recommended Changes in Core Strategies:

Recommended Changes in:

Long-Term Priorities (Program and Management/Operations Goals and Objectives)	**Short-Term Priorities (Program and Management/Operations Goals and Objectives)**

Appendix B: Sample Workplans for Abbreviated, Moderate, and Extensive Planning Processes

HOW TO USE THE WORKPLAN TEMPLATES

There are three workplan templates for each of the three planning processes: abbreviated, moderate, and extensive. Once the Planning Committee has chosen which process they are going to use, the workplan should be modified to reflect the specific needs of the organization. Changes will probably need to be made on the format or activity that will be undertaken, who should be involved, and which worksheets and templates the Planning Committee wishes to use. Finally, times will vary, and should be adjusted accordingly, with specific dates or time frames added to the time commitment section indicated in gray.

Template: Abbreviated Planning Process Workplan: One-Day* Retreat Agenda

Participants: Entire Board, Executive Director, and all staff

Proposed Agenda Topics	Process and Personnel Responsible	Time Frame
Introductions, meeting agreements, and agenda review • State of the organization and update on the external forces impacting the organization (presentation on trends, funding environment, competitor situation, statistics on client needs) • Organizational history† • Program services currently being offered • Future needs of clients and future challenges	Facilitator Presentation by ED Either presentation by designated individual or entire group recreate on wallchart Staff presentations	9:00–9:15 A.M. 9:15–10:15 A.M.
Mission Statement†† • Purpose • Values, beliefs, and assumptions • Business	Discussion of each component by all attendees	10:15–10:50 A.M. Break 10:50–11:05 A.M.
Vision the possible: Our preferred external and internal vision	Brainstorming session by Board and staff; summary of agreements and disagreements	11:05–11:30 A.M.
Program and management/operations SWOT (strengths and weaknesses: opportunities and threats)	Brainstorming session by Board and staff; if time, identify priority items	11:30 A.M.–12 noon
Identification of key issues/challenges facing the organization	Discussion by all	12 noon–12:30 P.M.
Lunch		12:30–1:30 P.M.
Discussion of key issues. Agreement on overall core strategies and short-term and long-term program and management/operations priorities • Prioritized list of current and future programs (short-term and long-term importance; whether to maintain, expand, eliminate, decrease, or modify) • Prioritized list of short-term and long-term management/operations priorities to support programs	Small groups or large group discussions	1:30–4:15 P.M. Including 15 minute break
Identification of issues that need further discussion by Board and/or staff, and any additional information needed to help clarify priorities (such as client survey, etc.)	All	4:15–4:50 P.M.
Next steps, responsible personnel, time		
Evaluation of the day	♦ what worked ♥ didn't work/suggested changes	4:50–5:00 P.M.

* Because of the number of programs or number of issues to discuss, a second day may need to be scheduled.

† If a presentation of the organization's history was done recently, an alternative presentation might include: Where we are in relation to our prior Strategic Plan (accomplishments, disappointments, effectiveness of prior strategies)

†† If there is already a mission statement, then the mission statement should either be reaffirmed or modified.

Template: Moderate Planning Process Workplan

Proposed Format	Who Involved	Possible Worksheets and Templates to Support Achieving Outcomes	Time Commitment
Meeting to assess organization's readiness, begin to identify issues to be addressed as part of the planning process and who to involve in the planning process May start to discuss what information is needed to help inform the planning process and how that information should be gathered. Or, may wait until after planning retreat to see what information needs to be gathered	Executive director, board president or designated representative, and consultant*	Worksheet 1: Planning Process Outcomes and Issues Worksheet 2: Check Your Readiness to Plan Worksheet 3: Participation in the Planning Process Worksheet 4: Organizational History and Profile Worksheet 5: Information Gathering Plan	Two to three hour meeting
Meeting to plan retreat	ED, Board president, and/or chair of Planning Committee, consultant, and other Board and staff as deemed necessary		Two to three hour meeting
Board/Staff Planning Retreat to discuss: • History of organization and/or state of the organization • Mission Statement review or creation • Vision Statement • Environmental Assessment (SWOT) • Key issues, SWOT grid, and possible future program and management/operations priorities • Next steps, who responsible, by when	If smaller organization, usually will include entire Board and staff; if larger organization, usually entire Board and staff representatives (management team). Line staff input to be gathered ahead of retreat through either questionnaires or department meetings. Consultant to facilitate retreat Some external stakeholders may also be invited to attend this meeting	Worksheet 6: Creating a Mission Statement Worksheet 7: Vision Statement Worksheet 8: Previous and Current Strategies (optional) Worksheet 9: Staff and Board Perceptions of SWOT Worksheet 13: Interplay of SWOT	Eight hour retreat

* The organization may choose not to use an external consultant to facilitate the planning process, but instead may choose to have a consultant act as a neutral facilitator during some of the large group meetings.

(Continued)

Template: Moderate Planning Process Workplan *(Continued)*

Proposed Format	Personnel Involved	Possible Worksheets and Templates to Support Achieving Outcomes	Time Commitment
Meeting of Planning Committee to review notes from Planning Retreat and assess what additional information needed to be gathered. Information might include: client satisfaction and needs surveys, Elements of an Effectively Managed Organization (EEMO™), staff assessment of programs and organization in relation to client needs and competitive position; program evaluation; interviews or surveys of key stakeholders	Planning Committee has discussion. May delegate responsibility for gathering information to individual members of the Planning Committee and/or staff	Will depend on information that Planning Committee deems as needed to have informed discussions regarding future strategies and priorities. Possible worksheets may include: Worksheet 10: External Stakeholders Perceptions and Expectations; Worksheet 11: Staff Assessment of Programs and Organization; Worksheet 12: Program Evaluation	Two- to three-hour meeting
Meetings of Planning Committee to assess previous and current strategies, discuss issues, agree on criteria for prioritizing programs, and on long-term and short-term priorities Discussion by members of the Planning Committee as to what the final format for the strategic planning document may look like (for example, whether a list of long-term and short-term priorities will suffice, or whether the Planning Committee wants those priorities to be translated into formal goals and objectives language Planning Committee may identify that an additional half- or full-day Board/staff planning retreat may be needed to complete discussion of key issues and setting priorities	Planning Committee (with consultant if needed) has discussions. Some discussions may be delegated to appropriate groups (for example, board of directors should discuss setting its long-term and short-term priorities, fund-raising staff and Resource Development may discuss funding strategies, etc.)	Worksheet 14: Selection Grid for Prioritizing Programs Worksheet 15: Core Future Strategies Worksheet 16: Long-Term and Short-Term Priorities Worksheet 17: Summary of Program Scope and Scale	Will depend on number of issues that need to be discussed: usually two to five two- to three-hour meetings

Proposed Format	Personnel Involved	Possible Worksheets and Templates to Support Achieving Outcomes	Time Commitment
Write formal goals and objectives for inclusion in strategic planning document (optional)	Those individuals designated by the Planning Committee to develop goals and objectives	Worksheet 18: Setting Goals and Objectives (optional)	
Meeting of Planning Committee to review strategic planning document; Strategic Planning circulated to staff and board	Planning Committee	Strategic Plan template	Two- to three-hour meeting
Meeting of board of directors to approve strategic plan	Board of directors		Board meeting
Development of annual operating plan to implement Strategic Plan	Staff	Annual Operating Plan template	Depends on size of organization
Evaluation of plans and the strategic planning process, celebration of the completion of the planning cycle	Planning Committee	Worksheet 20: Evaluation of Plans and the Strategic Planning Process	Two- to three-hour meeting
Monitor the Strategic Plan through the use of an annual planning retreat for the next planning cycle	Planning Committee coordinates and plans retreat	Worksheet 21: Monitoring the Strategic Plan	One-day retreat and time to plan retreat

Template: Extensive Planning Process Workplan

Phase	Key Outcomes Achieved During Each Planning Phase	Possible Worksheets and Templates to Support Achieving Outcomes	Proposed Format/Responsibility	Time Commitment
Phase 1: Getting Ready	Agreement that the organization is ready to initiate a successful planning process	• Worksheet 1: Planning Process Outcomes and Issues • Worksheet 2: Check Your Readiness to Plan	Consultant and agency representatives meet to begin to identify issues to be addressed as part of the planning process and assess organization readiness	Two- to three-hour meeting
	Agreement on who to involve in the planning process and what their involvement might be; a detailed Plan for Planning, including agreement on how to proceed through all the phases of the planning process, planning outcomes, possible activities, personnel responsibility, and time frame	• Worksheet 3: Participation in the Planning Process • Extensive Workplan template	Consultant, Executive Director, and Board President meet to clarify who to involve in the planning process and draft an initial Plan for Planning Consultant discuss possible revisions of Plan for Planning with Board/Staff Planning Committee, and make necessary workplan revisions. Agreement on roles, responsibilities, processes to keep Board and staff informed of the planning process, products to be delivered, and time frame	Two- to three-hour meeting
	Planning team members knowledgeable about planning; agreement on terminology to use in the planning process; common base of knowledge about the organization's history and programs	• Worksheet 4: Organizational History and Profile	Consultant orient Planning Committee regarding the planning process Nonprofit organization staff to assemble pertinent documents regarding agency budget, service statistics, organizational charts, previous mission statement, and other documents clarifying the organization's mandates, history, and operating trends	Two- to three-hour meeting
	Agreement on initial critical issues facing the organization and an initial plan for gathering information that will help the organization make its strategic decisions	• Worksheet 5: Information Gathering Plan	Consultant meet with Planning Committee to review/agree on critical issues and a plan for gathering information	Part of above mentioned orientation meeting

Phase	Key Outcomes Achieved During Each Planning Phase	Possible Worksheets and Templates to Support Achieving Outcomes	Proposed Format/Responsibility	Time Commitment
Phase 2: Articulating Purpose, Mission, and Vision	Agreement on a mission statement for the organization	• Worksheet 6: Creating a Mission Statement	Discussion at Board/Staff Planning retreat, facilitated by consultant. Small representative group to work on draft of revised statement	Part of eight-hour Board/Staff Planning Retreat
			Planning Committee and Consultant meet to review and approve revised mission statement for the organization	Two- to three-hour meeting
	Agreement on vision statement	• Worksheet 7: Vision Statement	Discussion at Board/Staff Planning retreat, facilitated by consultant. All participants to fill out Mission Statement and Vision Statement. Worksheets in preparation for retreat	Part of eight-hour Board/ Staff Planning Retreat

(Continued)

Template: Extensive Planning Process Workplan *(Continued)*

Phase	Key Outcomes Achieved During Each Planning Phase	Possible Worksheets and Templates to Support Achieving Outcomes	Proposed Format/Responsibility	Time Commitment
Phase 3: Assessing the Environment	Database of information to help inform decisions regarding responsibilities, comprehensive services: sufficient information about the organization so as to be able to make informed choices about long-term and short-term priorities	• Worksheet 8: Previous and Current Strategies	Planning Committee and Consultant discuss previous and current strategies so as to assess their future applicability	Two- to three-hour meeting
		• Worksheet 9: Staff and Board Perception of SWOT	Initial discussion at Board/Staff Planning retreat, facilitated by consultant. All participants to fill out worksheet Assessing Strengths, Weaknesses, Opportunities, and Threats in preparation for the meeting	Part of eight-hour Board/Staff Planning Retreat
		• Worksheet 10: External Stakeholders' Perceptions and Expectations	Planning Committee and consultant meet to agree on process for involving external stakeholders in the planning process. External stakeholders surveyed as to their perceptions of the organization (such as organization's strengths, weaknesses, opportunities, and threats; current and future client needs; and organization's reputation in the community	Two- to three-hour meeting
			Staff, Board, and/or consultant gather information regarding stakeholders' perception of the organization Empirical data collected by either staff, board, or consultant to support perceptions about client needs and trends	Depends on extent of information that needs to be gathered
	Evaluation of nonprofit organization's past performance and future program needs	Appendix: EEMO™; Self-Assessment Survey on Governance • Worksheet 11: Staff Assessment of Programs and Organization in Relation to Client Needs and Competitive Position	Staff complete in-depth analysis of the organization as a whole and all programs, and present to Planning Committee. May have outside evaluator assess programs	Depends on number of programs/ services
		• Worksheet 12: Program Evaluation	Planning Committee and consultant meet to review data collected above, identify additional strategic issues, and any additional research that needs to be undertaken	Two- to three-hour meeting

Phase	Key Outcomes Achieved During Each Planning Phase	Possible Worksheets and Templates to Support Achieving Outcomes	Proposed Format/Responsibility	Time Commitment
Phase 4: Agreeing on Priorities	Agreement on core strategies and long-term and short-term program and administrative priorities	• Worksheet 13: Interplay of SWOT	Planning Committee and consultant meet to discuss interrelationship of strengths, weaknesses, opportunities, and threats. Initial discussion of SWOT grid may take place at Board/Staff Retreat	Two- to three-hour meeting
		• Worksheet 14: Selection Grid for Prioritizing Programs • Worksheet 15: Core Future Strategies • Worksheet 16: Long-Term and Short-Term Priorities	Staff complete competitive analysis of programs Planning Committee and consultant meet to discuss overall core future strategies and agree on long-term and short-term program and organizational priorities. Some of the discussions of strategic issues and priorities may take place at Board/Staff Planning Retreat described above	Number of additional Planning Committee meetings will depend on complexity of issues, usually two to eight two- to three-hour meetings
	Agreement on overall program and organizational goals Agreement on specific objectives that the organization wishes to accomplish in the immediate and long term	• Worksheet 17: Summary of Program Scope and Scale • Worksheet 18: Setting Goals and Objectives • Worksheet 19: Long-Range Financial Projections	Staff develops and presents to Planning Committee suggested program portfolio (scope and scale of future programs) and identification of resources needed to support the achievement of program objectives Appropriate individuals write program and management/operations goals and objectives Executive Director, along with appropriate resource development staff and Board, assess current fund-raising base in relation to resource needs (sources of stability and solvency; trends in funding, etc.), and implications for organization's future. Discussion of various fund-raising approaches available, and fund-raising objectives and overall strategies. Consultant available to assist, as necessary	Number of staff hours to prepare data will vary. Two- to three-hour meeting of Planning Committee to review recommendations

(Continued)

Template: Extensive Planning Process Workplan *(Continued)*

Phase	Key Outcomes Achieved During Each Planning Phase	Possible Worksheets and Templates to Support Achieving Outcomes	Proposed Format/Responsibility	Time Commitment
Phase 5: Writing the Strategic Plan	Approval of a Strategic Plan!	• See Table of Contents suggestions in Phase 5	Executive Director and/or designated writer develop first draft of strategic plan. Consultant available to help as necessary	Number of hours to write plan will vary with size and complexity of organization
			Seek input from key stakeholders; circulate plan and get feedback from staff, Board members, and consultant. Planning Committee and consultant review draft(s) and make comments	One or two meetings to review Strategic Plan
			Submit final draft of Strategic Plan to Board for approval	Approval at regular Board meeting
	Written report to the community		Executive summary of plan developed by Executive Director and/or designated writer, and distributed to the community	Will depend on document

Phase	Key Outcomes Achieved During Each Planning Phase	Possible Worksheets and Templates to Support Achieving Outcomes	Proposed Format/Responsibility	Time Commitment
Phase 6: Implementing the Strategic Plan—Creating an Annual Operating Plan	A detailed annual operating plan	• Template: Annual Operating Plan	Staff develops detailed annual operating plans to ensure the successful implementation of the strategic plan during the upcoming year	Number of hours will depend on size and complexity of organization
Phase 7: Monitoring and Evaluation	An in-depth system to monitor and evaluate implementation of the plan(s) and achievement of success factors	• Worksheet 20: Evaluation of Plans and the Strategic Planning Process	Planning Committee and consultant meet to evaluate completed strategic Planning process, including identifying benchmarks and milestones	Two- to three-hour meeting
			Planning Committee and consultant meet to discuss processes to monitor and evaluate implementation of plan, including defining key success factors	Once or twice a year
	Processes in place to ensure that the plan(s) are modified as needed and that the Strategic Plan continues to provide guidance for the setting of current priorities for the following year	• Worksheet 21: Monitoring the Strategic Plan	Planning Committee coordinates a yearly strategic planning meeting to assess and validate current strategies, and ensure that the current Strategic Plan gives guidance to the development of upcoming annual operating plans. The Planning Committee may decide that the current Strategic Plan needs to be modified or significantly changed, and/or it may be time to start the strategic planning process again	At least every three to five years some formal strategic planning process should be undertaken

Appendix C: Elements of an Effectively Managed Organization (EEMO™)—A Self-Assessment Tool

HOW THIS SELF-ASSESSMENT TOOL CAN BE USEFUL

- This tool focuses on the elements of managing an organization. It is useful as a basis for discussion. For example, as part of a management retreat, strategic planning process, or as a stand-alone exercise, using the EEMO assessment tool can help staff compare notes about the strengths and weaknesses of the various dimensions in management of an organization.
- Because the tool requires subjective judgments, it can only be completed usefully by people who have an opinion about the questions asked. Some, like the questions about mission are quite general. However, others, like the questions about structure and systems require familiarity with the internal workings of the organization.
- Finally, the tool focuses on management, as opposed to governance. The Board would need to use a separate tool that focuses on governance in order to assess its effectiveness.

HOW TO COMPLETE THE SURVEY

Step One

Decide who should fill out the survey. For small organizations (less than 25 staff), all staff might be invited to complete the survey. For larger organizations, only department or senior managers might fill out the survey, although they might ask their staff for input regarding the relative strengths and weaknesses of the elements described. Alternatively, a team (for example, the management team) might discuss each of the elements and as a group decide whether the element is primarily a strength or a weakness.

Step Two

If EEMO is being used as a survey instrument, people should be asked to complete the survey anonymously, although they should state their position within the organization (for example, senior management, program manager, line staff, support staff, etc.). To complete the survey, individuals are asked to rate each of the eight elements and its related dimensions on a scale of 4–1 relative to whether they perceive it as a strength or a weakness of the organization. They are also asked to add any comments and recommendations regarding their responses.

Step Three

Collate the results, either an outside consultant or someone within the organization should tally the number of responses for each rating, as well as the average score. Comments and recommendations about the ratings should be summarized.

Sample

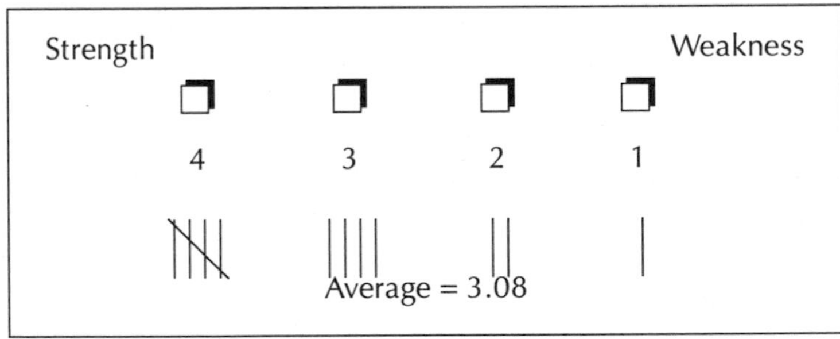

If EEMO is being used as part of a strategic planning process, then the senior management team should summarize key findings and present them to the Planning Committee. The Planning Committee would then use the data as part of its Assessing the Environment Phase and as a vehicle for not only assessing key organizational strengths and weaknesses, but also for help in identifying possible organizational responses.

If EEMO is being used as a stand-alone exercise, senior managers could either use the tool as a framework for discussing the organization's strengths or weaknesses, or they could survey individuals, review the findings (sometimes prepared by an outside neutral consultant), and then use the findings as a basis for discussing what needs improvement or attention within the organization, and what should be done regarding how to proceed next.

Elements of an Effectively Managed Organization (EEMO™)

Mission
Clearly articulated and agreed upon purpose; agreed upon values and beliefs; consensus on organization's primary business(es); agreed upon vision of what the organization is trying to accomplish

Planning
Agreement on priority clients to be served by the organization; three to five year strategic plan is in place; an annual planning process occurs; a written annual operational plan; agreement on overall major strategies for the allocation of resources

Structure
Well-defined organizational structure that ensures work gets delegated and accomplished, including clear lines of authority and responsibility; a decision-making structure supports decisions being implemented; lines of communication support the flow of information and feedback; well-run meetings; personnel policies and procedures in place

People
Sufficient and appropriate staff, able to attract and retain qualified employees; clear roles and responsibilities for paid and volunteer staff; staff evaluation process; effective governance that supports effective management; ongoing professional development; appropriate rewards and recognition; Board and staff feel valued and appreciated

Systems
Realistic short-term and long-term fund development programs; adequate financial resources; accurate and timely financial records; budgeting process in place; attention to financial management activities; effective use of appropriate technology and management information systems

Results and Quality
In-depth program evaluation is conducted; feedback mechanisms to assess client satisfaction and client needs; clients are satisfied with the services; programs are effective and efficient, and quality programs are offered that support the organization's mission

Leadership
The organization's management is a model for effective leadership; the ED and management team take responsibility for creating an environment where people feel supported and motivated. Leadership is a shared function among many people; the Board President models effective leadership by taking responsibility for ensuring that the Board is performing its governance and support roles; the organization takes a leadership role in the community, both by advocating on behalf of its constituencies and by fostering cooperation among agencies offering similar services in the community.

Relationships
There is a constructive climate where people can voice differences of option. There is effective problem solving and meetings; creativity and risk-taking are rewarded; people are committed to working as a team; individuals are willing to work through conflicts; there are systems to support effective formal and informal communication.

ACHIEVEMENT OF YOUR PURPOSE—THE ULTIMATE MEASURE OF YOUR EFFECTIVENESS

INSTRUCTIONS ON FILLING OUT THE EEMO SURVEY

(To be given to all individuals completing the survey.)

There are eight elements of an effectively managed organization: Mission, Planning, Structure, Systems, People, Results and Quality, Leadership, and Relationships.

For each of the eight elements there are descriptions of its specific dimensions. You are being asked to rate each of the elements, and its related dimensions, on a scale of 4–1 relative to whether you perceive it as a strength (rating of 4) or as a weakness of the organization (rating of 1). Remember, this is a subjective judgment, so precision is impossible!

Sample

Strength				Weakness
	❐	☒	❐	❐
	4	3	2	1

If you have any specific recommendations regarding any of the dimensions, or comments about why you gave it the rating that you did, please print or write legibly your responses; short, succinct statements are appreciated.

Your responses will be considered confidential, although it would be helpful to know your position within the organization—circle one: senior manager; department or program manager; line staff; support staff; other (specify:).

Please write legibly or type your responses. Specific recommendations in response to your ratings are extremely important.

__________________ will be collecting the survey.

Put your survey in a sealed envelope and return the survey to the individual named above, no later than the following due date: ____________.

MISSION

	Strength			Weakness
1. The organization has a clearly articulated and agreed upon purpose (a statement that describes the ultimate result the organization is working to achieve). Specific recommendations/comments:	☐ 4	☐ 3	☐ 2	☐ 1
2. There is a consensus on the primary business(es) primary services the organization should provide. Specific recommendations/comments:	☐ 4	☐ 3	☐ 2	☐ 1
3. There are shared values and beliefs that guide the organization and its members. Specific recommendations/comments:	☐ 4	☐ 3	☐ 2	☐ 1
4. There is a clear and agreed upon vision of what the organization is trying to accomplish and what it will take to make that vision happen. Specific recommendations/comments:	☐ 4	☐ 3	☐ 2	☐ 1
Mission: Overall Assessment	☐ 4	☐ 3	☐ 2	☐ 1

PLANNING

	Strength			Weakness
5. There is agreement on clients the organization should be serving. Specific recommendations/comments:	☐ 4	☐ 3	☐ 2	☐ 1
6. A three to five year strategic plan is in place. The plan is reviewed yearly and modified as needed to reflect trends in the environment, current and future client needs, and the organization's capacity to meet those needs. Specific recommendations/comments:	☐ 4	☐ 3	☐ 2	☐ 1
7. There is an annual planning process to set program goals and budget. Specific recommendations/comments:	☐ 4	☐ 3	☐ 2	☐ 1
8. There is a written annual operational plan that includes timelines and identification of who is responsible for which outcomes or activities. Specific recommendations/comments:	☐ 4	☐ 3	☐ 2	☐ 1
9. There is agreement on overall major strategies that the organization will use for the allocation of resources. (Strategies are priority responses that an organization will use to best accomplish its purpose.) Specific recommendations/comments:	☐ 4	☐ 3	☐ 2	☐ 1
Planning: Overall Assessment	☐ 4	☐ 3	☐ 2	☐ 1

STRUCTURE

	Strength			Weakness
10. There is well-defined organizational structure (work gets delegated and thus accomplished in an efficient and effective way, and there are clear lines of authority and responsibility including reporting relationships). An up-to-date organizational chart accurately reflects the reporting relationships. Specific recommendations/comments:	☐ 4	☐ 3	☐ 2	☐ 1
11. There is a decision-making process and structure that supports decisions being implemented (including clarity as to who has input and who has responsibility for making various decisions). Specific recommendations/comments:	☐ 4	☐ 3	☐ 2	☐ 1
12. Lines of communication encourage and support the flow of information and feedback between and among managers, staff, and the Board. There are communication structures in place to support this information flow. Specific recommendations/comments:	☐ 4	☐ 3	☐ 2	☐ 1
13. Meetings are well-organized and well-run. Specific recommendations/comments:	☐ 4	☐ 3	☐ 2	☐ 1
14. Personnel policies and procedures are in place and followed. Specific recommendations/comments:	☐ 4	☐ 3	☐ 2	☐ 1
Structure: Overall Assessment	☐ 4	☐ 3	☐ 2	☐ 1

PEOPLE

	Strength			Weakness
15. The organization is sufficiently and appropriately staffed with paid and volunteer personnel who are able to meet the needs of the clients. The organization is able to attract and retain qualified, competent, and committed employees. Specific recommendations/comments:	☐ 4	☐ 3	☐ 2	☐ 1
16. Roles and responsibilities for paid and volunteer staff are clear and understood; there are accurate and up-to-date written job descriptions for all staff. Specific recommendations/comments:	☐ 4	☐ 3	☐ 2	☐ 1
17. There is a staff evaluation process that includes established performance expectations, periodic work review sessions, and an annual evaluation. Specific recommendations/comments:	☐ 4	☐ 3	☐ 2	☐ 1
18. There is effective governance that supports effective management: governance responsibilities for the Board of Directors are understood; there are written job descriptions for the Board and all committees; specific expectations of members are clearly articulated; the Board annually evaluates its performance. Specific recommendations/comments:	☐ 4	☐ 3	☐ 2	☐ 1
19. There is ongoing professional development of all personnel (training opportunities to enhance current skills, learn new skills, and career planning). Specific recommendations/comments:	☐ 4	☐ 3	☐ 2	☐ 1
20. There are appropriate rewards and recognition for all personnel. Staff and Board feel valued and appreciated. Specific recommendations/comments:	☐ 4	☐ 3	☐ 2	☐ 1
People: Overall Assessment	☐ 4	☐ 3	☐ 2	☐ 1

SYSTEMS

	Strength			Weakness
21. A realistic short-term and long-term fund development program is in place. Specific recommendations/comments:	☐ 4	☐ 3	☐ 2	☐ 1
22. The fund development activities secure adequate financial resources for the organization. Specific recommendations/comments:	☐ 4	☐ 3	☐ 2	☐ 1
23. Accurate and timely financial records are maintained. Specific recommendations/comments:	☐ 4	☐ 3	☐ 2	☐ 1
24. A budgeting process is in place that ensures the effective allocation of resources. Specific recommendations/comments:	☐ 4	☐ 3	☐ 2	☐ 1
25. Financial management activity adequately attends to such items as cash flow, internal controls, cost analysis, and tax compliance. Specific recommendations/comments:	☐ 4	☐ 3	☐ 2	☐ 1
26. There is effective use of appropriate technology, computers, and other management information systems. Specific recommendations/comments:	☐ 4	☐ 3	☐ 2	☐ 1
Systems: Overall Assessment	☐ 4	☐ 3	☐ 2	☐ 1

RESULTS AND QUALITY

Item	Strength 4	3	2	Weakness 1
27. In-depth program evaluation is conducted as part of the planning process. This includes assessment based on identified benchmarks for quality and specific outcome and process objectives. The analysis of outcomes and processes are integrated into the monitoring and adjustment of the organization's long-range and operational plans. Specific recommendations/comments:	☐	☐	☐	☐
28. The organization has feedback mechanisms in place to assess client satisfaction and client needs. Specific recommendations/comments:	☐	☐	☐	☐
29. Clients are satisfied with the services offered by the organization. Specific recommendations/comments:	☐	☐	☐	☐
30. Programs are effective and efficient. The organization provides quality programs that support the organization's mission. Specific recommendations/comments:	☐	☐	☐	☐
Results and Quality: Overall Assessment	☐	☐	☐	☐

LEADERSHIP

	Strength			Weakness
31. The organization's management is a model for effective leadership (including inspiring shared values and a shared vision, holding people accountable for achieving results, and leading by example. Specific recommendations/comments:	☐ 4	☐ 3	☐ 2	☐ 1
32. The ED (and management team if applicable) takes responsibility for creating an environment in which all personnel feel supported and motivated to produce quality results. Specific recommendations/comments:	☐ 4	☐ 3	☐ 2	☐ 1
33. Leadership is not just personified in one person, but is a shared function among many people. Specific recommendations/comments:	☐ 4	☐ 3	☐ 2	☐ 1
34. The Board President models effective leadership by taking responsibility for ensuring that the Board is performing its governance and support roles, that Board committees are operating effectively, and that individual Board members are fulfilling their commitments. Specific recommendations/comments:	☐ 4	☐ 3	☐ 2	☐ 1
35. The organization takes a leadership role in the community, both in advocating on behalf of its constituencies and playing a key role in fostering cooperation among agencies offering similar services in the community. Specific recommendations/comments:	☐ 4	☐ 3	☐ 2	☐ 1
Leadership: Overall Assessment	☐ 4	☐ 3	☐ 2	☐ 1

RELATIONSHIPS

	Strength			Weakness
36. There is a constructive climate in which people are able to feel free to express unusual or unpopular views without fear of personal attack or reprisal. Specific recommendations/comments:	☐ 4	☐ 3	☐ 2	☐ 1
37. Individuals and groups have developed effective ways to be creative, innovative, and solve problems together. Specific recommendations/comments:	☐ 4	☐ 3	☐ 2	☐ 1
38. There is a strong commitment among all employees to working effectively as a team. Team spirit within and among departments is encouraged and supported, and there is effective coordinated services among departments. Specific recommendations/comments:	☐ 4	☐ 3	☐ 2	☐ 1
39. People are willing to work through conflicts. Difficult issues are discussed within an atmosphere of supportiveness and constructive criticism. Specific recommendations/comments:	☐ 4	☐ 3	☐ 2	☐ 1
40. Effective formal and informal communication systems are in place that encourage support, trust, and cooperation among groups and individuals. Specific recommendations/comments:	☐ 4	☐ 3	☐ 2	☐ 1
Relationships: Overall Assessment	☐ 4	☐ 3	☐ 2	☐ 1

Overall, how well is the organization doing in achieving its purpose?	Excellent	Good	Fair	Poor
	☐ 4	☐ 3	☐ 2	☐ 1

Elements of greatest strength? How can we take advantage of this strength?

Which element is holding the organization back from achieving its purpose the most? What should we do to respond to this weakness?

Confidence that your assessment is widely shared?

Other comments:

Thank You!

Appendix D: Board Self-Assessment Survey

Please rate your assessment of the board-of-directors' performance in each category as **N**ot **S**atisfied, **S**omewhat **S**atisfied, **S**atisfied, or **V**ery **S**atisfied.

How satisfied are you that the board:

		(Circle one)			
1.	Understands the mission and purpose of the organization?	NS	SS	S	VS
2.	Ensures legal compliance with federal, state, and local regulations?	NS	SS	S	VS
3.	Ensures that government contract obligations are fulfilled?	NS	SS	S	VS
4.	Has a strategic vision for the organization?	NS	SS	S	VS
5.	Is knowledgeable about the organization's programs and services?	NS	SS	S	VS
6.	Monitors and evaluates the performance of the executive director on a regular basis?	NS	SS	S	VS
7.	Provides financial oversight for the organization, including adopting a realistic budget that maximizes use of resources?	NS	SS	S	VS
8.	Monitors financial performance and projections on a regular basis?	NS	SS	S	VS
9.	Has adopted a fund-raising strategy to ensure adequate resources?	NS	SS	S	VS
10.	Has a clear policy on the responsibilities of board members in fund-raising?	NS	SS	S	VS
11.	Acts as ambassadors to the community on behalf of the organization and its clients?	NS	SS	S	VS
12.	Understands the role that volunteers play in the organization and the organization's philosophy of volunteer management?	NS	SS	S	VS

		(Circle one)			
13.	Understands the respective roles of the Board and staff?	NS	SS	S	VS
14.	Currently contains an appropriate range of expertise and diversity to make it an effective governing body?	NS	SS	S	VS
15.	Effectively involves all Board members in Board activities and responsibilities?	NS	SS	S	VS
16.	Regularly assesses its own work?	NS	SS	S	VS

Once all the survey answers have been tallied, the compiled information should be presented to the board. Here is an example of how the results for one question were presented to a board that has ten members, all of whom completed the self-assessment survey:

Exhibit A-1 Self-Assessment Question

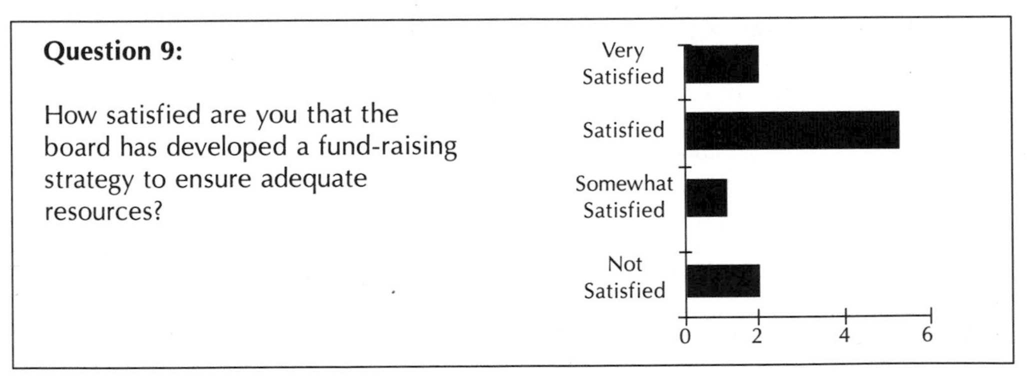

Based on the survey results, the board can see which areas call for greater attention over the coming year. For example, if some board members are satisfied that the board is adequately informed about the organization's programs and services, while others are not, perhaps a tour of the facility and a briefing can be held for the hour preceding a board meeting for those board members who would like to be better informed.

Appendix E: Sample Techniques Used in Program Evaluation

Formal program evaluation is a highly developed field with an extensive body of literature. Evaluation of major programs such as Head Start can cost millions of dollars and take place over many years. While program evaluation is important to agencies in the strategic planning process, a full discussion of program evaluation is beyond the scope of this Workbook. And, because program evaluation often involves tracking clients over time, an agency that does not have an existing program evaluation process will likely be unable to do a significant evaluation during the relatively short period during which the strategic plan is developed.

Here is a sampling of techniques used in program evaluations.

1. **Written survey of clients related to client satisfaction**

One of the questions asked in a written survey of parents of middle school students who participated in a program for at-risk students was:

Would you recommend this program to other parents?

☐ Yes ☐ No ☐ Not sure

Two of the questions asked in a written survey of participants in a CPR class, conducted at the conclusion of the class:

How would you rate your confidence in your ability to deal with an emergency first aid situation . . .

	Not at all confident			Very confident	
Before the class?	1	2	3	4	5
After the class?	1	2	3	4	5

Was this class fun?

2. **Written survey of clients related to outcomes**

The following question was asked on a written survey mailed to clients six months after they had completed a four-session job-seeking course:

Please indicate your job status at the time you took the course and today:

My job status:	Time of the course	Now
Employed full-time	☐	☐
Employed part-time but wanting full-time or more work	☐	☐
Employed part-time and satisfied with part-time	☐	☐
Unemployed	☐	☐
Full-time student	☐	☐
Part-time student	☐	☐
Other:	☐	☐

3. **Telephone survey of clients**

Three months after attending a "New Dads" workshop, participants were telephoned and asked the following, among other questions:

Looking back on the workshop, what was the most valuable thing you got out of it?

Would you recommend the workshop to other new fathers?

4. **Collection of objective data**

As part of an evaluation of an elementary school garden project, the change in science grades and CTBS scores of students participating in the program were compared with changes in grades and scores of students who did not participate in the program.

After Neighborhood Recycling Week activities, the total weight of recycled materials brought to the recycling center each week was compared with the total weight received before Recycling Week.

5. **Example of combining objective data and telephone survey**

After 120,000 booklets on senior services were distributed in a local community, telephone interviews were conducted with a random sample of the households that had received booklets. One of the questions was:

Have you recently received a booklet on services to seniors available in our neighborhood? [If not: Is it possible that someone else in your household received the booklet and you weren't aware of it?]

At the same time, calls to the Senior Central Information Line were tracked before and after distribution of the booklet. The program found that although only a minority of phone respondents remembered having received the booklet, calls to the Information Line took a dramatic jump upward in the two weeks following the booklet distribution.

6. **Focus group**

In a focus group, approximately five to twelve individuals are brought together to discuss aspects of the program. In an evaluation of an awards program made to unsung community heroes, past recipients of the award were brought together for a lunch where questions were posed to the group by an outside facilitator. One of the questions asked was:

Looking back on receiving the award, which aspects of the award had the great impact on you? For example, was it the cash award? The awards ceremony? Articles in the newspaper about the award? Other aspects?

A focus group for a program training new Board members of arts organizations was held one evening. Among the questions asked were:

Of the speakers you heard in the program, which ones do you remember? What sticks in your mind about any one of them or what they said?

Did you like having a light dinner available at the beginning of the sessions? Some people have said they would have preferred having the sessions earlier and shorter, while others have said they found the dinner a great opportunity to meet others. What are your reactions?

7. **Interviews with competitors and potential collaborators**

An AIDS organization serving Asian/Pacific Islanders with HIV conducted interviews with selected leaders from both other AIDS organizations and from Asian/Pacific community organizations. Two of the interview questions for those from other AIDS organizations were:

When Asian or Pacific Islander clients come to your agency for AIDS services, do you ever refer them to the AAA agency? Under what circumstances, and why? Why not?

If there were just one thing you could change about the AAA agency, what would it be?

In an interview with the head of a Filipino neighborhood association:

Are members of your association generally aware of the AAA agency's services? When AIDS comes up, is the AAA agency mentioned? What is said about the AAA agency? What other agencies are mentioned and what is said about them?

8. **Tests**

Post-test. In a post-test, participants in a learning program are given a test at the end of the program to evaluate whether they have learned the new knowledge or skill.

In an empowerment program for high school girls, participants learned how to change car tires. At the end of the program, each had to change a tire by herself, observed by the instructor and two other participants.

Pre- and post-test. The same test is given to participants before and after the learning program. A workshop that trains hospice volunteers asked the following question in a written test given both before the workshop and at the conclusion of the workshop:

Name three precautions that should be taken by hospice volunteers related to touching patients:

-
-
-

9. **Observation**

Open-ended observation. In an evaluation of an infant care training program for mothers, staff the homes of children whose mothers had participated in the program and observed home life in gene including physical environment, interaction between mother and child, etc.

Focused observation. In a focused evaluation done the second year of the infant safety program visited homes with checklists, including the following:

- Is there a working smoke detector present in the home?
- Did you observe electric outlet covers in place? Did you observe any electric outlets at child without outlet covers??
- Was there a pillow present in the infant's sleeping area?

Appendix F: Techniques and Tools for Managing Group Process—A Toolbox of Meeting Process Tools and Techniques

Since so much of the work of strategic planning takes place in meetings, here are some meeting process tools and techniques to help you have more effective meetings.[1]

SETTING UP MEETINGS FOR SUCCESS: CREATING EFFECTIVE AGENDAS

Agendas for all meetings should be prepared and distributed to all participants ahead of time. Agendas should include the following:

- Date and time frame of meeting
- Location of meeting
- Outcome(s) of meeting
- List of meeting attendees
- List of materials people should bring to the meeting
- Detailed proposed agenda

[1] This is by no means a complete list of all the meeting process tools and techniques that you could use. For additional help in running meetings, the following three books are recommended: Michael Doyle and Davis Straus, *How to Make Meetings Work* (New York: Jove Books, 1983); Roger M. Schwarz, *The Skilled Facilitator* (San Francisco: Jossey-Bass, 1994); and Sam Kaner, *Facilitator's Guide to Participatory Decision-Making* (Philadelphia: New Society Publishers, 1996).

Exhibit A-2 Example of Detailed Proposed Agenda

Agenda Topic	Time Allocated	Process to Be Used	Personnel Responsible
History profile	3:00–3:30 P.M.	Presentation	Executive Director
Previous strategies	3:30–4:00 P.M.	Brainstorm list Discuss prior and current effectiveness	All
External stakeholder involvement	4:00–4:45 P.M.	Brainstorm list of who to involve in the planning process Discuss what questions they should be asked, and how to best gather that information	All
Next steps, personnel responsible, and by when Evaluation of meeting	4:45–5:00 P.M.	List and agree	All

SETTING UP MEETINGS FOR SUCCESS: MEETING AGREEMENTS

To ensure successful meetings, it is a good idea to get the group to agree on basic meeting agreements (ground rules) as to how to work together. These meeting agreements might include:

- Listen as an ally
- Meetings will start and end on time
- No side conversations
- Focus on issues, not personalities
- Be specific and use examples
- Share all relevant information
- Short, succinct statements
- Keep to the point, keep the discussion focused

- Focus on interests, not positions
- No interruptions
- Okay to disagree—constructively
- All participate fully
- Seek first to understand, then to be understood
- Work to create decisions you can support
- The past has a vote but it doesn't have veto power

SETTING UP MEETINGS FOR SUCCESS: CLARIFY ROLES AND RESPONSIBILITIES FOR THE MEETING

Make sure there is clarity as to who is going to facilitate the meetings, who needs to be present at the meetings, and how information is going to be recorded (minutes).

Clarify in advance who makes decisions and how decisions are to be made; those involved in the planning process should know in advance whether they have the power to make a decision, or whether they are being asked for their input.

Decide whether it is most effective for the President of the Board, Chair of the Planning Committee, or Executive Director to run the meeting, or whether it is appropriate and useful to bring in an outside facilitator.

GENERATING IDEAS: BRAINSTORMING

Brainstorming is a commonly used meeting process. The outcome of brainstorming is to come up with as many ideas as possible within the time allowed. Guidelines for brainstorming include:

- During brainstorming, all ideas are okay
- There should be no discussion of ideas until the brainstorming is complete
- Build on others' ideas
- Creativity is encouraged

Consider the use of the *Round Robin* technique as a way of encouraging everyone to speak rather than anyone calling out an idea when they think of one: go around in a circle and have everyone make one comment on the topic at hand; people have the option of passing. At the end of the round robin, go back to those who

Exhibit A-3 File Chart

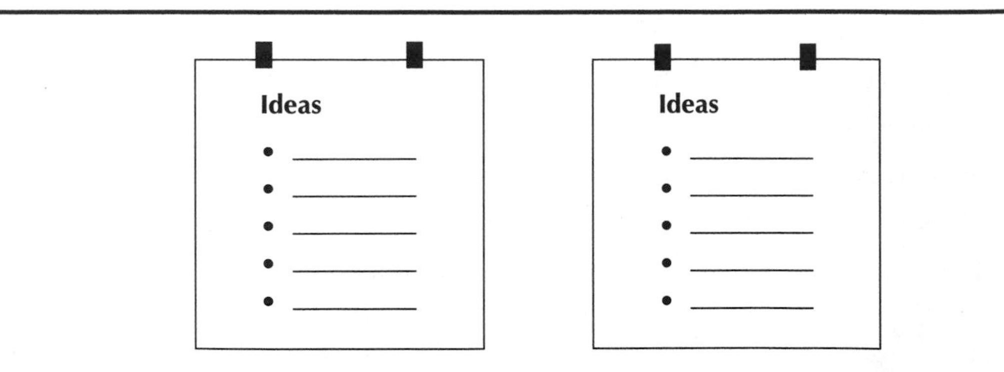

have passed and ask if they have anything to add. People who have offered ideas can add additional ideas only after the round robin is completed.

It is best to record ideas on a flip chart so that they can be seen and remembered by all on the team.

ORGANIZING IDEAS: SORT BY CATEGORY

After all ideas have been generated, it is sometimes useful to group them into larger categories. The actual process of grouping is usually done best by an individual or small group and then presented back to the larger group for changes and approval.

For example, after a group has brainstormed a list of strengths and weaknesses, the meeting leader might suggest that, during the break, the group should sort the ideas into the following categories: program service delivery; program evaluation; staffing and benefits; Board (governance); communications and decision-making; fund-raising; image/public relations; organizational structure and information systems; other (Note: Post-its are a useful tool—put each idea onto a Post-it and then sort the Post-its into the groupings).

ANALYZING IDEAS: RANK ADVANTAGES/DISADVANTAGES (FORCE FIELD ANALYSIS)

This tool allows you to assess the advantages and disadvantages of a particular suggestion, or look at the forces working for or against something happening.

Exhibit A-4 Force Field Analysis

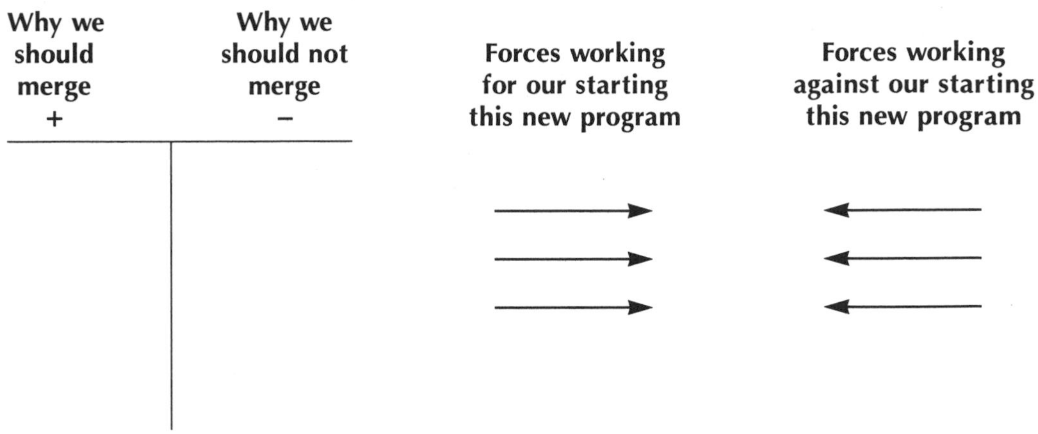

Why we should merge +	**Why we should not merge** −

Forces working for our starting this new program	**Forces working against our starting this new program**
⟶	⟵
⟶	⟵
⟶	⟵

ANALYZING IDEAS: EVALUATE USING CRITERIA

A criteria grid can be used to help analyze an idea based on an agreed set of criteria. To use to criteria grid, list and agree on criteria for a successful solution. Then the group evaluates alternative solutions against the criteria. The facilitator might say, "Let's agree on the three major success criteria that will meet our information needs. Then we can check equipment options against the criteria." (See Exhibit A-5.)

Exhibit A-5 Criteria Grid

Alternatives \ **Criteria**	1	2	3
A			
B			
C			

PRIORITIZING IDEAS: ASSIGNING AN A, B, OR C PRIORITY

Use the same process suggested by time management experts. List all ideas and then record whether the idea is an "A," "B," or "C" priority. (A, highest priority/most important; B, moderate priority; C, lowest priority/least important).

The colored paste-on dots sold in most stationary stores are very helpful: give everyone some red, blue, and green dots. The red dots represent an "A" priority (most important); blue dots represent a "B" priority, (something to consider, but not the highest priority); and green dots represent a "C" priority (it's a nice idea, but probably not all that important in relation to A and B). To make sure that not everything gets considered an "A" priority, you might give people an equal number of red, blue, and green dots, the total of which adds up to the number of ideas.

PRIORITIZING IDEAS: RANK ORDER TECHNIQUE (SOMETIMES KNOWN AS N/3)

This is a useful tool for narrowing down a large list of ideas. For example, you have just brainstormed a list of thirty different services you are either currently offering or would like to consider offering. How do you quickly do a straw poll with a large group to find out which of the services are most important? A quick way to find out which services the group thinks are important is to take the total number of items on your list (N = number of ideas) and divide by three. Give everyone that number of votes.

For example, with a list of fifteen items, divide 15 by 3, which equals 5. Each person votes for five of his/her highest priority items. The facilitator would say, "Let's see which of these items have the highest priority for you. There are fifteen different services you could offer, but you will probably not be able to do them all. Let's brainstorm a list of the criteria we should use to choose our top third, and then I will ask each of you to use that list of criteria to select your top five. Okay, so how many selected service A? How many for service B? (etc.) Now, let's see which alternatives got the highest votes."

PRIORITIZING IDEAS: MULTI-VOTING OR WEIGHTED VOTING

Multi-voting is a similar tool to N/3, and like N/3, it is used to narrow down lists of ideas generated through brainstorming. Unlike N/3 where individuals are given one vote for each idea, in multi-voting individuals are able to assign weights or different values to their votes. For example:

- Each individual has 10 total votes which may be distributed any way he or she chooses on the particular list of ideas being evaluated.
- No particular idea can receive more than four (4) votes from an individual. In other words, one might choose to assign four votes to Choice A, four votes to Choice B, two votes for Choice C, or any other combination as long as he or she does not exceed four on any single choice.

Exhibit A-6 Tally Sheet

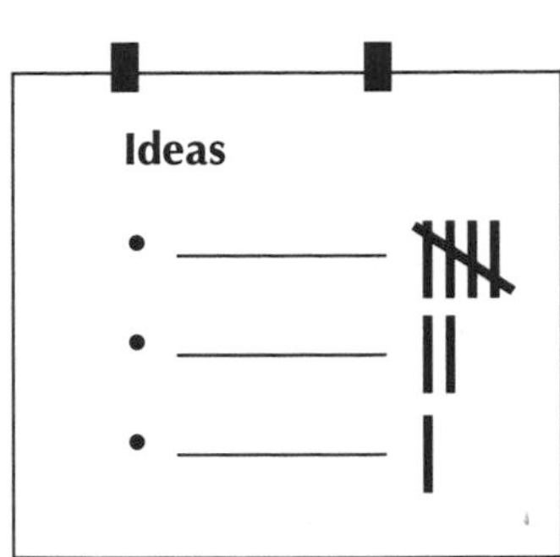

- The ideas being voted are written on flip chart paper. Individuals can then write their vote next to the issue they have chosen. (Or, each individual can be given 10 adhesive-backed dots that he or she could place besides the list of ideas.)
- The total number of votes are tallied. It is best to narrow the list to the top five to eight choices, depending on the size of the list.

KEEPING THE MEETING FOCUSED: USE OF THE "BIN" OR "PARKING LOT"

The "bin" (also known as the "parking lot") is a way of capturing ideas or issues which arise in a meeting but don't fit into the agenda or the part of the planning process on which the team is working. Rather than discussing these ideas and losing valuable time, or losing the idea by not discussing it at all, the Planning Committee can create a "bin." This is merely a flip chart sheet on which the idea or issue is listed. The sheet is affixed to the wall in subsequent meetings, and issues may be discussed when appropriate or identified as future agenda items. Prior to the end of this process, all issues listed on the "bin" should be resolved.

Appendix G: Template for an Action Plan

Strategic plan goal:

Strategic plan objective (if applicable):

Annual operating plan objective:

Benchmark(s) and method of measuring success:

Action Steps	Personnel Responsible	Time Frame or by When	Status: As of (date)

Feedback mechanisms:

Appendix H: Selected References

Barry, Bryan W. *Strategic Planning Workbook for Nonprofit Organizations* (St. Paul, MN: Amherst H. Wilder Foundation, 1986).

Bean, William C. *Strategic Planning that Makes Things Happen* (Amherst, MA: HRD Press, 1993).

Below, Patrick J., George L. Morrisey, and Betty L. Acomb. *The Executive Guide to Strategic Planning* (San Francisco, CA: Jossey-Bass, 1987).

Bielefeld, Wolfgang. "Funding uncertainty and nonprofit strategies in the 1980s." *Nonprofit Management and Leadership,* Jossey-Bass, Vol. 2, No. 4, Summer 1992.

Bryson, John M. *Strategic Planning for Public and Nonprofit Organizations: A Guide to Strengthening and Sustaining Organizational Achievement.* rev. ed. (San Francisco, CA: Jossey-Bass, 1993).

Doyle, Michael and David Straus. *How to Make Meetings Work.* (New York, NY: Jove Books, 1983).

Drucker, Peter F. *Managing the Nonprofit Organization: Principles and Practices* (New York, NY: HarperCollins, 1990).

Hax, Arnold C. and Nicholas S. Majluf. *Strategic Management: An Integrative Perspective* (Englewood Cliffs, NJ: Prentice Hall, 1984).

Kotler, Philip and Alan Andreasen. *Strategic Marketing for Nonprofit Organizations, 4th ed.* (Englewood Cliffs, NJ: Prentice Hall, 1991).

Kearns, Kevin P. "Comparative advantage to damage control: clarifying strategic issues using SWOT analysis." In *Nonprofit Management and Leadership,* Vol. 3, No. 1, Fall. Jossey-Bass.

McNutt, Paul and Robert W. Backoff. *Strategic Management of Public and Third Sector Organizations* (San Francisco, CA: Jossey-Bass, 1992).

Mintzberg, Henry. *The Rise and Fall of Strategic Planning* (New York, NY: Free Press, 1994).

Nanus, B. *Visionary Leadership: Creating a Compelling Sense of Direction for Your Organization* (San Francisco, CA: Jossey-Bass, 1992).

Osborne, David and Ted Gaebler. *Reinventing Government: How the Entreprenuerial Spirit Is Transforming the Public Sector* (Reading, MA: Addison-Wesley, 1992).

Peters, Thomas J. and Robert H. Waterman, Jr. *In Search of Excellence: Lessons from America's Best-Run Companies* (New York, NY: HarperCollins, 1982).

Porter, Michael E. *Competitive Strategy: Techniques for Analyzing Industries and Competitors* (New York, NY: Free Press. 1980).

Schwartz, Peter. *The Art of the Long View* (New York, NY: Doubleday, 1991).

Steiner, George A. *Strategic Planning: What Every Manager Must Know* (New York, NY: Free Press, 1979).

Tregoe, Benjamin B. and John W. Zimmerman. *Top Management Strategy: What It Is and How to Make It Work* (New York, NY: Simon & Schuster, 1980).

United Way of America. *Strategic Management and United Way* (Alexandria, VA: United Way Strategic Planning Division, 1988).

Index

K

M

N

O

P

R

S

ABOUT THE DISK

Disk Table of Contents

Introduction

The enclosed disk contains 21 forms saved in Microsoft Word version 2.0 format. In order to use the files you need to have Microsoft Word version 2.0 or higher, or other word processing software capable of reading Microsoft Word 2.0 files.

After installing the files to your hard drive (see instructions below), you can open the files in your word processor and print the forms or begin customizing them to suit your needs. You may want to add or delete text, adjust the formatting, reset margins and tabs, change fonts, etc. Refer to the user manual that came with your word processing software for instructions on how to make these changes.

System Requirements

- IBM PC or compatible computer with 386 or higher processor
- 3.5″ floppy disk drive
- Windows 3.1 or higher
- Microsoft Word version 2.0 or higher, or other word processing capable of reading Microsoft Word 2.0 files.

How to Install the Files onto Your Computer

The enclosed disk contains files saved in Microsoft Word version 2.0. Running the installation program will copy the files to your hard drive in the default directory **C:\NPFORMS.** To run the installation program, do the following:

1. Insert the enclosed disk into the floppy disk drive of your computer.
2. Windows 3.1: From Program Manager, choose File, Run.
   Windows 95: From the Start Menu, choose Run.
3. Type **A:\INSTALL** and press Enter.
4. The opening screen of the installation program will appear. Press Enter to continue.
5. The default destination directory is C:\NPFORMS. If you wish to change the default destination, you may do so now. Follow the instructions on the screen.
5. The installation program will copy all files to your hard drive in the C:\NPFORMS or user-designated directory.

Using the Files

In order to use the files you need to load your word processing program. Instructions are provided below.

Note: Most popular word processing programs are capable of reading Microsoft Word 2.0 files. However, users should be aware that some formatting might be lost when using a program other than Microsoft Word. Some users will need to readjust tabs, page margins, fonts, or table features.

Using the Files with Microsoft Word for Windows

To use the files with Microsoft Word for Windows, do the following:

1. Load the Microsoft Word for Windows program.
2. When the blank document screen is displayed, select Open from the File menu.
3. The Open dialog box will appear. Make the appropriate selections for the drive and directory. If you installed to the default directory the files will be located in the **C:\NPFORMS** directory.

4. In the file name list, double click on the file you want to open. You can make any changes or revisions to the document.
5. To print the file, select PRINT from the FILE menu.

Using the Files with WordPerfect for Windows
To use the files with WordPerfect for Windows, do the following:

1. Load the WordPerfect for Windows program.
2. When the blank document screen is displayed, select Open from the File Menu.
3. The Open dialog box will appear. Make the appropriate selections for the drive and directory. If you installed to the default directory the files will be located in the **C:\NPFORMS** directory.
4. To see a list of all files, under Type of Files select ALL FILES (*.*).
5. In the file name list, double click on the file you want to open.
6. The file will immediately load into WordPerfect for Windows. You can make any changes or revisions to the document.
7. To print the file, select PRINT from the FILE menu.

Saving Files
When you have finished editing a document, you should save it under a new file name before exiting your word processing program.

User Assistance

If you need basic assistance with installation or if you have a damaged disk, please call our product support number at (212) 850-6194 weekdays between 9 AM and 4 PM Eastern Standard Time.

To place additional orders or to request information about other Wiley products, please call (800) 225-5945.

MacIntosh Users

For those who use MacIntosh hardware and software, a disk can be made available. Please send $5.00 to:

Support Center for Nonprofit Management
Attn: Strategic Planning for Nonprofit Organizations Workbook
706 Mission Street
5th Floor
San Francisco, CA 94103

CUSTOMER NOTE: IF THIS BOOK IS ACCOMPANIED BY SOFTWARE, PLEASE READ THE FOLLOWING BEFORE OPENING THE PACKAGE.